The Spirited Life

Little Sunapee
New London
Kearsarge Mountain
Lake Sunapee
Concord
Alstead Centre
NEW HAMPSHIRE
Crotched Mountain
Manchester
Mount Monadnock
Peterborough
East Derry
ATLANTIC OCEAN
MERRIMACK RIVER
Newburyport
Haverhill
PARKER RIVER
Plum Island
Mason
Georgetown
Rowley
Ipswich
Rockport
Ashburnham
Essex
Gloucester
South Ashburnham
Danvers
Petersham
MASSACHUSETTS
Swampscott
N
W
E
S
CHARLES RIVER
Weston
Boston
Wellesley Hills
Milton
Worcester
Dedham

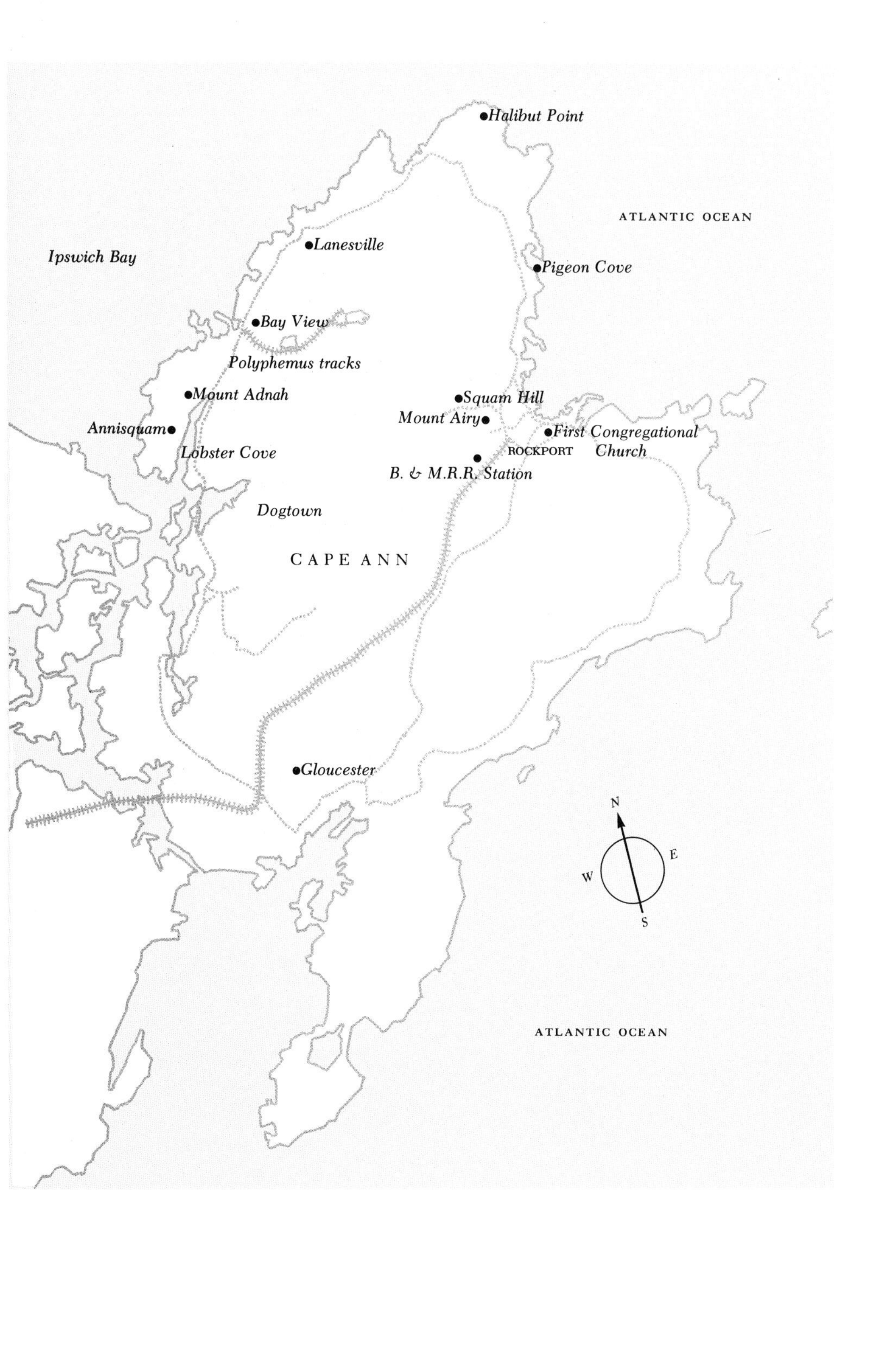
Halibut Point
ATLANTIC OCEAN
Lanesville
Ipswich Bay
Pigeon Cove
Bay View
Polyphemus tracks
Mount Adnah
Squam Hill
Mount Airy
Annisquam
First Congregational Church
ROCKPORT
Lobster Cove
B. & M.R.R. Station
Dogtown
CAPE ANN
Gloucester
N
E
W
S
ATLANTIC OCEAN

The Spirited Life

BERTHA MAHONY MILLER AND CHILDREN'S BOOKS

BY EULALIE STEINMETZ ROSS

SELECTED BIBLIOGRAPHY

COMPILED BY

VIRGINIA HAVILAND

THE HORN BOOK, INCORPORATED

BOSTON, MASSACHUSETTS

1973

Permission to reprint selections from the following material is acknowledged with thanks:
From "Two Tramps in Mud Time" from THE POETRY OF ROBERT FROST edited by Edward Connery Lathem. Copyright 1936 by Robert Frost. Copyright © 1964 by Lesley Frost Ballantine. Copyright © 1969 by Holt, Rinehart and Winston, Inc. Reprinted by permission of Holt, Rinehart and Winston, Inc. From ANIMAL STORIES chosen, arranged and in some part rewritten by Walter de la Mare. Copyright, 1939, 1940 by Charles Scribner's Sons. Reprinted by permission of The Literary Trustees of Walter de la Mare, and The Society of Authors as their representative and by permission of Charles Scribner's Sons. From a review of HORN BOOK REFLECTIONS in *The* (London) *Times Literary Supplement*, reproduced by permission.

Printed in the United States of America.
Great Britain: B. F. Stevens & Brown, Ltd., Godalming
Library of Congress Catalog Card Number: 73-84132
International Standard Book Number: 0-87675-057-9

Designed by Larry Webster
Printed by Thomas Todd Company

To

Elinor Whitney Field

Acknowledgements

"WE MAKE OF OUR THANKS a bundle of good wishes at your feet. We make of our thanks a wind of good fortune to run before you. We make of our thanks a blossoming of luck in house and hearth and homestead." Mrs. Miller often used that Irish litany from Ella Young's *The Unicorn with Silver Shoes,* which McKay now publishes, to express her appreciation for an especially fine creative effort by a writer, illustrator, or publisher of children's books. I follow her pattern to acknowledge my gratitude to the vast number of generous people who have helped me write her biography.

I am particularly grateful to have been able to talk with Mrs. Miller's brother, Daniel Mahony, before his death. Shaken at first by his looks, which were startlingly like his sister's, I was soon put at ease by the gentle courtesy of his ways. Charles Alden Peabody, the son of Mrs. Miller's beloved Aunt Nellie, shared with me the memories of his cousin and childhood companion. Using Mrs. Miller's memoir material for reference, Homer G. Orne, then President of the Sandy Bay Historical Society and Museum, Inc., mapped for my feet the Rockport walks she took as a child with her father. The letters of Marguerite Haskell and Abby Merchant gave substance to the elusive adolescent Bertha of Bay View.

In Boston, Sherwood Allen Barrow, the Registrar of Simmons College, found for me the facts of Mrs. Miller's year at the school. Mildred A. Frank, the Recording Clerk of the Women's Educational and Industrial Union, opened the file of the Union's annual reports to me and led me through the maze of corridors and rooms where Mrs. Miller had worked for so many years.

In Ashburnham, Jeanne Schoonmaker Jarmon added appreciably to my understanding of her aunt, Celena Whitney Miller. Gordon Manthorne did the same for his uncle, William Davis Miller. Indeed they, and everyone else in Ashburnham, made me so welcome, with such good talk about Mr. and Mrs. Miller, that I now consider the community to be my second home. Mary Lydia Nims made my visits there especially pleasant by allowing me to stay with her in her lovely old New England home. The staff of Mr. Manthorne's Hitchcock Shop, where I read Mrs. Miller's files, lent a collectively appreciative ear when treasure was discovered and offered comfort when a day's research yielded only aridity.

For their summaries of the unique relationships they enjoyed with Mrs. Miller, I am particularly grateful to Carolyn G. Norris, Elizabeth C. Reed, Momoko Ishii, Esther Averill, Elizabeth Orton Jones, Mildred Lawrence, Kit Jarmon Porter, Alice Miller Morse, and Nancy Dean Kingman. Mrs. Kingman also took the pictures of the rooms of the Ashburnham home which are reproduced in the illustrated section of this book. I would thank particularly Beulah Folmsbee, who not only responded at length to my initial letter of inquiry, but patiently answered question after question as the writing of the book progressed.

Elinor Whitney Field, Louise Seaman Bechtel, and Frances C. Darling offered invaluable factual help as well as sympathetic counsel, when the woman about whom I was writing tended to get lost in her own record.

Mary Manthorne, as President of The Horn Book, Incorporated, asked me to write this book. Her faith and confidence have supported me when my own were in short supply. Lee Kingman Natti, as my editor, has used a blue pencil with good effect, delicately balancing criticism with encouragement.

Elizabeth S. Halbrooks, the Business Manager of The Horn Book, Incorporated, and Mary Ramon Kinney, Associate Professor of Library Science at Simmons College (now retired), operated as Boston researchers for me, tracking down names, dates, and places with good-will and astonishing results. Elliott Hardaway, the Librarian of the Clearwater Public Library, and his young, zippy staff have also done yeoman detective work for me. Paul Heins, the present Editor of *The Horn Book Magazine*, and his staff helped me courteously and kindly in every way they could.

To those publishers, societies, and persons who allowed me to quote from books, magazine articles, and letters I am most truly grateful.

My thanks make a very special bundle of good wishes to lay at the Beacon Hill doorstep of The Thomas Todd Company. Thomas Todd, Larry Webster, who designed the book, typesetters, proofreaders — all were patient and helpful as my manuscript pages became printed ones of distinction and beauty.

I have written this book from a studio in the Bruce Taylor Building which looks out over Clearwater Bay to the beach. The view of sky and sand and water, framed by palm fronds, has offered ease to the eye and balm to the spirit. It is just such a long view as delighted Mrs. Miller from the piazza at Mount Airy and the sleeping porch at Ashburnham.

Eulalie S. Ross

Clearwater, Florida
January 19, 1973

Contents

The Spirited Life

Introduction

BECAUSE BERTHA MILLER engaged in so many pursuits, it was difficult to keep the various threads of her life running simultaneously and smoothly through this biography. Then, when various arbitrary divisions were decided upon in the interest of organization and for the sake of clarity, considerable movement backward and forward in time was inevitable. To keep the record straight chronologically, and for the benefit of those readers who may be coming freshly to an acquaintance with a great bookwoman, a résumé of Mrs. Miller's life follows.

She was born Bertha Everett Mahony in Rockport on Cape Ann, Massachusetts, in 1882. She was the oldest of four children in an Irish-New England family of modest means. In 1902, as a special one-year student in its Secretarial School, she entered Simmons College, newly founded in Boston to provide young women with the kind of education that would lead to decent and gainful employment. In 1906, as Assistant Secretary, she joined the staff of the Women's Educational and Industrial Union, a Boston institution organized to protect and promote the status of the working woman.

Ten years later Miss Mahony established for the Union the Bookshop for Boys and Girls which, under her direction, became a Boston institution in its own right and a dependable source of revenue for the parent organization's philanthropic undertakings. In 1924, with Elinor Whitney, a co-worker in the Bookshop, she founded *The Horn Book*, a unique magazine in America — then and now — devoted solely to the consideration of children's books and reading. The Union published the magazine.

Bertha Mahony became Bertha Miller in 1932, marrying William Davis Miller, the President of the W. F. Whitney Furniture Company of South Ashburnham, Massachusetts, and the widower of her good friend, Celena Whitney Miller. Celena and Elinor Whitney were distant cousins. In the spring of 1936 Elinor Whitney followed her friend into matrimony, marrying William L. W. Field, the Headmaster of Milton Academy in Milton, Massachusetts.

In June of the same year the two women withdrew from the Bookshop and in October assumed the publishing of *The Horn Book Magazine*, forming to do so a close corporation with their husbands and their printer, Thomas Todd. Mrs. Miller edited the magazine from its inception through 1950; from 1951 to 1963 she served as the President of The Horn Book, Incorporated; from 1963 until her death she was Chairman of the company's Board of Directors.

In 1944 The Horn Book, Incorporated, entered the book publishing field with a major publication, a translation from the French of Paul Hazard's *Books, Children and Men*. Other volumes, equally distinguished, followed regularly through the years, all illuminating some aspect of children's literature.

In 1955 the Women's National Book Association gave Mrs. Miller its Constance Lindsay Skinner Award in recognition of her contribution to the world of books. At its 1959 annual meeting the Children's Services Division of the American Library Association passed a resolution saluting Mrs. Miller for the role she had played in the development of children's literature in America. In 1967 the Catholic Library Association bestowed upon her its Regina Medal in appreciation of her life's work on behalf of children and their books.

Mrs. Miller died in 1969 at her home in Ashburnham. Her ashes rest on a hilltop in a Cape Ann cemetery where the view is far and wide and the solitude complete.

* * *

This story of one woman's life can be read for its relation to the first wave of the Women's Liberation Movement that broke across the country at the turn of the century leaving its mark on the education of women and their position in the labor market. It can be read as the chronicle of an inspired bookseller who anticipated by fifty years the reaching-out approach currently advocated by bookshop directors. It can be read as the record of a pioneer in the children's book world whose magazine was a major force in creating a body of distinguished books for American boys and girls. It can be read as the romance of a woman to whom spring came late, but was none the less beautiful for its tardiness.

The biography can be read — and this is its primary purpose — as an introduction to Mrs. Miller's writings, which are as pertinent today as when they were written. When Ruth Hill Viguers, then the editor of *The Horn Book*, accepted the Regina Medal for Mrs. Miller, she did so in the first editor's own words, quoting from her *Horn Book* editorials. When Mrs. Miller died, quotations from the same editorials were read at her Memorial Service. In both instances, the audiences remarked on the applicability of the passages to the world of the 1960s. The applicability has not diminished in this decade of the 1970s.

Much of Mrs. Miller's writing has been included in this book, hoping it will lead young parents, librarians, booksellers, educators — all who are concerned with the welfare of children — to search out back issues of *The Horn Book* and discover for themselves the full measure of a great woman's spirit as she poured it unstintingly into the pages of her magazine. Time so spent will be enriched by meeting a woman whose simple and straightforward approach to life anticipated youth's current trend back to basics.

* * *

The Horn Book Magazine, particularly Mrs. Miller's writings in it, was a major source of research for this book. A complete reading of Mrs. Miller's files was also made, with the discovery of such treasures as Bookshop scrapbooks and the dummies of the earliest Horn Book, Incorporated, publications. The rarest find was a folder of memoir material that Mrs. Miller had worked on over the years. None of the sketches is complete, nor has any been published. Mrs. Miller began afresh with each writing so that the repetitive emphasis is on her childhood and on the Bookshop years. She had total recall and something of Pepys' gift of catching the essence of a character or an incident in a brief storytelling paragraph. "The Cape Ann Years" in this biography and the chapter describing the founding of the Bookshop would have been sterile indeed without the memoir material.

The files yielded other primary source material: an envelope containing the papers of Captain David Lane mentioned in "The Cape Ann Years"; a diary kept intermittently by Mrs. Miller from 1914 through 1918; unpublished sketches by her about

Henry and Bertha Greene, with whom she and Mr. Miller enjoyed Canadian fishing expeditions; and a notebook account of her visit to England with her sister in 1936.

Mrs. Field generously made available the diary she and Mrs. Miller wrote jointly of their 1924 European trip, and Frances Darling, a Bookshop co-worker, loaned the one she kept of her summers on the Bookshop Caravan. Mrs. Field also allowed me to read and use "The Story of a Friendship," an unpublished essay she wrote for her own pleasure about her relationship with Mrs. Miller.

As much as possible has been quoted from these original sources to allow those concerned with a time or an event to describe it themselves.

* * *

I have known *The Horn Book* and the publications of The Horn Book, Incorporated, all of my professional life, which began in 1935. Until 1963 my acquaintance with Mrs. Miller herself was largely through correspondence over the occasional articles for her magazine that I wrote as Supervisor of Storytelling in The New York Public Library and Coordinator of Children's Services in The Public Library of Cincinnati and Hamilton County. 1963 marked the first of my six summers teaching at Simmons School of Library Science. Mrs. Miller was kind enough to invite me to spend a weekend in her lovely old home in the hill town of Ashburnham during each of those summers. A visit to Cape Ann was also included in every summer's program because I came to love it so. When in 1965 I joined my parents to live in Florida, it was possible to pay seasonal calls on Mrs. Miller at her home in Winter Park.

Thus I came to know the scenery of Mrs. Miller's life as well as the woman herself. With her spirit I had long been familiar, distilled as it is in her *Horn Book* writings. It is the spirit of Bertha Miller that I have tried to evoke in this biography, avoiding the nostalgic and the worshipful. With neither approach would Mrs. Miller have much patience, for she had an innate, almost fastidious, dislike of personal vainglory and her sights were always firmly in the future. This biography is for those of today who are shaping the children's book world of tomorrow with vision derived from and strengthened by a knowledge of its yesterdays.

The Cape Ann Years

If anyone should ask me what element out of my childhood had the greatest influence on my life, I should answer, "A sense of wonder." By this I mean an atmosphere, an attitude of mind which made life significant to a small child and gave it unending interest and sparkle even to this day.

—Bertha Mahony Miller. From a Memoir written when she was seventy[1]

Childhood in Rockport

BERTHA EVERETT MAHONY, the first child of Daniel and Mary Lane Everett Mahony, was born on March 13, 1882 in a white clapboard house on King Street in Rockport, Massachusetts.

The town of Rockport is an internationally famous art center on the ocean side of Cape Ann where it thrusts out into the Atlantic some thirty miles northeast of Boston. The village of Pigeon Cove shares the sea coast with Rockport; Lanesville, Bay View and Annisquam drop down the back shore from Halibut Point, the northernmost tip of the Cape, and look across Ipswich Bay to Plum Island and the low-lying hills of Essex, Ipswich, Rowley and Newburyport on the Massachusetts mainland. The city of Gloucester is on the south shore with its fishing fleets snug behind a long protective peninsula of land. A road encircles the Cape binding all the coastal communities together.

The center of the Cape is a wild upland expanse where gigantic glacial boulders, the empty cellar holes of Dogtown — an early Cape settlement — and water-filled granite quarries offer mute testimony to the Cape's geological, historical and industrial pasts.

In the nineteenth century the excellent train service from Boston brought a new industry to Cape Ann: tourism. The summer visitors quickly fell under the same spell the Cape had cast upon the native New England stock, fishermen from Italy and Portugal, skilled quarry hands from Finland, and Irish laborers. Nowhere is that enchantment stronger than in Rockport.

The town lies in a hollow bowl that slopes down from wooded hills to a rocky shore. The woods are of beech and evergreen with an abundance of bird and plant life in season; the rocky shore gives over in places to sandy beaches and sheltered coves. The streets of the town follow the slope and contour of the hills; they are shaded by maples and elms and lined with trim white New England houses and weather-beaten fishermen's shacks. The white spire of the First Congregational Church, rising above the trees and the rooftops, is a benison on the scene below. The town has a blue and green look to it and a wonderfully tangy smell compounded of salt breezes, fishermen's gear, and evergreens warm in the sun.

And, because the town has managed to retain its essential character without stultification or self-consciousness, Rockport can be seen today much as it appeared to Bertha Everett Mahony when she lived there as a child in the 1880s and 1890s.

She was named Bertha after her mother's older sister who had died at seventeen, and Everett because she was the ninth generation of that American First Family, descending from Richard Everett of Essex County in England and Dedham, Massachusetts, in the New World.

Young Daniel was born two years after Bertha; their brother, George Everett, the following year. Named after his maternal grandfather, Major George Washington Everett, the boy was called Everett, shortened in the family to Ev. In 1887 Mary Mahony had her last child, a second daughter, Ruth Ellen; both grandmothers were Ellens and so was Mary's younger sister.

The Mahony family was unusually close. Some of Mary's relatives had not approved of her marriage to an Irishman, so that social intercourse within the family groups was limited. The children, so near in age and so happily divided into boy and girl pairs, were natural companions, sufficient unto themselves and requiring little of neighborhood friends to round out their play circle at home or in the Rockport woods. Bertha, by age and by nature the leader of the group, was often responsible for it as well, because of the frequent illnesses of her mother.

Yet in spite of Mary's frail health, it was she and Daniel who were the chief cohesive forces in the Mahony household. With gaiety, affection, and true gentleness, with a zest for life and a wonder at its beauties, they gave the children such a happy and interesting family life that there was little reason for them to turn elsewhere for security or excitement.

Mary Lane Everett was the daughter of Ellen Frances Lane of Annisquam and George Washington Everett of New London, New Hampshire. Already a farmer, George had proposed to become a barrister as well and, to finance his legal studies, had accepted a temporary teaching post in Annisquam. There he had met Ellen, married her in 1849 and soon thereafter carried her back with him to his farm in the foothills of the White Mountains some 125 miles northwest of Cape Ann. After a distinguished career as farmer, lawyer and civil servant — county solicitor and state legislator — Major Everett had died in the Civil War following the participation of his battalion, the Ninth Regiment of New Hampshire Volunteers, in the Siege of Vicksburg.

Mary, the middle child of the Everett five, was eight at the time of her father's death. She showed a marked talent for the piano and, helped by a Lane aunt and uncle, was able to study music in private schools in New Hampshire, learning to play both the piano and the organ. When she was ready to teach music herself, Mary chose to do so in Rockport rather than in New London, returning to the Cape where her mother had her roots and where so many members of the Lane family still lived.

Mary was not in the mold of the neighborhood piano teacher of the day. In addition to the learning of exercises and parlor pieces, she required her students to keep notebooks on the grammar of music: harmony, counterpoint, etc. Whatever her methods, she must have been a good teacher, for when she married Daniel Mahony in 1881 she had fifty pupils.

Daniel, at the time of his marriage, was the passenger agent and telegraph operator at the Boston and Maine Railroad Station in Rockport. He had had a hard childhood, the very antithesis of his wife's. His father, Patrick Mahony, had come to America from Cahirciveen in County Kerry, Ireland, in 1848 during the terrible potato famine. He left his wife Ellen behind, with his infant son, to follow him when he could send them passage money. It took him a year to save the required amount for, although he had had a good education by Irish standards, in Rowley, Massachusetts, where he chose to settle, Patrick could only find work upon the land. When he did send the money, Ellen, in complete ignorance of American geography, booked passage on a ship that landed her in Canada. It took her literally another year to work her way south to Patrick at Rowley. There, two more sons were born and at the birth of the third child, Daniel, in 1854, the mother died.

Daniel lived with various widows and maiden ladies all of his boyhood years, doing chores for the women in return for the shelter they gave him. He had the reputation of being a good boy and helpful, so foster homes were always open to him. He tried to put himself through Dummer Academy, but could not manage the combined expense of tuition, supplies and clothes to keep himself neatly dressed — always a matter of importance to him. He worked in the salt marshes in his adolescent years and attributed to that gruelling labor the tremor that was both a physical and psychological handicap in his later years.

The vignettes of Bertha's parents that follow are composites, made from several of her autobiographical sketches.

> The father — black-haired, heavy black eyebrows, and blue eyes — was a person of unusual quiet. His presence controlled the children without effort or oppressiveness for he was kindness itself. Though habitually quiet, grave and serious, he was capable of witty turns of phrase, flashes of fun, and on rare occasions a memorable storyteller. He was a careful person who disliked wastefulness or extravagance in any form. His judgment was so good and so fair that Town disputes of one kind or another were sometimes submitted to him for settlement. He had a passion for books, particularly history and poetry. He loved the world of out-of-doors and had green fingers [in the growing of flowers].
>
> Now the mother of this family was completely different from the father. She was a straight, slender woman with dark brown hair and grey-blue eyes. Her face was thin and her features clearly defined. She was gay, generous and extravagant, and loved sociability and fun. She was full of stories and merry conversation. Her very presence created for the children a kind of sparkle. And when she played the piano, as she did constantly and brilliantly, she seemed to be expressing in music the sparkle in herself.[2]

The Mahony house was filled with music, night and day. By day the students and their gifted teacher performed; by night a trio played in the parlor with Mary at the piano, her younger brother Johnny on the flute or the clarinet as was required, and a neighbor on the violin. It was good music they played; the mother's musical library included the works of Chopin, of Haydn, of Mozart and of Beethoven. In addition Mary sang about her household chores, a pleasant habit she passed on to both daughters.

From Bertha's infancy, Mary Mahony chanted Mother Goose

rhymes to her and sang the folk songs of the nursery. She had an unlimited supply of both to fit any occasion, to brighten a sour face, to banish a fear, or, most frequently, just for fun. From the chanting and the singing it was a natural step to the telling of the old folk and fairy tales. "Sleeping Beauty," "The Babes in the Wood," "Cinderella," "Tom Thumb" — Mary knew them all. In the children's favorite story their mother had her own special way of handling the fearsome line, "The better to eat you with, my dear!" At the words she would bend down to whatever child was in her lap at the time and with nibbles and kisses "eat" him or her into helpless laughter.

Mary also told the children about her own childhood in New London, giving them their first lesson in geography as well as a sense of their continuity with the past. She told them of farms on the slopes of Kearsarge Mountain, of picnics on Lake Sunapee and Little Sunapee, of snows far deeper and longer-lasting than those of Cape Ann, of studying at Colby Academy in New London and Miss Taylor's school in East Derry.

To help her children recall past Christmas celebrations and so put an edge on their anticipation of the returning holiday, Mary told them from Thanksgiving Eve to Christmas Eve a whole series of stories associated with the holy time.

> These firelit Christmas talks filled the children's minds with much wonder and with lovely images: — the strange journey of the shepherds led by the star to that stable in Bethlehem; Santa's reindeer and sleigh against the evening sky. Then there was the magical quality of the pine-scented sitting-room early on Christmas morning with the bulging Christmas stockings, the fascinating things placed about the chimney and the fairy feeling of Santa's having been there in the night. Every one of the four children now holds those days as a bright memory.[3]

Sometimes while Bertha and her mother were companionably engaged with bread or pie dough, Mary would spin out of her own fancy stories about one Violet Armstrong, a creature of irreproachable character and conduct. Violet was so real to Bertha that she was genuinely affronted when her sister was not named after the ravishing story friend.

The father told stories to the children, too. They were about his boyhood in Rowley: of the blueberry pastures there, of the marshes along the Parker River and the salt meadows where it flowed into Ipswich Bay, and of all the wonders of Plum Island. There was no bitterness in his stories at the hardships he had endured; indeed, there was no mention of hardships at all. He gave the children kindly stories of people, a feeling for their own personal history, and a third geographical area to add to the two they already knew: Cape Ann and New London.

Mary's storytelling was natural, bubbling, artless, as much a part of herself as singing and playing the piano. Daniel had more of the conscious storyteller's art: each story had a point; it was carefully constructed with a beginning and an end and travelled briskly in between; just before the point near the end he would hesitate, catch the children up in suspense and hold them there before releasing them to laughter with the climactic line.

If Daniel could only be persuaded to tell his stories "on rare occasions," he was ready at all times to read aloud to the children from the volumes of poetry he owned and loved. His taste ran to the sad and sentimental but, with teamplay born of long practice, the children learned how to divert him from such lugubrious selections as "Annie and Willie's Prayer" — which made their throats uncomfortably tight — to something more sprightly like "Darius Green and His Flying-Machine."

The storytelling was as constant in the Mahony ménage as was the mother's piano playing. Both were responsible in a way for Bertha's learning to read just before she was five. She had demanded piano lessons from her mother at that time, so that she, too, might make beautiful sounds from the family instrument. Mary was willing enough to teach the insistent little girl, but said that in order to play the piano, it was necessary first to know how to read. Both were easy to do; they would start the reading lessons at once. That was agreeable to the child, for in the family storytelling and reading-aloud she had known a reading-readiness program all the years of her short life. So, doubly motivated, Bertha settled down with her mother to acquire the skill that would be forever after a major source of joy to her. They used for their study a primer from the household's small library and they chose to sit for the daily lessons at the child's favorite window, where the ocean could be glimpsed diagonally down and across a meadow and a town street.

Every day they sat for a while at the window engaged
with the never-ending fascination of letters and words.

> The two younger brothers learned to read in the backwash of Bertha's excitement. Letters on the kitchen stove, on street signs, on locomotives [supplemented their lessons in the primer]. At seven, when Bertha went to school she could read, really read.[4]

Once acquired, the reading skill had to be put to use. There were few children's books in the Mahony home, but the father allowed Bertha to read from his cherished volumes of poetry cautioning her each time she removed one from the bookcase, "Handle it carefully, Bertha." Finally, after long examination, four of the books became the children's favorites:

> *A Treasury of the Poets* in two volumes with wood engravings, Thomas Moore's *Poems*, and a volume of Longfellow. The *Treasury* had one disadvantage: one volume contained a picture of the fearful end of the farmer at Bingen on the Rhine who hoarded his grain in time of famine. This picture could not be borne. Its location was carefully observed, and a goodly portion of the book sacrificed in order to pass it safely. Thomas Moore was bound in bright blue with a good deal of gilt, very small type and engravings; but in spite of the fine print, "Lalla Rookh" was read and re-read and some of the songs in it learned. . . . Longfellow was worn to pieces. "The Spanish Student" was dramatized and the production given on the carpenter's bench in the cellar and repeated Christmas Eve in the parlor for the family — by request of the players.[5]

It was a Christmas that brought the Mahony children the first book that was entirely theirs, a gift from Charles Bond, who sold Daniel the cigars for the station newsstand. It was a picture book about Indian life printed on coated paper. The children opened it out on the floor and told themselves stories from the pictures. The text had been read to them, but they abandoned it for the more satisfying details of the pictures and their own imaginations.

Bertha's real possession by books began when she was ten. She wrote movingly of the occasion in a *Horn Book* editorial:

> It was early on a Saturday morning in late winter years ago. Breakfast was just over but a little girl of ten had withdrawn to the parlor with a book. She was no sooner

settled than the door opened a little and a rich Irish voice said, "Since you've won the book as a prize, your mother says you may read it and not do your tasks." Then followed one never-to-be-forgotten day, a day filled to the brim with bliss, surprise and high excitement. The reading of *this* book was a revelation. She had not known before that one could by reading be transported so deeply into another world.

The book was *Little Women*. That special joy and delight have been had since from books, and from books only. There has been deep pleasure in solitary places in woods near the sea or in the country. There has been joy in friendship and love, and satisfaction in creative work. But the joy and delight in books have gathered up all these other joys and carried one into a wider, richer, freer existence; they have re-vitalized life.[6]

* * *

The sunny family life of her Rockport childhood was a well-spring experience from which Bertha took refreshment throughout her adult years. The out-of-doors country days that she enjoyed on the wooded hills of the town with Dan and Ev and Ruth — when the little sister was old enough — was another such experience, rich and ever-flowing. In writing in *The Horn Book* of others who had known similar joy, Bertha described her own:

> This reminded me of three children in another part of New England who also spent most of their free time during seven months of the year in the woods. . . .
>
> These woods were warp and woof of the three children's lives. . . . The sea was always there, as a part of the picture, a little remote, and very mighty. Occasionally a high and rare festival took place on its sands, arranged by grown-ups. But the woods were the children's own. They lived in the midst of the changes wrought by spring, summer, and fall. They came to know the brook by heart, and each year they followed it deeper and deeper into the woods. This yearly penetration farther up the brook, up the paths away from home, was one of the excitements of each summer.[7]

The brook, the trees, and the ever-present glacial boulders were the natural equipment of the children's playground. The brook, their road to adventure, was beautiful in itself with clear-flowing water and banks covered with ferns, jewelweed, and wild flowers in season. The boys quarried the outcroppings on the banks, calling them "ledges." Glacial boulders provided questing feet with stepping-stones in the brook and, under the trees, made furnishings for the girls' playhouses. They were also the props for a wild game the children had devised which they called "Duck on a Rock." It was similar to leapfrog except that the flying jumps were made over rigid boulders instead of the more yielding human back. The gray trunks of the beech trees marked off rooms in the playhouses, the branches offered shade, and the strong green leaves could be pinned together with twigs to fashion collars, caps and belts.

Bertha's first adventure in dressmaking concerned those leaves. She decided they would make costumes out of them to wear in the Horribles Parade on the Fourth of July. They used real pins but, alas, the leaves dried out and the pins slid out. Undaunted, Bertha soaked the garments in water the night before the parade, but that only added to their general state of disrepair. But the children wore them, clammy and tattered as they were.

On occasion, the familiar wooded playground took on fresh wonder. One January day when Bertha was quite small, she was carried into the woods and out upon the frozen brook. There was no sunshine; snow lay on the ground; the brook murmuring under the ice was the only sound in the profound stillness. Bertha longed to be put down, have her friends go away and leave her alone in the mysterious beauty of that gray, winter world.

Sometimes fear came into the woods, but, because it was self-induced, it was more enjoyed than otherwise.

> A certain reverberation of the earth, undoubtedly quarry blasting a few miles away, was said with great unction to be "a 'n'elefunt coming this way." Such was the power of suggestion that this picture dwelt on would send feet scurrying homeward — no reasons stated.[8]

Similarly, if a dog barked at night the children, safe in their beds, shivered with delicious fear and told each other that it was surely one of the wild dogs from Dogtown. That fear was half real and was only fully dispersed when, as teenagers in Bay View, they came to make the deserted village their second playground.

It was a rare Sunday for the children when Mary and Daniel Mahony went with their brood for a summer picnic in the woods. The outings were always held at The Third Pine on the Hill, the family's very own private picnic spot. After lunch the mother rested in a hammock strung between the beech trees and the father set forth with his children for a walk through the woods. Daniel walked gravely and silently, as was his nature, but his eyes were alert to the marvels of the natural world around him. These he pointed out to his children, not always able to call a flower or bird or tree by name, but that was of small consequence: there was no mistaking his wonder at the color of a flower, the sweep of a bird's flight, or the lacy pattern of a tree's branches. The children sensed the wonder and their own grew accordingly. Daniel Mahony, by example, taught his children not only to see nature's marvels but to behold their wonder as well. Bertha never forgot the lesson.

It was not so much the individual adventures that made the life out-of-doors in Rockport so wonderful for the Mahony children, but the fact that they were allowed to partake of it freely, on their own imaginative terms, with a minimum of adult supervision or interference.

To Bertha the woods also offered sanctuary where, if she chose, she could be alone. She sensed at an early age that the most ordinary experience had a deeper meaning for her and that she had to be alone to discover what the meaning was. She had to find herself in relation to the experience and from the revelation somehow dream or think or will her individuality into complete being.

Her favorite place to dream Longfellow's long, long thoughts of youth was on the brow of Squam Hill where Sadie Butman's cottage stood, little bigger than a birdcage among the beeches and called appropriately enough, Mount Airy. A great split boulder rested just outside the cottage's side door, its flat top accommodating easily a sitting or a standing child. From it Bertha had a great, wide sweeping view of the whole town of Rockport and the sea beyond and presently from the beauty of the scene came the inner quietude necessary even to a child's meditations.

> Childhood is the time when the eye to see is keenest; and impressions are deepest. . . . A child must be alone in the fields and woods for long periods of time to feel that oneness with nature which brings the truest joy. . . . Solitude may seem too mature a word to use with children, but . . . my own experience makes me know that some solitude is as necessary to children as it is to grown-ups.[9]

The town of Rockport itself offered adventures to the Mahony children, most of them centered around the station on Railroad Avenue where their father worked. All of the houses the family lived in on King Street, Summit Avenue and Granite Street were within short walking distances of the station. This was appreciated by the children who often, in a fit of boredom, ran to the station to see if a band had come in on a train. Why a band should so come or why it never did was unimportant: the power of suggestion was enough to send imaginations soaring and feet flying, much as it did when elephants trumpeted in the beech woods and dogs howled from Dogtown.

The children knew the names of all the locomotives at the station, even before they could read, and were on rare occasions allowed to ride in them when they were shifted at the roundhouse. At the roundhouse, in summer, they looked with pleasure — and some puzzlement — at the flower garden Daniel grew there after the fashion of station agents of the time. What puzzled the children was that only the engines could see the beautiful beds of lobelia, candytuft, sweet William, verbena, and fuchsia — so they called them "the locomotives' garden." The garden was Bertha's first experience with flowers planted formally with an eye to color and form.

Sometimes Bertha walked to the station alone to expound to the long-suffering apprentice telegrapher on the plans she had for giving plays there. After the spatial restrictions of cellar and parlor, the possibilities of the great cavernous shell seemed endless to the stage-struck child. Years later Bertha's interest in play production would lead indirectly to the establishment of her Bookshop for Boys and Girls, but nothing ever came of the earlier Rockport fantasy.

The Mahony children loved to walk the streets of Rockport with their father, for the same reasons that they enjoyed tramping with him through the woods: he made them aware, he taught them to see, and when needful he let them quietly alone to take what they could from a visual experience.

There was one walk Bertha took with Daniel the essence of which stayed with her all her life, much as did the memory of the wintry day in the beeches. She was very young at the time and only she and her father were involved. They had walked up and down and over the town's hilly streets until they reached the Miner Allen house on Pleasant Street. A black hitching-post boy stood in front of the house, at the curb. Bertha had never seen it before and the small figure fascinated the equally small child. She looked at it from every angle, felt of its substance, examined the detail of dress and form until at last she had figuratively made the statue a part of herself. Daniel Mahony waited patiently and silently until his daughter had completely satisfied herself. It was Bertha's first knowledge of black skin.

* * *

At just about the same time as the hitching-post boy incident, and while she was struggling through the primer lessons with her mother, another profound experience came to Bertha. When she was not yet five, she began regularly attending church services at the First Congregational Church. The experience was as much a source of wonder in her childhood as the reading skill and it helped Bertha, when she grew up, to evolve a personal faith and philosophy of life that had significance for her and were the bedrock upon which her bookshop and her magazine were founded.

Although Patrick Mahony had been a devout Catholic, walking ten miles from Rowley to Newburyport to attend Sunday Mass, he was also a liberal and admonished his son to respect all religious persuasions as different people's beliefs in the same thing. Possibly because of the pillar-to-post circumstances of his childhood, Daniel Mahony had no church affiliations at all. When it was time to consider a church for his own children, Daniel examined those at Rockport and, in his judgment, found the First Congregational Church "offering the best influences"—as he told his daughter in later years.

Bertha went to church each Sunday with Mr. and Mrs. Scripture who lived next door. The Scriptures were pillars of the church and somewhat awesome, but they let the little girl alone, so she felt comfortable with them. The mysticism of Bertha's Irish heritage responded at once to the beauty and the mystery of the new experience.

> The first impression received in church was that of many quiet, thoughtful faces. After that there were numerous things to absorb the interest of a child. The strange experience of hearing the united voices of a church filled with people reciting the Apostles' Creed, the gradual emergence of those words and their unconscious memorizing . . . like lines of nursery rhymes or phrases of a song. Often there was story interest in the scripture

> reading and always there was an arresting beauty, majesty, and mystery to the words.
>
> The choir and the organist were as endlessly interesting as a drama. A child loved the singing of hymns. And when it came to the sermon there were often bits which were clearly within her grasp. As for the rest, she reached for it — an important thing — and when she was tired reaching, she went off on thoughts and imaginings of her own.[10]

On occasion, because she was after all a very human little girl, Bertha's wayward thoughts led to amusing complications. Once she came out of church and, in a fine burst of Christian charity, invited every child in sight to the afternoon birthday party Mary Mahony was preparing for four children. Another time she emerged with a full-blown plan whereby an aquarium might be placed in every classroom in her school — she had been reading a book about aquaria the day before. On Monday morning she lay in wait for her teacher, who walked from her home in Pigeon Cove to the school in Rockport, to dazzle her with the brilliant scheme. A young man walked with the teacher, trying to court her. On Tuesday morning Bertha met the teacher at a point before she was joined by her suitor. On Wednesday morning Mary Mahony firmly put an end to the whole business.

Yet the memory of what she had heard in church stayed with Bertha to be examined in solitude as was her way with all experiences, all impressions.

> The biggest gains to this child were the mysteries she heard, the constant stirring of the impulse to wonder. And there was also the steady enlargement of understanding, the unconscious building of word sense and vocabulary. . . . The stories heard, the great wonders or mysteries could be carried out into the quiet woods and pondered. At night after supper, the child would make a point of finishing before the others in order to have some quiet time in the dark sitting-room to stand at her favorite window. There she would look across a meadow in the moonlight and get a glimpse of the ocean a half-mile away. Or, if the night were dark, would watch the stars, talking to herself and trying to grasp the sense of meaning and immensity; striving to penetrate all wonders, all mysteries.[11]

Shadows

UNTIL SHE WAS ELEVEN BERTHA'S happy childhood knew only three shadows: fear that all the trees in the world would be cut down to make room for the people, shame in her Irish name, and terror lest her mother die.

The ecological concern was minor, though important to the child. It was a great satisfaction to her to have a visitor assure her that where he lived there were many trees and that no one was cutting any of them down at all.

Her first brush with prejudice was not so easily disposed of, particularly since those responsible for it loved the child dearly and were equally beloved by her. They were her Grandmother Everett and her Aunt Nellie, as Mary's younger sister Ellen was called in the family. The widow and her unmarried daughter had left the New Hampshire home to live at first in Georgetown and then in Danvers, both in Massachusetts and both within easier travelling distance from Cape Ann than the New London farm had been.

Bertha felt the presence of the women in the Mahony home long before she was old enough to visit them in their own establishments. The grandmother wrote the child letters illustrated with pencil drawings and water-colors. To help the family during Mary's frequent illnesses, the women sent boxes of food, all the work of their own hands: graham bread, cookies, jellies and candies. Sometimes the boxes also yielded a beautifully knitted cap for Bertha or a new costume for her doll.

When Bertha did go to her grandmother's home she found there a rare understanding of children and their interests. Both grandmother and aunt, like Mary Mahony, were natural-born storytellers and they added the fine, rousing stories of the Old Testament to the child's growing collection.

The grandmother also told Bertha stirring tales of the sea captains who were a part of her Lane heritage: Captain David Lane and his cousin, Captain George Lane. Captain David was the grandmother's father and, as she told Bertha about him, she allowed the little girl to look at some of his papers: bills of lading, letters of recommendation, moving letters to his dear wife and children. They were all brown with age, the writing was fine and spidery, and the spelling highly individualistic. They were also tangible, dramatic links with Bertha's past.

Captain David Lane had been a highly respected master mariner who sailed merchant ships out of Boston to ports all over the world. In 1846 he had had a fearful crossing to Rotterdam and the following year saw the ship he desired to sail commissioned to his cousin. The Lane family believed it was those two factors that led him to take his own life in 1848. To provide a grave for the Captain's body, a group of Cape Ann citizens bought Jack's Hill, made of it a private cemetery, and re-named it Mount Adnah. The Captain lies just over the brow of the entrance hill in the burial ground; the great-granddaughter, who came to own his documents that she had fingered so carefully as a child, rests at the top of the hill.

Captain George Lane had not experienced the terrible 1846 gales that had so unnerved his cousin. He chose that year to marry Major Everett's sister, Mary, and abide at home with his bride. When he returned to sea he took his wife with him on all his voyages, sailing mostly to ports in the Orient. Mary Mahony was the namesake of Mary Everett Lane and both aunt and uncle were fond of their talented niece; it was they who had helped her gain her musical education. From Eastern bazaars the aunt sent beautiful materials back to her niece; there was a whole trunkful of the precious stuff in the Mahony sewing room and Bertha had many dresses from it made by her mother's skilful fingers. Her Great-Aunt Mary had died in India before Bertha was born, but the treasured yardage made her a living personality to the little girl.

In the Everett home there was another link with Mary Lane. She had once brought Nellie Everett an exquisite doll from Paris, with a dainty Parian head and dressed in pale green silk with an over-dress of lace. When Bertha visited, the doll was brought out, not to be played with, but for a wondering examination of its garments, so perfectly and so delicately made.

There *were* dolls to play with at the grandmother's. The aunt had cut a whole boxful of them from the colored fashion plates in *Godey's Lady's Book,* mounting them first on thin cardboard so that Bertha's small fingers might safely handle them. Queen Victoria was among the dolls with a variety of regal costumes; so were Tom Thumb and his wife — P. T. Barnum's real-life Tom Thumb, not he of Mary Mahony's storytelling.

Then, in the midst of so much loving-kindness, the shadow fell and Bertha Mahony tasted for the first time the bitterness of prejudice.

> There was something else gleaned at Grandmother's which was to trouble the child's later years, particularly the teens. She sensed in both Grandmother and Aunt a pride in family, and gathered as the years passed that Father was not important enough in this way.
>
> She observed that her last name was seldom spoken. She observed that Irish people and Catholics were looked down upon. And yet she knew that Grandfather Everett had helped some Irishmen to come to America, and they had repaid their passage money by work on his farm.
>
> As a result of the feeling engendered by Grandmother and Aunt, the child came to feel ashamed of her Irish name.[12]

Bertha was so baffled by the prejudices she could not understand that when she was eleven she determined to change her name just as soon as she came of age. Of course she did nothing of the sort, for shame does not sit well on a New England-Irish conscience and, when she went to live in Boston, she moved in a more sophisticated society that placed less importance on the circumstances of birth. Then, too, the general feeling in New England about Irish Catholics changed as the years went by. Whatever the reason, Bertha came in time to equate with pride both the New England and the Irish parts of her heritage, and the hurt caused by the earlier prejudices gradually fell away.

> There was another grief of the years before eleven — the fear that her mother would die. This fear began in her fifth year and continued until the dread event happened. . . . It waked her in the night as a recurring night-

> mare, and dogged her days. At night she stood at her mother's bedside and was enfolded and comforted. By day her mother sang or chanted [the fear away].[13]

Then, when Bertha was eleven, the shadow under which she lived for so many years became a tragic reality: Mary Mahony died just ten days before her thirty-eighth birthday. The death of the gay young mother who had made life sparkle for her children was a terrible blow to Bertha. The world became a changed place to the grieving child, clothes felt stiff and unnatural, even the sunshine was of a strange distillation. The mother died on September 20, 1893; the day marked also the end of Bertha Mahony's childhood.

ALMOST SIMULTANEOUSLY with the death of Mary Mahony another shock came to Bertha. Daniel Mahony left his agency with the Boston and Maine Railroad to work for the Rockport Granite Company. His new offices were in Bay View and, in order to be closer to them, Daniel moved his family to a company house in the back-shore village. Squam Hill, the beech woods, the brook, the station, the First Congregational Church, the distant sea — the whole familiar Rockport scene was gone, even as the mother who had been the most important part of it.

Yet Bertha discovered the new home was not without its own peculiar attractions. The house sat isolated on a drumlin hill left by the glacier and, from under a mansard roof, the front windows and a side piazza looked out over Ipswich Bay to the Massachusetts mainland. Hill, porch, windows and Bay gave Bertha a new wonder: magnificent sunsets over water. After dark, the navigational lights then on Plum Island shone through the night.

Directly below the hill during the day was an equally fascinating scene. There Polyphemus, the one-eyed railway engine of the Rockport Granite Company, brought the great granite slabs from the quarries for loading on the waiting boats. Docks and ships were covered with gray dust from the cutting, polishing, and loading of the granite; the blue Bay lay beyond them. When Bertha redecorated the sitting room of the new home, she did so in soft grays and blues, borrowing her colors from the granite-gray sea-blue view.

Woods and rocky, wild pastures came right up to the stone wall behind the house and the children ran in them as freely as they had in the beech woods in Rockport. Dogtown Commons became their second playground with the boulder-hopping game a real challenge there. On occasion, their cousin, Charles Alden Peabody, roamed the woods with the children and Bertha experienced for the first time the pleasure of showing a child the wonders her father had discovered to her. There were abandoned quarries in the woods, filled with water. In the winter the water froze and provided the Mahony children with private skating ponds.

Because Ipswich Bay was closer than the sea had been to their Rockport homes, the children added another dimension to their out-of-door life, traveling the length of the back-shore paths from Annisquam to Halibut Point. The horizon was wide at Bay View; the natural scene wild and varied. When the children ranged the woods and pastures and shores there, they came to feel that they owned the world.

Still, the Bay View years were difficult ones for Bertha. There were housekeepers at first, but the responsibility of the homemaking fell more and more upon her as she grew older, a grievous burden for an adolescent in high school. Her Aunt Nellie tried to help by continuing to send beautifully packed boxes of food, but she had married after the grandmother's death and was busy with her own family. Charles Alden was the younger of her two children, both boys. The uncle who had played the flute and the clarinet in Mary Mahony's trio came often on Sunday afternoons to visit the "little family," as he called it, always with a pocketful of peppermints for the children.

Daniel Mahony, aware of the troubling time his older daughter was experiencing, tried to help in his own sensitive way. Once he sent Bertha out into the woods with a quiet word so that she might have, alone, her first glimpse of a blue heron. Another time he directed her to the elderberry bushes by the stone wall so that she might see — again for the first time, and again alone — a flock of cedar waxwings feeding on the berries.

The sight of blue herons and cedar waxwings did indeed lift Bertha's spirit, as all out-of-door beauty did, and the concern of aunt and uncle supported her in her determination to keep the family home as her mother would have wanted it. The physical effort to do so, however, was more than her growing young body could sustain. In her junior year she was forced to withdraw from high school under pressure of the work and worry at home and the state of her own uncertain health. Daniel Mahony, a sensible man, could not allow that and he made arrangements whereby Bertha could return to her classes the following September.

The classes were at Gloucester High School, to which Bertha went and returned each day by trolley. The trolley schedule, the isolation of the Bay View house, and the responsibilities at home tended to restrict Bertha's social life. She was not without friends, however, for later in Boston her circle of acquaintances consisted in large part of former classmates from her high school days. In the final analysis, the limited social life may have been a blessing in disguise, for Bertha managed to graduate with her class in 1901 in spite of time lost, an outstanding student, maintaining a yearly average of 94 academically and 100 in deportment. She knew what she knew with a beautiful accuracy, so much so that the school's principal, Albert W. Bacheler, who was given to characterizing his pupils, called her "Little Saint Certainty."

There is in *The Horn Book* an appealing picture of Bertha struggling with one of her high school assignments:

> What the book would have meant to a girl of fifteen some years ago, on the afternoon of the first day of her second year of high school. On that particular day the girl was trying to make a beginning in her new year's Latin, and she was stuck fast in the opening lines of the *Aeneid.* The page looked so different from any of the pages of Caesar's *Gallic Wars.* She knew it was poetry, of course, but who Virgil was or what the *Aeneid* or why one read it, she knew not. What wonderful light and increased interest would have been cast upon the whole year's study if *The Winged Horse* [a study of poets and poetry] had been available to her![14]

Abby Merchant, a friend from the high school days, remembers Bertha as she appeared then: "She was a round-faced, pink-cheeked little person with exactly the same manner and way of talking that she carried through life. Her father and brother Dan were the same Irish type — black hair and blue eyes, although Bert's hair was modified to brown. All three had the same charm."[15] "The manner and way of talking" was brisk and eager in a light voice that was inclined to quaver.

After graduation from high school at nineteen, Bertha entered the Training Class of the Public Schools of the City of Gloucester to become a pupil-teacher. The purpose of the class was refreshingly direct as a statement from the *Fifty-Ninth Annual Report* of the school system indicated: "They [the pupil-teachers] are learning how to get acquainted with children — also the necessity of it. They are wrestling with one of the most difficult of school problems, that of bridging the chasm of years that separates the growth to which they have attained from the immaturity of the children whom they would serve."

Bertha spent a year in the Training Class but never went on to a teaching career, for late in 1901 Mr. Bacheler showed her the prospectus he had received from Simmons College for Women in Boston which proposed to hold its first classes in the fall of 1902. The kindly and discerning principal urged Bertha to apply for admittance to the College's School of Library Science which he felt would be just right for her. Bertha thought so, too, but there were no funds in the Mahony family to sustain a four-year program of college studies. It was essential that Bertha become self-supporting just as soon as she possibly could. Therefore she applied instead to be admitted to the College's School of Secretarial Studies as a special one-year graduate student. In its early years, the College encouraged such students with advanced standing and accepted Bertha, in part because of her excellent scholastic record, and in part because of the pupil-teaching experience.

The College held its opening-day exercises on October 9, 1902 in the assembly hall of the dormitory building on St. Botolph Street. The President, Dr. Henry Lefavour, welcomed the students to a college that "is unique, in that it is the first to stand in New England for a utilitarian education for girls, while aiming not to neglect any influence that may broaden the students' outlooks and deepen their lives. What our idea may accomplish, however, will be determined by you young women."[16]

There were in the hall before Dr. Lefavour one hundred and twenty-five of the young women to whom he referred, the first daughters of Simmons College. Bertha Everett Mahony was one of them, eager for the new experience and the promise it held out to her of early financial independence. No one in the Convocation could have known then how the idea of the College would be accomplished in her distinguished career.

College and "University"

But yield who will to their separation,
My object in living is to unite
My avocation and my vocation
As my two eyes make one in sight.
Only where love and need are one,
And the work is play for mortal stakes,
Is the deed ever really done
For Heaven and the future's sakes.

— Robert Frost. From "Two Tramps in Mud Time"

Simmons College

IT WAS PARTICULARLY RIGHT that Bertha Mahony should have been in the first class at Simmons College, for she was to be a self-made woman as the school's founder had been a self-made man.

John Simmons was a nineteenth-century Boston merchant whose industry and sagacity enabled him to make two fortunes in his lifetime. The first derived from his men's clothing store, where in the 1830s he began to manufacture ready-made suits for men, a revolutionary idea in the clothing industry. The second came from the downtown Boston real estate in which he shrewdly invested the profits of his clothing business after he retired from it in 1854. When he died in 1870 at the age of seventy-four, John Simmons left an estate totaling almost two million dollars.

Tragically, there were no male heirs to carry on the Simmons name. It was that circumstance, according to Kenneth Mark in his history of the school, that led John Simmons to found a college. "It is generally agreed by the family that he wished the name of Simmons perpetuated . . . and that he found in the establishment of Simmons Female College a means of accomplishing his desire."[1]

Dr. Mark suggested an explanation of why Simmons was designated specifically and exclusively "female." When John Simmons manufactured his ready-made suits, he had them cut in his shop and the pieces sent out to be sewn by women in their homes. He took a personal interest in the women and often visited them in Roxbury and the South End, thus coming to know well the circumstances of the untrained and uneducated female worker of the day. By founding Simmons Female College, John Simmons was able "to make a return to that class of women by whose labor as seamstresses he had laid the foundation of his own fortune."[2]

Delayed by the great fire of 1872 which destroyed many of the Simmons' properties, the College was not founded until 1899. Three years later it offered, in rented quarters, its first curricula as organized in four schools: Household Economics, Library Science, General Science, and Secretarial Studies.

The School of Secretarial Studies gave a four-year course for undergraduates and a one-year advanced course for college graduates to prepare them for such positions as office assistants, private secretaries, registrars and teachers of commercial subjects. Both graduate and undergraduate courses were, in the vernacular, "stiff." The one-year students were expected to maintain the same standard of excellence and achieve the same degree of accuracy as the four-year matriculants. Degrees were not awarded the graduate students until they had completed six months of satisfactory work, vouched for by their employers. "Insistence on a meticulous discipline was the outstanding characteristic of the School."[3]

Excellence, accuracy and discipline were not foreign to Bertha Mahony's educational pattern; still, it was remarkable that with only a high school diploma and one year of pupil-teaching, she was able to complete the advanced course with college graduates and do so with distinction. In the vault of Simmons College is one small three-by-five card that records, in fine Spencerian handwriting, Bertha's scholastic achievements at the School as well as the chief events in four years of her life:

Mahony, Bertha Everett
Secretarial adv.
Oct. 1902 20½

Shorthand	A	A
Typing	A	A
Sec. Subjs.	B	B
Lib.	C+	

Special Student for 1 year
1/30/04 Clerk, Rockport Granite Company
10/04 New Library, 591 Boylston Street
12/06 Women's Educational and Industrial Union

Yet the record card does not tell the whole story of Bertha's year at Simmons for she had experiences other than scholastic. During the school year, despite the weight of the abstracting and cataloging chores included in the "Lib." course, she found time to read. On Copley Square, convenient to her classrooms on nearby Huntington Avenue, was the New Library, a lending library with an unusually good selection of non-fiction as well as fiction titles. Bertha borrowed books constantly from the library and became well acquainted with its owner.

Bertha also joined the Women's Educational and Industrial Union. "It gave me a wonderful sense of pride to join this organization. It seemed to me I had somehow allied myself with wide social and educational forces of the world."[4] The Union, at 264 Boylston Street, was within easy walking distance from Bertha's classes as well as the New Library, and offered the college student, whose finances were limited, free lecture series, discussion groups, and special classes as well as restaurants with reasonable prices.

Friendships, too, were made at Simmons. One, especially long-enduring, was with Mildred Barber who came to the College like Bertha as a one-year advanced student, but in the School of Household Economics where she took a special course in Institutional Management. Mildred was a Smith College graduate with an A.B. degree. The differences in their ages and educational backgrounds did not prevent the two women from becoming warm friends and remaining such for fifty-one years.

"Since secretarial work was not my real interest, after finishing the year at Simmons, I found it difficult to place myself in a business office."[5] Because of that difficulty, Bertha went back to Cape Ann after her graduation to be with her father in the offices of the Rockport Granite Company. Then, in October of 1904, the proprietor of the New Library offered her a position as assistant in the bookshop. That was more to Bertha's liking and she returned to Boston to work in the library she knew well from her student days.

The library had a large clientele of good readers attracted by its excellent stock and Bertha had there her first heady taste of working with people and books. Her efforts must have been satisfactory for, after only eight months in the shop, she was left in charge while the owner went off on extended vacations at her summer home in New Hampshire.

The experience would have been completely satisfying to

Bertha except for one jarring note: her employer, in spite of her apparent confidence in her young assistant, treated Bertha as an inferior. The treatment may have derived from Bertha's youth, the name Mahony, or just from the small spirit of a woman who took advantage of an inexperienced girl. In any case, the indignity was a bitter one for Bertha to bear, especially since she had not yet fully recovered from the Irish-Catholic prejudices of her youth. "A new experience, this caused me so much unhappiness that it darkened my life."[6] Fortunately it was not to be endured for long.

Among the patrons of the New Library was the Secretary of the Women's Educational and Industrial Union, Harriet I. Goodrich. One day Miss Goodrich told Bertha of an opening in her office for an Assistant Secretary and suggested that she apply for it. Bertha had great respect for the organization to which she already belonged and she felt that there would be real purpose to secretarial work done within the framework of the Union's educational and social service program. Then, too, Mildred Barber had gone from Simmons to become the director of the Union's numerous lunch rooms and Mary Eager, another Simmons classmate, had become her assistant. If Bertha went to the Union, the three college friends and classmates would also be co-workers — a pleasant prospect indeed.

Bertha applied for the position at once and was accepted. She took up her duties in 1906 thus beginning "an association which was to prove of first importance in my life. The Union proved to be a kind of University to me."[7]

The Women's Educational and Industrial Union

THE UNION where Bertha Mahony ultimately earned the title of Bookwoman was a venerable and honorable Boston institution, a non-profit social service agency that had served the city's women well for twenty-nine years. Concern for the working woman had been a motivating force in the founding of Bertha's "university," as it had been with her college. It seemed singularly right for her, a working woman, to attend Simmons; it seemed equally so for her to become associated with the Women's Educational and Industrial Union.

The Union had come into being on the first wave of the Women's Liberation Movement which swept across the country in the 1870s. The reform and feminist groups of those days were made up of women of means and education who deeply resented the economic and social barriers that kept so many of their less fortunate sisters untrained, uneducated, and impoverished. In Boston a pioneer woman physician, Dr. Harriet Clisby, determined to do something about women's plight in the city and in 1877 persuaded forty-seven other public-spirited women to join her in founding the Women's Educational and Industrial Union for the stated purpose "of increasing fellowship among women in order to promote the best practical methods of securing their educational, industrial and social advancement."[8]

In its work on behalf of women the Union established early two patterns of operation: to give the formidable weight of its support to any needed social or educational reform, and to all city and state legislation concerned with the welfare of women and children; and to demonstrate itself how a piece of work could and should be done, turn the functioning operation over to a responsible agency, and move forward to fresh experimentation in new areas. Simmons' School of Household Economics had been the Union's School of Housekeeping; the Legal Aid Society of Boston had begun as the "law" part of the Union's Law and Thrift Department. The pioneering policy kept the Union from becoming static through the years, continuously moving forward with the times, and sensitive to the changing needs of the community it served.

The Union helped Boston's women in two other ways: it established consignment shops to provide outlets for the products women made in their homes, using its share of the profits to support its social service and educational projects; it conducted all manner of programs and offered all kinds of services of interest and benefit to its membership. The membership stood at 400 when the Union's first rooms were opened on Park Street; when Bertha Mahony became its Assistant Secretary, the Union was providing programs and services to a membership of 4,000 from its Back Bay buildings on Boylston Street across from the Public Garden.

At that time Mary Morton Kehew was serving the Union as its third president. Mrs. Kehew was a prominent Boston woman of forceful character and tremendous energy, who was sought after by every important educational and social service institution in the city to serve on its board of directors. She had been a member of the Corporation responsible for the organization of Simmons College. The innumerable board associations made it possible for her to channel the energies of the Union into promising activities as she became aware of them. Her capacity for leadership and friendship assured the success of any endeavor she proposed at the Union, for during the quarter century she served it she gathered around her loyal and enthusiastic women eager to bring her plans to fruition.

The administrative body of the Union was an Executive Committee which met twice a week under the chairmanship of Mrs. Kehew. One of Bertha's secretarial responsibilities was to record the minutes of the Committee's meetings, a task that proved to be a combined course in organizational methods, group management, and executive procedures. It also brought her to the attention of Mrs. Kehew who, characteristically, made time to listen to the ideas of the Union's youngest and newest employee and to encourage her in her work.

At the Committee meetings Bertha also came under the influence of Helen Peirce, a Cape Ann compatriot from Gloucester and the Treasurer of the Union. Mrs. Peirce's business judgment was sound; her business ethics impeccable. By simply listening to her at the meetings Bertha learned much about prudent financial management. Since she herself said she had inherited her mother's extravagant ways rather than her father's careful thriftiness, the "course" in economics and finance was helpful.

Bertha also recorded the meetings of the Advisory Committees of the Union and since every department, every endeavor, and every committee had its own Advisory Committee of knowledgeable Bostonians to guide it, the task was Herculean. Yet the meetings were never routine to her in her early secretarial years; through them she came in contact with some of Boston's finest minds and to a clearer understanding of the full extent of the Union's involvement in the welfare of the city's women and children. To understand better the work of the various committees, she began to read widely in the fields of economics, sociology and education.

The extent of Bertha's capabilities was quickly recognized at the Union, particularly her essential creativeness. So that she might bring that to bear upon her work, a new responsibility was given to her: the handling of the Union's publicity and advertising and the preparation of its informational leaflets. Bertha had to gather the data for the latter, write the copy, and then see it printed by either the Union's own press or that of Thomas Todd. The Todd establishment was, and is, diagonally across the Garden and the Common from the Union at the crest of Beacon Hill. Mr. Todd, a discriminating printer and a gentle man, taught Bertha the physical make-up of a printing job and how to talk with him about it in the terms of the printing trade.

Bertha was also encouraged in her creative plans to give plays for children under the sponsorship of the Union's Employees' Association. The Association was a particularly lively and self-expressive group during Mrs. Kehew's presidency and Bertha served it in various official capacities, as did her Simmons classmate, Mary Eager. The plays began modestly in 1910 with a series of Alice-in-Wonderland divertissements. The sketches were so well received that The Children's Players was created to present a real play the following year in one of Boston's commercial theatres — a far cry from Bertha's Rockport cellar and parlor presentations and the play-in-the-depot fantasy.

Bertha acted in the Alice sketches and in the first play; thereafter she withdrew from the stage to become the Associate

Chairman of the Executive Committee of the little company. Skilled amateurs took over the acting roles, recruited mostly from the ranks of the drama students at Radcliffe and Harvard. Professor George P. Baker, the Director of The 47 Workshop of Harvard, was on the Advisory Committee of The Children's Players.

One of the responsibilities of Bertha's Executive Committee was to discover good plays for the annual productions. The Committee found there was a dearth of such material and forthwith launched a playwriting contest to produce some. Until the contest brought results, the Committee members began to search in children's books for material suitable for dramatization. That search exposed Bertha Mahony for the first time in her life to the whole field of modern children's literature. It was a burgeoning field, even in the early 1910s, due in large part to Mary Mapes Dodge and her *St. Nicholas Magazine*, that seedbed of children's books.

The search produced results, but not those anticipated: it yielded no dramatic possibilities, but instead brought about the demise of The Children's Players in 1915. Bertha explained how that happened in a paper she read before the American Booksellers Association in 1917:

> Those who had most to do with this work finally came to feel that children do not need the theatre, that good reading taste gained by them as children and their very occasional attendance at the best dramatic productions for grown-ups will take care of good adult dramatic taste. They came to feel that "the book's the thing." They were aided, no doubt, in arriving at this conclusion by their study of children's books during those four years [of giving plays] and by the discovery that the field of good books for children is such a rich one.[9]

The Children's Players was gone, but the interest in children's books haunted Bertha until a simple event in the late summer of 1915 brought it out of the shadows into sharp focus, to become thereafter one of the major concerns of her life. She read an article by Earl Barnes, "A New Profession for Women," in the August *Atlantic Monthly*. The profession Mr. Barnes described was that of bookwoman, the female owner and proprietor of her own bookshop.

Mr. Barnes found a discrepancy in America's culture between the people who could read and the number of those who bought books to do so, and attributed that discrepancy to the inadequate distributive facilities of the book trade. He also found a great number of young women unemployed after college graduation because they did not care to teach, become librarians, or enter social service. Those women would make perfect bookshop proprietors, Mr. Barnes stated: they came from good families, were esteemed in their communities, and were bookish by background and education.

The last paragraph of Mr. Barnes' article spoke directly to Bertha. The language was that of the Union, the philosophy of service to others was in complete harmony with her own.

> It [a bookshop] would give young women of ability and devotion a wide range of useful exercise for their talents. As industrial agents they would be handling goods that would make for larger intelligence and for social betterment. They could help individuals and the community at large. The work would be active and varied but not too laborious; and they would be meeting men and women under conditions of freedom and security which might naturally lead to their largest possible life. Even if it did not, it would still be an interesting and useful life, independent of the caprice of directors, and admirably fitted for youth, middle age, and old age.[10]

Bookwoman. That was the profession for Bertha Mahony. She knew it instantly and irrevocably after reading Mr. Barnes' article. All that was in her past was prelude to the recognition of this absolutely right career for her: the love of the word instilled in her from childhood by the constant storytelling and reading aloud in the family circles, the training in office skills at Simmons, the work with books in the New Library, the observation of administrative and financial ways at the Union, and the introduction to children's literature through The Children's Players.

Bookwoman. That was the "real interest" Bertha had been searching for from her graduation day at Simmons. She was already a bookwoman by avocation; now she should become one by vocation as well, uniting interest and work in one career. The idea that the career should be devoted to children's books was a little slower to surface, but surface it did in its own good time, and with its realization Bertha Mahony was launched at last on her life's work in behalf of children and their books.

The Bookshop for Boys and Girls

It does not seem possible that there can be any profession with greater satisfactions, a higher daily excitement or a more vital sense of the surging tides of life than that of a bookman in a bookshop. Everything is grist which comes to his mill. And his commodity, his stock in trade, is unique, because between the covers of his books are records of life; records made significant by means of art.

Because of the peculiar character of books and the joy of work with them, the profession of books lays a special obligation upon bookmen, the obligation to understand and to know; to develop an awareness for varied human needs, and a special appreciation of creative power.

Fjeril Hess's new book . . . carries to the reader the joy of work in a bookshop when the bookman's obligation is discharged with taste, resourcefulness, and imagination. Then the bookshop stands a glowing spot in the community, making for the increase of understanding, good will and art.

— Bertha Mahony Miller. From a *Horn Book* editorial [1]

A Time of Change

BERTHA'S PAST SEEMED a perfect prelude for a future as the proprietor of a bookshop; moreover, there were indications in 1914 that she was in need of a change of occupation, possibly even of scene. In the diary she kept fitfully from 1914 through 1918 Bertha often referred to being "so weary," "depressed," "tired to death," and "heart as heavy as lead." That behavior pattern of exhaustion and low spirits was totally uncharacteristic of a woman usually full of fun and an eager zest for life. It had its roots in both her work and in certain circumstances of her personal life.

The weariness was frequently noted following sessions with Union committees. Clearly, after ten years at the task, Bertha had grown beyond the mechanical recording of committee meetings, however interesting their subject matter might be. In 1914 she felt such a vague dissatisfaction in the restrictive secretarial work — The Children's Players and the publicity duties notwithstanding — that she wrote to the State Superintendent of Schools in Maine about teaching opportunities there. Nothing came of the inquiry, but it was a straw in the wind of her discontent.

In 1914 also she was obliged to become involved in a Union project that troubled her exceedingly. The Union proposed to run Saturday morning movies for children in order to give them the best efforts of the new communication medium. Bertha was asked to direct the project, but declined because she thought it was too big an undertaking for the Union to handle. She could not dissociate herself entirely from the activity, however, for she was responsible for its publicity and she had to record the committee meetings held in relation to it. Each meeting left her more depressed than the one before. Her judgment that the project would eventually sink under its own weight was predicted by an entry from her diary: "Pictures for children started with a whoop this A.M. 1,800 present."[2]

The feeling of restlessness was intensified in 1915, when two of Bertha's friends and co-workers announced they were leaving the Union. Abby Merchant's sister, Helen, planned to withdraw from the Law and Thrift Department and set up her own investment service agency in New York City; Mildred Barber expected to assume her new duties as Manager of the Boston Women's City Club on January 1, 1916. Helen and Bertha could continue to meet during summer vacations on Maine's Monhegan Island, which they both loved, and Mildred would only be across the park from the Union on Beacon Street. Still, the easy, casual, day-by-day relationship of women in the same work scene would be gone and its loss was not anticipated with pleasure.

There had been a great loss in Bertha's own personal life. In 1911 Daniel Mahony had died, the gentle father who had given his older daughter such intuitive understanding and had taught her to see and wonder at all natural beauty. Family responsibilities had sloughed off, too, with the passing of the years. Dan and Ev had both married and were preoccupied with their own households and businesses. Ev worked for a time for the Rockport Granite Company and continued to live in the Bay View house; then he established his own insurance agency in Gloucester and moved there with his wife, the former Kathryn Cleary. Dan was making a career for himself with the New England Telephone Company; he and his wife, Abigail Whelton Mahony, lived in the Back Bay area of Boston near the Simmons College building on The Fenway.

Ruth was busy with social service work for the Boston Children's Aid Society and independent of the sister whose concern she had been for so many years. That Ruth could work at all was a major miracle accomplished primarily by Bertha's devotion, patience and determination, for Daniel Mahony's familial tremor had appeared in Ruth in her adolescent years in a greatly aggravated form. A Boston neurologist diagnosed the tremor as an incurable degenerative lesion of the physical nerve centers and predicted that the young girl would be an invalid in six years' time.

After twelve months had passed with no further deterioration apparent, Bertha refused to accept the neurologist's prognosis and persuaded Ruth to come into Boston for a series of psychiatric treatments with Dr. James Jackson Putnam, one of the first American psychiatrists to study in Europe with Freud. Ruth was withdrawn and anti-social at the time, but she consented at last to the analysis, which consisted of daily interviews with Dr. Putnam over a five-month period.

The psychiatrist, disagreeing also with the neurologist's prediction, proposed to lead Ruth to an understanding of how she might live a useful and rich life in spite of the tremor, and to an unselfconscious acceptance of the handicap. The first he accomplished; the latter he could not. When Dr. Putnam felt he had done all he could for Ruth, he talked with Bertha about possible work for her and liked the suggestion of social service work with children. Ruth proved to have a natural aptitude for the work as Bertha had anticipated and, after various courses and training periods, moved from volunteer assignments to work with the Boston Society for the Care of Girls and then to the Children's Aid Society. There she quickly gained a reputation as one of the Society's most able field workers.

Madge Haskell of Annisquam knew both of the Mahony sisters from the time of Bertha's high school days. She wrote the following thoughtful sketch of Ruth and of her relationship with Bertha: "Ruth resembled Bertha but she was prettier and taller. She had big blue eyes with heavy dark lashes and brown hair that looked black because her skin was very white. She was slender, giving the impression of frailty, but had a strong, positive voice especially when she brought Bertha back to earth from her dreaming. A brief remark or question would cut off Bertha's imagining; the sisters would look at each other, then burst into laughter. She balanced Bertha, though not influencing her."[3]

In 1914 Ruth's dependence on Bertha had eased as she went about her social service assignments with increasing confidence and pride. It seemed possible that Bertha might even entertain thoughts of leaving Boston to work elsewhere, if she so chose. The thought of teaching in Maine had come from that realization.

Bertha did want to get away from Boston to escape from a frustrating romance that had gone on for years, but refused to resolve itself one way or another. She was deeply in love with a man who was destined to find his happiness with another woman. Bertha and R. had met in high school and were frequently together at the Union where R., a lawyer, served on the Advisory Committee of the Law and Thrift Department.

The bittersweet, very feminine story runs through almost the whole of the five-year diary: an encouraging evening at the theatre with R. sent Bertha flying out the next day to spend fifteen dollars on a second hat which she did not need at all; a letter from him was cherished unopened all morning to be savored alone at lunch; evening walks on the Charles River Esplanade brought about "chance" meetings — the meetings made Bertha "all feeling and no mind," as she put it; when R. joined the army for service in World War I, Bertha knitted him yards of neck scarves and socks by the gross.

When the end finally came to the one-sided romance in 1917, it was not unexpected, as a poignant entry in the diary indicated:

> I'm trying to make myself drink down the bitter draft, drink it thoroughly that R. does not care at all for me. It seems like cutting off a very important part of me. Is just now unbearable. Then, too, I pity myself because I realize, or I feel, that if this could work out as I want that I sh'd be a different person — full of life and fun and joy. I seem now like a good enough house but with neglected grounds. I know under other conditions I could grow most lovely gardens. Now the thing which concerns me is how to grow the gardens in spite of discouragement. I must turn my mind first of all toward my work & then toward my friends.[4]

The friends were largely co-workers at the Union and a small circle of men and women who had been together in the Gloucester High School. Mildred Barber was unquestionably closest to Bertha during those years. Besides working together, the two women for years had rooms in the same house on Acorn Street, a narrow cobblestone way that plunges down Beacon Hill in the general vicinity of Louisburg Square. When Ruth came in for her analysis with Dr. Putnam, Mildred made room for the younger girl in her quarters, since Bertha's hall bedroom could scarcely accommodate her own single bed. Later, when Ruth began to work in Boston, the three women took a comfortable apartment together on the level part of the Hill area where Ruth could get around more easily.

Mildred shared Bertha's zest for life, with an added flair for the unusual adventure. In 1914 she persuaded Bertha to take a canoe trip with her on the Charles River over the Labor Day weekend. They paddled sixty miles in the four-day period, waded rapids dragging their full canoe behind them, made two carries, camped out at night, and recorded in Bertha's diary long Whitmanesque catalogs of the wildflowers they were seeing. It was a strange, brave journey for two young women to undertake alone in 1914, especially since one of them — Bertha — could not swim.

Bertha was used to being on the Charles in boats, however, with either R. or with two other friends from the Gloucester school days: Harry Burnham, a lawyer like R., and Charles Hodgkins, an architect. Besides Bertha and Ruth, Harry and Charles and R., the Gloucester circle included Abby and Helen Merchant and Madge Haskell.

The Cape Ann friends found their pleasure in the theatre; in shared summer holidays on Monhegan Island; in walks around Boston and out into the country; in outings on the Charles; in dining at The Women's City Club or The College Club on nearby Commonwealth Avenue, or at Moseley's Boathouse in West Roxbury; in talking about the books they were reading, or, increasingly, as the shadow turned into substance, about World War I.

In 1915 some of the talk concerned Bertha's idea of establishing herself in a bookshop of her own, possibly outside of Boston, even outside of New England. Washington or Oregon was suggested, because the Pacific coastal states were reputed to look like New England. Harry Burnham, more sensitive than the others to Bertha's need to leave Boston, urged her to have the courage to go West, even offering to loan her the capital she would need to start her business. Accordingly, Bertha wrote to the Chamber of Commerce of Portland and of Tacoma, asking about the cities as possible locations for a bookshop.

Scarcely were the letters posted, when the thought of leaving New England "shook the foundations of life completely," as Bertha described it in one of her autobiographical essays. She continued:

> An immediate decision was made: this new bookstore must be in New England. Various important New England cities were visited with the result that another decision was reached: the new bookstore must be in Boston. But Boston was well served with bookstores. . . . Suddenly, on account of the work with plays for children, I thought, "Why not have a bookshop for children in Boston?" The moment the bookshop was thought of in this way it came clear. . . . The dream took on a kind

> of substance and vigor. It seemed bound to come into being. The ways and means were not nearly so clear as the vision![5]

It was the Women's Educational and Industrial Union that provided the "ways and means" for Bertha to translate her vision into splendid reality.

The Founding of the Bookshop for Boys and Girls

NONE COULD COUNSEL Bertha more wisely on the ways and means of a business venture than Mrs. Kehew and Mrs. Peirce. Because they had always encouraged her confidence, Bertha had no hesitancy in asking for their advice on the practical aspects of her bookshop dream. At first the two Union executives were dubious of the whole thing, fearful of financial entanglements for "the child," as they affectionately called their Assistant Secretary. Then as Bertha grew eloquent, inspired by her own vision and their responsive listening, their interest quickened and they came finally to believe in the soundness of the plan. Indeed their faith was so strong that they asked Bertha to establish the bookshop under Union sponsorship, seeing it as a valid piece of fresh educational effort and an additional source of income for the Union's social service work.

Since Bertha's persuasiveness had won them over, Mrs. Kehew and Mrs. Peirce cannily sent her to plead her own cause with the Union's Board of Government, which would have the final decision in the matter. That was a formidable task, for it would be costly to establish the shop and the Board members were conservative New Englanders. Bertha foresaw the difficulty and was able to present them with a plan whereby certain publishers had agreed to provide stock on a consignment basis for the first three years of the bookshop's operation. Moreover, Mrs. Kehew and Mrs. Peirce had volunteered to cover any initial deficits the shop might incur. Confronted by Bertha's contagious enthusiasm and her advantageous business arrangements, the Board capitulated and very late in the fall of 1915 approved of the establishment of the Bookshop for Boys and Girls as a Department of the Women's Educational and Industrial Union.

Monday, October 9, 1916 was chosen as the opening day of the Bookshop and toward the accomplishment of that felicitous event Bertha turned the concentrated power of all her energies. Her preparations fell into six categories: a study of children's literature, the placement of book orders with publishers, the compilation of a buying guide of selected children's books for the convenience of customers, the training of a staff for the shop, an exploration of the book field beyond the Boston area, and the procurement of quarters capable of being turned into the kind of bookshop Bertha had in mind.

The study of children's books was made under the direction of Alice M. Jordan, with whom Bertha had become acquainted in her search for play material in the Children's Room of the Boston Public Library on Copley Square. Miss Jordan's appointment, in 1902, as the Children's Librarian of the room, had been one of the first of its kind in the country. Miss Jordan used two lists to guide Bertha's reading: *Books for Boys and Girls*, compiled by Caroline M. Hewins out of concern for the children she served as Librarian of the Hartford Public Library in Connecticut; and *The Bookshelf for Boys and Girls*, prepared under the direction of Clara Whitehill Hunt, the Superintendent of Work with Children at the Brooklyn Public Library.

Each Saturday morning the two women met to discuss the books Miss Jordan had assigned for Bertha to read the week before. Bertha's judgment of children's books was formed in those tutorial sessions with a librarian who read widely in all fields; a woman whose clarity of self-expression derived from a disciplined mind and a serene spirit; and a critic who evaluated books objectively, associatively, and, above all, with wit and good humor.

From her study with Miss Jordan and with her two reading lists to help her, Bertha began to write orders for her book stock. The standards of book selection she had set herself were stringent. She had determined to have in the Bookshop only those titles that would provide children with the best of writing and the best of illustration. She could not be dissuaded from her support of excellence even by Miss Jordan, who doubted that a commercial establishment could exist under such a restrictive policy, noble and praiseworthy as it might be.

Bertha was helped in the clerical preparation of her orders

by the two Union employees who were to be her assistants in the Bookshop: Margaret E. Sayward and Alma W. Howard. Miss Sayward, a professional storyteller, had been connected with The Children's Players, as Bertha had suggested that before the presentation of each new play, Miss Sayward tell the story of the drama to the sponsoring group of patrons in an effort to stimulate ticket sales. Miss Howard took a summer course in children's literature at Simmons to prepare herself for the Bookshop duties.

When the books arrived from the publishers, the two assistants checked them against the orders they had written, and then made from them a card catalog for use in the Bookshop. The multiple handling of each title was fortunate, for it gave them a thorough knowledge of the stock, and since the books were to be arranged by subject in the shop, such a knowledge was imperative for easy selling.

Miss Sayward and Miss Howard also worked with Bertha on the buying guide of selected children's books, which she had determined to distribute simultaneously with the opening of the Bookshop. No such commercial list had ever been published. The list was to be her primary piece of publicity; it was expensive to do and she took much criticism for undertaking it before the shop was fairly established. Yet Bertha persisted, basing her judgment on the years of experience she had had in handling the advertising and publicity of the Union. She was convinced the list would repay its cost in book orders; she was hopeful that it would bespeak the spirit of the Bookshop in the careful selectivity of its titles.

The list was called *Books for Boys and Girls — A Suggestive Purchase List* and within its 110 pages some 1,200 children's books were grouped, first into two general age categories and then by subject matter. Most of the titles had brief descriptive notes, and the monotony of the listing was relieved by quotations and illustrations from children's books. While it was a sober list in appearance, in concept it was unique.

The next step in her Bookshop preparations was for Bertha to become acquainted with some of the pioneer personalities working in the field of children's books outside of The Hub area. In the spring of 1916, with the details of book orders and purchase list in the capable hands of her staff, Bertha left Boston for visits to Indianapolis, Chicago, New York and Hartford. That was her first journey alone beyond New England state lines and she "was really frightened. Friends came to see me off and as the train moved slowly out one friend called up to me, 'People are much the same everywhere, Bertha!' "[6]

The Stewart Bookstore in Indianapolis was the initial stop on Bertha's pilgrimage. She had been invited to spend a week with Frederic G. Melcher, the store's manager, to observe the mechanics of his operations and to examine the department of children's books which he had established. Mr. Melcher's interest in books for boys and girls was not new. It had begun during the eighteen years of his association with the Lauriat Bookstore on Washington Street in Boston. When he undertook the Indianapolis post in 1913, he carried this interest with him to the Midwest.

Bertha was welcomed by Mr. Melcher at the train after her thousand-mile journey; then the two New Englanders, bookman and aspiring bookwoman, plunged into a week of discussion, observation, and on-job training. Mr. Melcher described the experience in a *Horn Book* article he wrote years later:

> Such a happy week we had. Next to selling books for children, I like to find myself counseling others on how they can best be sold. The book selection standards for the Boylston Street Shop could be set at a more exacting level than those for a main street store in Indianapolis, but I sensed that new impulses and selling successes might come from this gentle enthusiast with all her useful background and good support at Boston. I probably gained as many useful ideas as I gave. I am sure of it. And that week began a lasting friendship.[7]

The only quarrel Mr. Melcher had with the "gentle enthusiast" was her reckless expenditure of a large sum of money for the printing of a book-buying guide. But even that kindly and experienced man's concern did not shake Bertha's faith in her list.

Bertha's original itinerary had not included Chicago; it was Mr. Melcher's suggestion that she go there with him to attend the convention of the American Booksellers Association. Mr. Melcher was active in the Association, with many official duties to perform; yet he found time to keep a prospective bookseller in mind: to see that she attended the most important meetings and that she met the most important people.

Three especially pleasant things made Bertha's first Booksellers' Convention memorable. She met May Massee, a former children's librarian, who was then the editor of the American

Library Association's *Booklist*, a professional publication designed to help libraries in their selection of current books. She was presented by an Omaha bookwoman with a copy of the beautiful Spielmann and Layard *Kate Greenaway* "just by way of speeding a new and green bookseller on her way."[8] She was taken by Mr. Melcher to "see a puppet production of 'A Midsummer Night's Dream' at the Chicago Little Theatre, an experience I have never ceased to remember with joy and gratitude."[9]

From Chicago Bertha went to New York, where she spent three weeks calling upon publishers and examining their children's books in sample rooms or house libraries. She had to work largely on her own, for in 1916 publishing houses did not yet have special editors for their children's books who might have welcomed and assisted a neophyte bookwoman. However, Bertha had come prepared with notes made from the Hewins and Hunt lists and her own growing familiarity with the literature of the field.

While in New York Bertha revisited the Children's Room of the Central Building of The New York Public Library at Fifth Avenue and Forty-Second Street. A friend had taken her there shortly after the library opened in 1911 and she had been deeply impressed by the Children's Room. Five years later when she began to visualize the physical appearance of the Bookshop, Bertha found herself drawing upon her memory of the room for guidance and inspiration. The 1916 visit clarified the memory, and strengthened the conviction that the Bookshop should have the same welcoming air of warm friendliness that characterized the Children's Room; the same harmony of decor that emphasized and dramatized the books on the shelves.

The person responsible for the creation of the Children's Room was Anne Carroll Moore. In 1906 Miss Moore had left the children's work she had started in the Pratt Institute Free Library in Brooklyn to become the first Superintendent of Work with Children of the entire New York Public Library system. She was, in 1916, an established authority in the field of library service to children.

Bertha naturally sought out Miss Moore during her New York visit and placed before her the Bookshop plans. Miss Moore listened attentively, but was characteristically noncommittal, withholding her approval until such time as the shop was in operation and she might judge its character and performance for herself. Later, Miss Moore explained to an American Library

Association audience her hesitancy in endorsing the Bookshop project. "I will confess that I felt a little fearful of the Bookshop itself lest it seem too precious, too educational, too much of the cult of the child. I had watched several experiments of book selling in the interests of children from prepared surroundings backed by excellent intentions and varying degrees of skill."[10]

While in New York, Bertha also visited Miss Hunt in her offices in the Brooklyn Public Library. She wished to thank the library administrator personally for her helpful list, and to ask for any advice that might contribute to the successful realization of the Bookshop plans. Miss Hunt was cordiality itself and most constructive in the suggestions she made. She spent the first part of the interview, however, in calming a terrified Bertha, who had fully expected to be blown out of the open cars of the Elevated as they crossed the windswept span of the Brooklyn Bridge.

On the return trip to Boston, Bertha stopped off at Hartford to call upon Caroline Hewins. She wrote of the occasion in a *Horn Book* editorial:

> That Hartford day in May is as vivid in my memory today as though it happened last month. We sat in Miss Hewins' office, where many volumes of early children's books filled the shelves on two sides of the room. We lunched at a historic club. We visited her central children's room to which she had brought treasures from her travels. It was on this occasion that Miss Hewins promised to write for our recommended purchase list a preface on John Newbery's "Juvenile Library," a first bookshop for children in London of the 1700's.[11]

Back in Boston at last, Bertha went to see Sidney Smith who had volunteered to make the Bookshop's colophon. Mr. Smith was an acknowledged bookplate artist whom Bertha had met through his daughter, a co-worker of Ruth's. She took with her the Spielmann and Layard keepsake from the Booksellers' Convention, hoping Mr. Smith might find inspiration from some of the bookplates Kate Greenaway had designed for children. He did, and in a later *Horn Book* article Bertha paid tribute to his contribution to the Bookshop:

> It was a quality of youthfulness and joy in him, combined with a quiet, genial friendliness, which made him a listener to the unfolding of plans for the Bookshop in

> the winter and spring of 1916. He looked over Kate Greenaway's bookplates with the prospective "director," especially a Locker-Lampson plate . . . and one day he came with the drawing now familiar to all who know the Bookshop for Boys and Girls, and also with the drawing for the design which has appeared for so long on Bookshop envelopes and book labels. It was a free gift.[12]

The colophon Mr. Smith designed for the Bookshop showed a girl and boy sharing a book as they sat under a shade tree. The turrets of a fanciful castle rose in the background. The legend at the top of the bookplate read: "The thoughts of youth are long, long thoughts," a line which Bertha had first met in the volume of Longfellow in her father's library at Rockport. The design for the mailing label was a graceful scroll bordered with flowers and bearing the necessary items of address.

Everything was in order by the summer of 1916 for the October 9th opening of the Bookshop for Boys and Girls, except the actual site of the shop itself. Mrs. Kehew was consulted. " 'Look about in this neighborhood and see if you can find a room that is satisfactory,' " she told Bertha. "She must have known pretty well what the possibilities were but what a sense of freedom and expansion this way of expressing it gave me!"[13]

Bertha chose for her location the second floor of an old dwelling house immediately adjacent to a similar one already occupied by the Union. The suite of rooms had served originally as a front and back bedroom with a bath off the connecting hall. There was a fireplace in each room and bay windows overlooked the Garden in front and a court in the rear. A complicated entry from the street by stair and hall was judged inadequate so a door was cut through to the Union building and a passageway created that led directly from the Union elevator to the Bookshop. The bath was converted into a stock room. White bookshelves were positioned along the walls of the two rooms in harmony with the white mantels and the old-fashioned white woodwork. Then Bertha was allowed to go to certain rooms in Mrs. Kehew's home on Beacon Hill and select what furnishings she found suitable for the shop. They were mostly antiques in mahogany and oak and contrasted beautifully with the white shelves and trim. Charles Hodgkins designed for his friend a combination display and storage unit and that, too, was constructed of dark wood. For the window hangings Bertha chose Pickwick chintz, a material at home with antiques and a design appropriate for a bookstore.

By the first week in October all was in order for the opening of the Bookshop for Boys and Girls. In Mrs. Miller's records and in those of the Union there is confusion as to the exact date when the Bookshop did open. Some say October 8; some, October 9. Since October 8 was a Sunday in 1916 it seemed reasonable to assume that date to be an "at home," when Bertha Mahony and her staff welcomed Union members, co-workers and friends to the Union's newest department. October 9, Monday, would then have been the first business day of the shop. The assumption is further supported by a similar double opening being recorded when the Bookshop moved to larger quarters in 1921. Moreover, a descriptive folder of the Bookshop's fall and winter activities, prepared for distribution on the opening day, gave that day as October 9, 1916. The point need not be labored, for, as Miss Sayward, who was present at the October 8—October 9 openings, wrote: "After all is the exact date so important? The fact that it was *there* is significant!"[14]

Three months later, at Christmas, Miss Moore and Miss Hewins visited the Bookshop together. What Miss Moore saw swept all her doubts away and she gave the Bookshop her support and her friendship. She reported the visit to the American Library Association, in conference in Louisville, Kentucky:

> The holiday rush was over when Miss Hewins and I entered the Bookshop, but there were all the evidences of a succession of busy days.
>
> Bright fires burned in the two fire-places and an atmosphere of coziness, of repose, and of appreciation — appreciation of books, of arrangements and of the visitor's mood — pervaded the place. The room felt as if it were being lived in. . . .
>
> "What do you think of the Bookshop?" asked Miss Hewins. "I think it is a dream come true and I wish every librarian might not merely see the room but realize what lies behind it," was my reply.
>
> For I believe that Miss Mahony has dramatized and produced in the Bookshop for Boys and Girls our old slogan for library work with children, "The right book for the right child at the right time," and that she has done it in a way to enlist the interest and inspire the confidence of a book-loving and book-buying public.[15]

Reaching Out

A YEAR AFTER BERTHA sat with the delegates to the American Booksellers Association Convention in Chicago, she stood before the same body as an honored speaker at its New York meeting. She was introduced by Mr. Melcher, who was proud of his one-time pupil and eager as always to advance the cause of children's books for, of course, Bertha was to speak about the Bookshop for Boys and Girls. In the paper that she read was a thoughtful statement of the Bookshop's raison d'être and her own belief in the value of good books in the life of the child.

> Our Bookshop for Boys and Girls exists, not simply to sell good books for children but to increase their love for books, because we believe that good books are so important as to be an essential part of life. We feel that the two main essentials are the power to think truly and the power to feel deeply, and that these two essentials result in "preparedness for worthy action." These are the things we all desire for children. While they can certainly be had in part through the experience of everyday living, they can be had in most satisfactory completion, we feel, only through worthwhile books.[16]

A month later, with Alice Jordan as a travelling companion, Bertha journeyed to Louisville to carry the message of the Bookshop to the librarians attending the American Library Association Conference. Her paper and Miss Moore's, mentioned earlier, nicely complemented each other. Bertha included in her talk a discussion of the two procedures whereby the Bookshop's altruistic philosophy was to be implemented; she had been with the

Union far too long not to know that a visionary, idealistic goal was dependent for its realization on shrewd, realistic business practices. In the Bookshop she and her staff expected to increase children's love of books *and* sell the same by two methods: reaching out into the community for customers, and providing the customers when they came into the Bookshop with highly specialized services.

That dual program for action had its roots in Bertha's observation of bookstores while she was preparing for the directorship of her own.

> They were then, generally speaking, backwaters, dead water. The booksellers *waited* for customers to come in; and they all *loved* books. The bookstore's stock in trade is life in essence, records of life. It is explosive material, capable of stirring up fresh life endlessly, but only when it is handled with living enthusiasm. It is not possible to sell books — especially children's books — as they should be sold, by sitting in the bookstore waiting for customers and dusting the stock. If the bookstore is to be full of life, active and imaginative people must be in charge, who will make the customers feel the vitality of the stuff they sell.[17]

There were additional factors that influenced Bertha's decision to go out into the community after business. The very newness of the Bookshop was one: it did not yet have behind it a body of regular customers to support it with equally regular orders. Then, it was admittedly hard to find: the hall and stair entrance would have challenged the White Rabbit; the elevator was easy enough, once found, only patrons did not expect to take an elevator in one building to reach a bookshop in another. But those circumstances were nothing compared to the one Bertha had to cope with scarcely a month after the Bookshop opened: a rival bookstore located directly next door, on the street level, run by two sisters, and offering patrons both adult and children's books.

The catastrophe came about in this way. In May of 1916, with natural pride in its newest venture and with the greatest good-will in the world, the Union instructed Bertha to send releases to the Boston papers about the fall opening of the Bookshop. The notices duly appeared in the press so that the plans for the shop were no more a secret. In the late summer, rumor had it that another bookstore was going to open in the neighborhood and rumor became bitter fact when in November 1916 the Gardenside Bookstore began operations. Naturally, there was much confusion on the part of the Bookshop's customers and just as naturally most of the confusion was resolved at the street level to the advantage of the Gardenside. The advent of the rival bookstore gave an added imperativeness, an added urgency to the plans Bertha had already formulated for the promotion of her fledgling enterprise.

Of foremost importance was a clarification of the shop's location among Union members and employees: Bertha discovered that the lunchroom waitresses were directing guests to the Gardenside in the belief that it was the Union's new bookshop. In 1917 Bertha took advantage of the Conference of Committees, held each spring by the Union, to speak about the Bookshop: its location, its credo, and its facilities and services. By the following spring the shop was so well established that the whole Conference was given over to a study of children's literature with Bertha in charge of the program.

The members of the Bookshop's own Advisory Committee were potential ambassadors of goodwill, particularly in the Boston area; Bertha chose them carefully. Education was represented by the principal of the Brimmer School, a staff member of Milton Academy, a representative of the Massachusetts State Board of Education and, in 1917, by Dr. Lefavour of Simmons. To speak for public libraries were the librarian of the Boston Public Library and Miss Jordan, his newly appointed Supervisor of Children's Work; Miss Moore joined them in 1917. Abbie Farwell Brown, a writer of children's books, acted for those laboring in the creative arts. The Committee changed from time to time, but the original pattern was held to with representatives from the educational, library and literary worlds.

To get the Bookshop known through Massachusetts, Bertha took to the rostrum, although public speaking was never easy for her. The light, quavering voice was a handicap until her audiences forgot it in the sincerity and enthusiasm of the woman behind it; there was a strain, though, until that point was reached. Nonetheless, Bertha undertook to speak up for her Bookshop to any women's organization in the state that desired her to do so. Letters were sent of her availability, not only to speak about the shop, but to bring a sampling of its wares to provide the talk with a background exhibit. The response was gratifying:

twelve talks in so many towns in the first three months of 1917. It was easy enough to tabulate the mail orders that came in as a result of Bertha's barnstorming; it was not so easy to identify the new customers who came in personally, for inevitably the Gardenside got its unfair share of them.

That unfortunate sharing did not pertain to the orders that poured in after the distribution of *Books for Boys and Girls — A Suggestive Purchase List.* Bertha's faith in her book-buying guide was completely justified, almost immediately after its mailing at the time of the shop's opening. She gloated a little when she addressed the 1917 Booksellers Association meeting:

> I know that some of you have considered this catalog . . . an extravagance, but from our standpoint it has been well worth while. It has been applied for by mail from all over the country and from places in Canada, England and France. It is used in class work at the University of Illinois, Pratt Institute and Teachers' College. It is on the desks of the New York Public Library branches where the Supervisor has suggested that it be recommended to parents as a practical list. Many persons from far away places have visited the Bookshop as a result of it and mail orders have been received from it.
>
> Our desire has been that mail-order business should come from places remote from good book centers and it is interesting that such orders *have* come from Nova Scotia, Canada, Florida, Tennessee, North Carolina, Delaware, California, Washington, Minnesota and Michigan.[18]

The list was so well received, in fact, that Bertha was obliged to prepare a second edition of it in 1917, a third in 1919, and a fourth in 1922. The lists carried as their distinguishing mark, on covers and title pages, the colophon Sidney Smith designed for the Bookshop.

Once lists or talks or friendly recommendations had brought potential customers to the Bookshop's hospitable rooms, they were quickly converted into steady and enthusiastic patrons by the special services Bertha offered.

From the beginning the Bookshop continuously sponsored programs for children, for young people, and for adults with general or special interests. The first was a series of six story-hours for three different age groups of children. Margaret Sayward gave all eighteen programs, while Bertha listened with the children by the fireside. "To this day — forty-seven years later — I can hear her voice telling 'The Three Billy Goats Gruff' " she recalled in a memoir.[19]

In March 1917 Bertha also presented Marie Shedlock in a series of programs for adults interested in the ancient folk art of storytelling. Miss Shedlock, a distinguished teacher and monologist from England, was in America to continue the work she had started during an earlier visit: the revival of storytelling as an effective and dramatic educational tool. Earl Barnes, whose *Atlantic* article had inspired Bertha to found the Bookshop, had been one of Miss Shedlock's sponsors in 1900 and when her book, *The Art of the Story-Teller,* was published by Appleton in 1915 he contributed an introduction to it.

Bertha had secured Miss Shedlock for five presentations. They were given in Mrs. Kehew's Beacon Hill residence, a singularly apt setting, for once the same home had been witness to the histrionic gifts of a former owner: Edwin Booth. Miss Shedlock chose to interpret the imaginative writings of Hans Christian Andersen and Laurence Housman and the folk tales of various national groups.

In 1934, on the occasion of Miss Shedlock's eightieth birthday, the May *Horn Book* was dedicated to the English storyteller. In the editorial of the issue, Mrs. Miller expressed her appreciation of Miss Shedlock's art and made a timeless plea for its practice by other creative artists.

> Because Marie L. Shedlock was a genuine artist in voice, diction, perception and dramatic power, she revived here the art of story-telling. She was in herself a revelation of the fact that when words selected and combined with genius are spoken by an artist, their effect upon the soul is incalculable. Those people who have bred their children upon a spoken literature have used a powerful character-building force, the more powerful because so filled with joy. Under the influence of the music of the voice, the body relaxes, words make deep entrance and take root, and grow into finer form than happens otherwise. The foundation of all music lies in the human voice.
>
> Moreover, the story-teller creates a hunger for the printed page. To many who have not a book tradition,

> the story-teller shows the meaning of the book, brings it to life, builds a bridge between listener and reader.
>
> Among peoples with a spoken literature, the story-teller was a special person, *is* a special person, *must be* a special person. Today when the story-teller in America may choose from the literature of many people, he must have background knowledge, judgment and taste for that choice. He must also have the proper voice, speech, manner, personality. We need more story-tellers, but only those story-tellers who are at the same time artists.[20]

To encourage young people to venture into the storytelling field, Bertha arranged a special series of lectures for them in 1920. They were given in the Union's auditorium, Perkins Hall, by John Cronan, assisted by his wife and his sister-in-law, Mrs. Margaret Powers. Mrs. Cronan and Mrs. Powers had been telling stories to children in the branches of the Boston Public Library since 1910; in 1927 Mr. Cronan would join his talents to theirs in a unique storytelling experience.

Like Miss Shedlock, they all three told folk and fairy tales, but their particular forte was telling in part, and in the authors' own words, the stories of great books. They hoped the storytelling introductions would make their young listeners want to read the entire books for themselves. The lectures in the Bookshop series were directed to that kind of oral interpretation, with four books examined for their storytelling possibilities: *Kidnapped*, *Captains Courageous*, *Great Expectations* and *Quentin Durward.*

The programs were well attended as a previous series for older boys and girls had indicated they would be. The earlier series, "Poetry Afternoons for Young People," was held in 1918 with area poets and local teachers of English reading and discussing poetry with the youthful audiences.

Bertha had also held similarly successful discussion programs for adults. Called "The Bookshop Special Evenings," they were concerned with the whole field of children's literature and were led by such authorities as Miss Moore, Marguerite Clement, a writer of children's books, and distinguished representatives from the field of education. There was no set program for any of those evenings; the pattern was completely informal with the discussions consequently lively and pertinent to the current scene.

"Saturday Morning Book Conferences" were established by Bertha in 1919, her first venture in serving a special professional group. The cooperating organization was the New England Association of School Librarians whose membership consisted primarily of high school librarians, there being almost no other kind in schools at that time. The group met monthly from January through June in Perkins Hall, with speakers such as Miss Jordan or Mabel Williams, of the School Department of The New York Public Library, talking about books of interest to high school students. In time the Conferences became traditional, with consistently large attendances. Out of the meetings was created a Reading Committee of Books for Young People. Bertha kept the reviews of the Committee on file in the Bookshop for consultation by school librarians or any one else interested in selecting good books for young adults.

In addition to a full calendar of programs, Bertha also provided Bookshop patrons with other special services. Although her stock-in-trade was children's books, she had one section, books about children and childhood, of particular interest to parents and teachers. She was ever mindful, too, of special book needs as they evolved from the current world scene. Accordingly, she offered a collection of adult books about World War I, including those that dealt with the problems of wartime housekeeping. When a fresh interest arose in Allied France and its language, she began to gather together a collection of French children's books.

A set of Zodiac bookplates, designed especially for the Bookshop by Frances Swan, were available in the shop, as was the artist's "Picture Map of Boston." The map, created for children, noted just enough historical and cultural sites to interest the child without overwhelming him. It folded neatly into a brown cover decorated by the Bookshop colophon and printed by Thomas Todd. On the copy of the map in Mrs. Miller's files an additional marking in red pencil noted the locations of The Hub's bookstores, including Lauriat's where Mr. Melcher began his bookselling career. The Gardenside was neither marked nor listed.

Framed pictures suitable for a child's room were for sale in the Bookshop, as were individual items in the exhibits local artists frequently hung on its walls. For the children there were special displays for the celebration of Boys' Week in November and to accompany the vacation reading lists that became as traditional in the shop as the long, lazy days of a child's summer.

But by far the most effective exhibit of all, so far as the children were concerned, was the Bookshop per se: the welcoming look of it, the freedom to browse among its treasures, and the friendly ladies who were never intrusive but helped if help was needed. The children were expected to handle the books on the shelves and tables, and, if they wanted to read before deciding on a selection, found comfortable chairs waiting with footstools under them for the easement of short legs. If it was desired to sit upon the floor rather than in a chair, that was understood, and the staff learned the art of stepping around sprawled children. Lee Kingman Natti, a writer of distinguished children's books and now a director of The Horn Book, Incorporated, was one of the "floor-sitting" patrons in her childhood.

> It was a long time before the faces of Miss Mahony and Miss Whitney became apparent to me. Because children were allowed to take books from the shelves themselves and I was a floor-sitting type, my first memories of the Bookshop staff are of their feet. What patient feet! They walked around me; they stopped to answer questions and to guide me to other shelves. I was happily content to follow wherever the eager feet led.[21]

For the Christmas issue of *The Horn Book Magazine* in 1946 Margaret Warren Brown recalled the special ambience the Bookshop held for her as a child. The great-aunt in her account was Miss Moore.

> This book [George Macdonald's *The Princess and the Goblin*] I treasured for another reason too. It was — and is — mine as no other book was. When I was ten, I went with my great-aunt to Boston. Any trip to Boston was interesting; any trip with my aunt was bound to be unusual. The combination offered unlimited possibilities and I set off with the highest hopes, which were more than realized. We went to the Bookshop for Boys and Girls, which was already a familiar place to us children. And, when we arrived, I was told that I could choose any book that I wanted . . . any book in that whole wonderful place. The possibilities were staggering; my stomach felt suddenly queasy. It was the *Princess* I chose, finally, and I have never regretted it.[22]

Storyhours for children and young people and adults, talks to women's clubs and speeches at booksellers' and librarians' meetings, Saturday Morning Book Conferences and Conferences of Committees, Bookshop Special Evenings and Poetry Afternoons, book-buying guides and vacation reading lists, art exhibits and special book collections — all those activities and services contributed to the establishment of the Bookshop for Boys and Girls as a Boston institution almost from the day of its opening.

But more important than any of them was the caliber of the Bookshop staff: "active and imaginative people" who made "the customers feel the vitality of the stuff" they sold with such "living enthusiasm." The reason they could so sell was the simple fact that they knew the books they were handling: they had read them, liked them, and desired to share their pleasure in them with others.

When the Bookshop opened, Bertha and her two assistants literally knew the stock from cover to cover because of their involvement with its preparation. They could talk easily and authoritatively about the books and it did not take the patrons long to become dependent on such rare and extremely personalized service. Bertha had not realized how quickly the dependence had been created, until the first Christmas rush was upon the Bookshop. Extra staff had been added to meet the demands of the season, but what was supposed to have been a help turned into a near-disaster. The limited and derivative sales talks of the seasonal employees were totally unacceptable to customers used to the first-hand knowledge and contagious enthusiasm of the Misses Mahony, Howard, and Sayward.

To avoid a repetition of the calamity, Bertha took on extra summer sales persons in 1917, trained them during the more leisurely vacation months, and then re-hired them for the rigors of the Christmas season. There was no dearth of candidates for such seasonal employment. Vacationing librarians, teachers on holiday, other bookstore saleswomen, college students from Wellesley, Smith, Vassar and Simmons — all were eager for a chance to work under Bertha Mahony in her Bookshop for Boys and Girls. Things were always happening there, everyone enjoyed what he was doing, and the air fairly sparkled with life — in and out of books.

Elinor Whitney

THERE SHOULD HAVE BEEN a fanfare of trumpets on the December day in 1919 when Elinor Whitney entered the Bookshop scene as one of the additional staff members engaged for the holiday season.

Elinor had come to the Bookshop in search of a job, sent there by Miss Jordan whose course in children's literature she had taken while a student at the Library School of Simmons College. After graduating from Simmons, Elinor had worked for two years in the Boston Museum of Fine Arts as assistant to the librarian, and then had returned to her home community, Milton, Massachusetts, to teach English in the Academy there. She had graduated from Milton Academy herself, having lived most of her life in the old Whitney homestead on Milton Hill overlooking the Neponset River.

Elinor was the granddaughter of Mrs. A. D. T. Whitney, a well-known writer of girls' books which used as their material "homes, neighborhoods, and the inner life of the people who made them what they were."[23] Mrs. Whitney's home, also on Milton Hill, was hospitably open to her young grandchildren and, although they "barged noisily into her house. . . . She always had a bright welcome for them and appeared untroubled by interruption."[24] She was not disturbed either by the carriages that stopped on the hill in front of her house while the drivers informed the occupants " 'This is the home of Mrs. A. D. T. Whitney who wrote *Faith Gartney's Girlhood, A Summer in Leslie Goldthwaite's Life, Hitherto,* and many other stories of New England life. Giddap!' "[25] The grandchildren found the performances very funny, for Mrs. Whitney was grandmother to them, not a local celebrity.

Elinor's great-grandfather, the father of Adeline Dutton Train Whitney, was Enoch Train, "one of Boston's leading merchants and shipowners. He owned the Diamond Line of packet ships which sailed between Boston and Liverpool. He also owned brigs, barks, and clippers for trading. Many of these ships were built by Donald McKay, whom Mr. Train brought to East Boston shipyards. Indeed, the famous clipper *Flying Cloud* was built by Mr. McKay on Mr. Train's order, but was sold by him before she left the ways."[26] During the same years that Enoch Train's ships were making their Atlantic crossings, Captain David Lane, Bertha's great-grandfather, was sailing merchant ships to ports all over the world.

So, on a winter's day in 1919 two women, with a picturesque era in American maritime history as a common heritage, met in the Bookshop for Boys and Girls amid the pleasant confusion of a busy Christmas season: Elinor Whitney, tall and slim and fair, and Bertha Mahony, "a blue-eyed woman, pink-cheeked, alert and neatly compact" with "an aura of clean air, sea breeze, and open horizons."[27]

There was immediate rapport between the attractive young applicant and the Bookshop's Director. Elinor recalled the meeting later for readers of *The Horn Book:*

> From the very first time I walked into the pleasant large room with its long center table where books were displayed in a more colorful and harmonious way than ordinarily seen in a bookstore, and my first meeting with Bertha Mahony, whose whole person radiated interest and vitality, I was sure that this was the place where I wanted to work and where I would find the greatest satisfaction and enduring delight.[28]

Elinor was engaged at once, walked out on the floor, and began to sell books as if she had been doing it all her life. After the holidays she remained at the Bookshop as a regular staff member. She also "remained" with children's books for the rest of her professional life: as Assistant Director and then Joint Director of the Bookshop, as co-founder and assistant editor of *The Horn Book Magazine*, as a founding member of The Horn Book, Incorporated, as a compiler of volumes about children's literature, and as a writer of distinguished books for boys and girls.

Elinor brought to the Bookshop a wide knowledge of children's books derived from her own book-enriched childhood and from the four years of teaching English to seven- to twelve-year-olds at Milton Academy. The latter experience had given her an understanding of boys and girls and a sensitive awareness of their book needs. She brought the gift of creativity also to the Bookshop for Elinor was, and indeed is, creative literally to her fingertips, being able to turn her hand to almost any art or craft form, in addition to that of writing. She wore her knowledge and her gifts lightly, however, and her warm personality, wit, and playful sense of humor quickly made friends for her among the Bookshop's customers and staff.

The friendship between Bertha and Elinor that had sprung so spontaneously into existence on that December day in 1919 continued uninterrupted until Mrs. Miller's death in 1969, nurtured through the years by shared work, mutual interests, and a common philosophy about the importance of good books in the life of the child. Forty years after the first meeting in the Bookshop, Elinor wrote an essay, "The Story of a Friendship," "to look back over the relationship and enjoy in retrospect its many highlights."[29] These lines from the account catch the essence of the relationship.

> Many friendships seem to hit snags at intervals, to be dislocated perhaps forever, but with our friendship I cannot remember any break. Often we went our own ways, enjoyed other friends and other pursuits, but we always found each other where we had parted, and no other attachment seemed to have lessened our enjoyment of each other's companionship or of the continuance of work on some compiling project.
>
> It is difficult to appraise a friend in terms of virtues or faults. Both are essential to the whole concept of congeniality. I think we both were tolerant, not losing our tempers, or arguing or disagreeing vehemently on anything. Like Mrs. Boffin we preferred to say, "Lor'! Let's be comfortable!"
>
> . . . I would like to wish for any possible reader a similar experience in her lifetime of such an enriching and enduring companionship and one of which she could say, "Isn't it interesting? Isn't it fun?" and "Lor'! Let's be comfortable!"[30]

The Book Caravan

WHEN ELINOR WHITNEY joined the Bookshop staff in 1919, she was just in time to get involved in Bertha Mahony's latest scheme to reach out into the community for converts to the reading habit and patrons for the Bookshop for Boys and Girls. In Bertha's new plan, the community was enlarged to encompass almost all of New England, not just Boston, and the reaching-out was to be quite literal, for it was to be accomplished by a travelling bookstore, a Book Caravan. The mobile unit was scheduled to roll over the highways of New England during the summer months of 1920, making its stops primarily in country towns and seashore villages where bookstores were generally non-existent.

According to an article in the Boston *Evening Transcript* of July 3, 1920, Bertha had had the notion of such a travelling bookshop as far back as 1916, with the elements of her vision a canvas booth, a Ford car, and a trailer. The Union did not look with favor on the notion, so Bertha laid it aside to concentrate on opening the Bookshop.[31] An increasing number of articles in magazines about public library service to rural areas by book trucks kept the idea alive and it was completely revitalized when Christopher Morley's *Parnassus on Wheels* was published in the fall of 1917.

Then Bertha suggested her Caravan idea to the Union once more. It seemed fitting to her that, since the Union had again and again taken the pioneer step educationally, its Bookshop should lead in the exploration of a potentially rich new field. Talk of the possible mobile extension of the Bookshop spread out from the Union to Boston's book world and presently McGregor Jenkins, of The Atlantic Monthly Company, led a group of publishers in an offer to underwrite the Union project. They proposed to guarantee the Union from loss by establishing a fund to cover the cost of the car and its running expenses, with the understanding that the car should stand as their asset. The Caravan should, in return, carry only the books of the contributing publishers, although orders might be taken for any publisher's books requested by customers. The Union could not afford to turn down so generous an offer and Bertha Mahony had her Caravan.

As soon as the financial details were completed in January of 1920, Bertha turned her organizational genius to getting her travelling bookshop on the road by the following July. She had to see that the Caravan was designed and built, that books were selected and ordered for its shelves, that arrangements were made for the delivery of fresh supplies from time to time, that staff was acquired to drive the truck and sell from it, that routes and stops were worked out with the cooperation of local officials, and that publicity for the whole adventure was written and placed.

A rough pencil sketch of the Book Caravan is in Mrs. Miller's files, marked in her handwriting, "Charles Hodgkins' first drawing for Book Caravan." The sketch looks remarkably like the completed Caravan as designed and constructed under the supervision of Lewis B. Abbott, an architect with a Boston firm. The Caravan was built on the body of a Stewart truck at a cost, roughly, of five thousand dollars. It was thirteen feet long, six feet wide, and a six-foot-two man could stand upright in it. It was painted gray and the side panels bore the names of the Union and the Bookshop in gold.

Doors in the middle of the truck, on either side, provided easy entrance as well as cross-ventilation. Windows at the sides and the back, curtained in orange silk gauze, could be opened for additional breeze. Inside the Caravan, bookshelves lined the sides and a cushioned seat stretched across the back for browsers. Above the seat, framing the window, were pictures and a basket for flowers. Carpeting on the steps and a rug on the floor dulled the noise of shuffling feet. Camp stools were available for reading out-of-doors in the shade of the Caravan's blue awnings which spread out like great wings when unrolled.

The shelves of the truck held twelve hundred books which were at first kept in place by brass rods while travelling; those proved to be lethal weapons on rough roads and were quickly replaced by less dangerous leather straps. Books for adults and children were carried on the truck. A small publicity folder about the Caravan listed twenty-two kinds of books on the shelves including those about farming, housekeeping, poultry, sewing, flowers, care of children, stars, insects, politics, history, travel, poetry, romance and art. A jingle on the back of the same folder, written by John Chipman Farrar, listed the wares of the Caravan more fancifully.

> A turquoise book for mid-day,
> A golden book for dawn,
> A calico book for kitchens
> And a green book for the lawn:
>
> Poetry for starlight
> Drama for the moon,
> And fiction for the hammock
> In the lazy afternoon:
>
> Love-songs for lovers,
> Mad songs for fools,
> Romance for the stay-at-homes
> And ghost-books for ghouls.

The design on the little folder was by Maurice Day, an illustrator of children's books. He had also advised on the decoration and the colors of the Caravan itself.

The first Caravaners were Mary Frank and Genevieve Washburn. Miss Frank, a Pratt Institute Library School graduate, was on leave from The New York Public Library where, as Head of the Extension Department, she was responsible for services to those communities at some distance from branch libraries. Because of the nature of her work, she was interested in the growing use of mobile units by other library systems to carry books to out-of-the-way neighborhoods. The Book Caravan experience gave her the opportunity to observe such a unit in operation — even though its purpose was to sell books, not just lend them.

Genevieve Washburn was a Wellesley graduate from Duluth, Minnesota, and Tryon, North Carolina, who had come to Boston looking for a job in a bookstore. Naturally, she applied at the Bookshop; she recalled later her interview with its Director.

> In no time flat, with her great supply of human interest and sympathy, she found out that I had recently spent a year driving cars of all conditions in France for the Fund for French Wounded, and before the hour or so was up she said suddenly, "Why, you're just the person

we are looking for. We have no driver for our Book Caravan we are sending out this summer." So shortly I began working in the shop, getting acquainted with stock, methods, etc., in preparation for the summer.[32]

The Caravaners were provided with minutely itemized schedules and instructions, though individual judgment had to be exercised under certain circumstances. These excerpts from one of the Caravan schedules give some indication of the mass of detail connected with the whole operation.

Thurs. July 28, Beverly. Start as early as possible in the morning from Boston. Location is at Oceanside Park, permission from the City of Beverly. Miss Katherine P. Loring of Prides Crossing has made the arrangements and placed the posters. Mrs. Cole will come in her car to meet you between five and six and will guide you to Wenham. You will spend Thursday and Friday nights with her.

Mon. Aug. 1, Magnolia. Drive to Magnolia as early as possible Monday morning. Location is on Lexington Avenue at any point that seems suitable to you. Try to leave in time to reach Annisquam for dinner Monday night. Rooms are engaged for you there . . . at Wonasquam Lodge.

Tues. Aug. 2, Annisquam. Location is in front of Village Hall, permission of Mr. Charles E. Cunningham, Postmaster. Mr. Ralph Hale has made arrangements and placed posters.

Wed. Aug. 3, Thurs. Aug. 4, East Gloucester. You will spend Wednesday and Thursday mornings at Bass Rocks bathing beach. This has not been advertised. The location at East Gloucester is opposite the Arcade, permission of the Hawthorne Inn. The Inn is very insistent about the ground being smoothed over after the car has been on it. It may seem best to stand on the side of the road. Rooms for Wednesday and Thursday nights have been engaged at the Harbor View, $4.50 per day American plan.

Sat. Aug. 6, York Harbor. You have two locations, one on the grounds of the Marshall House by the courtesy of Mr. and Mrs. Gilman L. Moulton, and the other on the Village Green, the driveway in front of the Town Hall, by permission of Joseph P. Bragdon, Chairman of

Selectmen. You can divide your time between them as you see fit. . . . From here on arrangements about rooms have not been made as yet. You will be notified later.

Mon. Aug. 8, Ogunquit. Location is near the Post Office on land of Mr. Ray P. Hancom. Mrs. S. J. Perkins of the St. Aspinquid Hotel has made all arrangements.

Tues. Aug. 9, Kennebunkport. Location is near Mr. Hoff's blacksmith shop. Miss Florence Blunt placed posters for us.

Thurs. Aug. 11, Prouts Neck. Location near Country Club beside boardwalk leading down to Club, permission from Miss Ethlyn W. Libby, Superintendent.[33]

Before the Book Caravan rolled out on its initial journey, notices were sent to the press about Bertha's "first." A number of feature stories appeared, due to the human interest inherent in the adventure and to Christopher Morley's advance publicity, so to speak. In fact, Charles Messer Stow called his article, already mentioned in the July 3, 1920 Boston *Evening Transcript*, "Parnassus Without a Pegasus Tours New England."[34] Only *The New York Times* struck a sour note. Confused perhaps by the participation of Miss Frank in the experiment, it grumbled that The New York Public Library had no business sending a book caravan out of the state and, furthermore, to carry books to New England was like carrying coals to Newcastle.

The Caravan took to the road on July 5 and Bertha, with a keen sense of the dramatic and the newsworthy, scheduled its first stop at Gloucester. The Cape Ann papers outdid themselves in praise of the unique creation of a local girl. Later, at Falmouth on Cape Cod, the newly-organized National Association of Book Publishers arranged to have the Caravan's operations filmed by the four major motion-picture news services of the day: Pathé, International, Fox and Kinegram. The films were later shown in movie houses all over the country in connection with the Association's campaign to get "More Books in the Home."

During its first summer the Book Caravan missed only two of its forty-nine scheduled stops as it worked its way along the New England coast from Provincetown, Massachusetts, on the tip of Cape Cod in the south to Bar Harbor, Maine, in the north, then inland to the hill towns of Maine, New Hampshire, Vermont, and Massachusetts. Considering the state of cars and roads in 1920 that record is almost miraculous.

Unfortunately, the miracle did not carry over into the financial return of the Caravan. Although the average daily business of its sixty working days was $120, the overhead was too high to admit of a profit and the contributing fund was almost exhausted at the summer's end. Unfortunately, too, and to Bertha's sorrow, the publishers who had underwritten the Caravan measured its "results entirely from a dollars-and-cents point of view — and this in spite of the fact that they do not so measure their expensive advertising in newspapers and magazines."[35]

In reporting to the Union on the Caravan's 1920 season, Bertha included a plea for another experimental year.

> There are, of course, ways in which the Book car can be made more effective a second summer. While the Bookshop Director does not feel that the returns to the Union or the Bookshop have yet been at all commensurate with the work that has been put into the Book Car's first summer, she does believe that the experiment has been the best kind of publicity for books. She also believes that in order to make the best use of the experience gained, the car should be conducted under the same management another summer. If the contributing publishers do wish the Bookshop for Boys and Girls to operate the car for another summer, the Director will, in conference with Mr. McGregor Jenkins, present definite plans for the future.[36]

The "dollars-and-cents" publishers capitulated and presently Bertha and Mr. Jenkins were making the arrangements for the 1921 trips of the Book Caravan.

The last stop of the Caravan in the fall of 1920 had been at the Lake Placid meeting of the New York Library Association, where it was on display for examination by conference delegates. Miss Frank and Miss Washburn, exhausted, were relieved of the exhibit assignment and it was undertaken by Frances Darling and Marion Harding, with Miss Harding acting as driver. (They almost didn't make the conference for the Caravan sank in a soft spot in the road. Luckily, a passing motorist pulled them out, and then identified himself as a director of the Brentano Bookstore in New York City.) Miss Darling and Miss Harding were also with the Caravan during the winter months of 1920-1921 when it was on display at various places in Boston. For those stops Miss Darling was obliged to obtain a license from the

Health Department where her name was recorded as a Pedler and a Hawker.

The Caravan cast its spell on all who travelled with it, making them feel at once like responsible missionaries and irresponsible gypsies — a combination hard to resist. It was not surprising, then, that one team of Caravaners for the 1921 season consisted of Miss Darling and Miss Harding. Frances Darling had joined the Bookshop staff during its first Christmas season, bringing to her work a graduate degree from the Carnegie Library School of Pittsburgh and several years of experience as a children's librarian in the Chatham Square Library which serves New York City's Chinese community. Miss Darling, an ebullient, out-going person, full of life and good humor, was exactly right for the larky adventures of a travelling bookshop. Both she and Miss Harding were from Chestnut Hill, near Boston, where they and their families had been friends for years.

In 1963 Miss Darling recalled for *The Horn Book* some of the adventures and misadventures of their Caravan journey: how they prepared for it — Miss Harding, who had a "very real mechanical ability" but was completely non-bookish, "plunged into a reading of books and publishers' catalogs, and *I* took a course at the Y.M.C.A. on automobiles and engines;" how *they* raised the book car's beautiful but recalcitrant awnings by looking helplessly at any passing male; how they shamelessly autographed copies of *Parnassus on Wheels* for delighted patrons; and how one of them hid a day's receipts in her shoes, and the other put the shoes out in the hotel corridor to be shined. "We were luckier than we deserved," Miss Darling observed dryly.[37]

Miss Darling's memory was jogged in her recollections by a diary she kept of the summer safari. The following entries from the diary demonstrate the variety of the Caravan work and the zest with which Miss Darling and Miss Harding undertook it.

> Monday, May 23. Caravan started its second season. Miss Harding and Miss Darling aboard. Drove from Boston to Bridgewater, Mass. (38 miles) with picnic lunch on the way.
>
> Tuesday, May 24. Bridgewater, Mass. Caravan stood in front of the old White Academy. Miss Darling spoke to 300 odd at the Normal School Chapel exercises. Deluged with Normal students and school children all day. Normal School came in classes — as well as separately. Geography class used our Japan books. Art class

we heard was much grieved at not being allowed to adjourn and sketch us.

Thursday, May 26. From Pomfret Center to Farmington (65 miles). Stopped at garage & found all these things wrong: point broken off magneto, choke not working (disconnected), leaky carburetor, grease cups on front wheel dry, foot brake disconnected, steering wheel needing grease. While waiting at the garage sold *Finger Plays* to woman who stopped and enquired for it.

Friday, May 27. Farmington, Conn. Connecticut library meeting held in Farmington. Miss Darling gave a twenty-minute talk at the morning session. After supper drove to Hartford (9 miles). . . . Miss Hewins met us and conducted us to stand on Niles Street.

Sunday, May 29. Had tea with Miss Hewins.

Monday, May 30. Stopped to buy "Margaret's Salted Nuts" and sold $13.75 in about ten minutes. Nicest family — all thrilled. Father found *What Really Happened at Paris* and ordered *Peace Negotiations.* One boy bought *Burgess Bird Book;* another, *Jack in the Rockies.*

Monday, June 20. Drove down from Boston in afternoon to Swampscott, for American Library Association meeting.

Tuesday, June 21. Librarians showed much interest in car, its work and its mechanism. Miss Caroline Hewins, always an interesting visitor, came to see us. She read a story (most charmingly) from *Picture Tales from the Russian* to a small barefooted boy who was entranced.

Wednesday, June 22. Caravan open all day. In the evening about seventy-five people sat on the lawn outside and listened to . . . Mr. Melcher of the *Publishers' Weekly* read poetry. [In 1918 Mr. Melcher had left Indianapolis for New York to become the editor of the book trade magazine.] After an hour of reading the mosquitoes made it desirable to be elsewhere, so the group moved up to the hotel and listened for another hour.

Thursday, June 23. Two small boys have been reading quietly all day long — going away only when I locked up for an hour at noon.

Friday, June 24. At last I feel satisfied that the librarians . . . know what Miss Mahony is trying to do and realize that more than an idealistic interest is necessary to make the car a success. If they only help to convince the publishers!

Friday, July 1. Drove in blinding rain storm fifty miles to Marion. Had a hard trip as car leaked and we had to remove more than half the books from the shelves to protect them.

Wednesday, July 20. Batteries were being charged, so we held shop by Japanese lantern light and bayberry candles, which was very effective.

Friday, July 29. Mr. Sheehan [Henry Beston, author of *Firelight Fairy Book*] read fairy tales in afternoon to a group of thirty odd.

Friday, August 12. Camping for the night directly under the Old Man of the Mountains.[38]

In spite of Miss Darling's hopes, the contributing publishers were not convinced that the Caravan constituted a legitimate business investment and, when the second year's safari was no more successful financially than the first, they felt justified in terminating their sponsorship of the book car. Ruth Drake, who had participated in the 1921 season as a librarian-driver, begged them to allow her to take it out alone in 1922 to cut down on the overhead, but neither the publishers nor the Union would countenance such an arrangement.

It was a great satisfaction to Bertha that when the car was sold to the School Department of Monroe County, New York, Ruth Drake went with it. She served the travelling library that the Caravan became with the same competence and enthusiasm that she had given to its career as a travelling bookshop.[39] It is interesting also to note that in 1922 Mary Frank sent out the first travelling library in New York City to serve the then rural areas on Staten Island.

It was inevitable, perhaps, that the Caravan could not endure, since its originator saw it primarily as a promotional medium for books and reading, while its sponsors looked upon it as a source of revenue. Yet it was visited by librarians from this country and abroad and did its fair share to stimulate the development of bookmobile service by public libraries in the next decade. Its saga, though short, had been a gallant one and during its brief existence it had made a lovely light over the roads of New England, with or without Japanese lanterns and bayberry candles.

With Books on Many Subjects for Grown-Ups

Although Bertha regretted the demise of the Book Caravan, she was not by nature inclined to waste time and energy in futile hand-wringing. Besides, she was preoccupied with a new project. On October 20, 1921 the Bookshop for Boys and Girls was scheduled to re-open in larger quarters and as a general bookstore.

Even if the Bookshop had continued to stock only children's books, more room would have been needed to accommodate the titles being produced by a rapidly expanding publishing field. The new quarters would provide the additional space needed, as well as suitable arrangements for the adult books.

The specialization of the expanded shop would be children's books. To make that clear, Bertha determined to keep the original name, adding a phrase to indicate the more comprehensive book coverage: The Bookshop for Boys and Girls — With Books on Many Subjects for Grown-Ups.

Bertha expected the move to eliminate one of the shop's severest handicaps: its hide-away location. Largely because of that, she felt, the Bookshop was still operating at a loss after five years. The losses were never great and they lessened each year, but losses they were nonetheless. Mrs. Peirce loyally covered them alone after Mrs. Kehew's death in 1918, but both she and Bertha knew that losses could not be accepted indefinitely from a shop that was supposed to help support the Union's social service work with its profits.

Bertha was confident that the expanded shop would produce those desired profits by offering patrons one general bookstore in which to make all of their reading purchases, adult as well as juvenile. Moreover, she planned to establish a lending library in the reorganized Bookshop, remembering the financial returns of the New Library's operation.

The expansion of book stock had a philosophical reason behind it also. Bertha had become convinced that a children's bookshop per se was not theoretically sound, isolating young readers as it did from the main stream of literature. Even though they were engaged with a tributary, so to speak, the children ought to sense the depth and richness of the current toward which they were reading themselves, and the current should be available to them when they were ready to enter it.

A second troublesome handicap, under which the Bookshop had labored almost from the day it opened, was neatly eliminated in the moving process. The Union bought the building in which the Gardenside Bookstore was located and ordered its proprietors to move.

Then, by shifting certain Union departments, the Bookshop was reopened at 270 Boylston Street, at street level, with a direct entrance from sidewalk to foyer. Under the direction of Lewis B. Abbott, who had designed the Caravan, two floors of the former home were ingeniously opened up to provide one floor for the adult books and a balcony floor for the children's. Each floor had various levels with odd steps up and down, which made for natural divisions of the book stock.

The longest flight of stairs led to the children's balcony and had a handsome Georgian balustrade that continued around the stairwell. A long gallery ran the length of the well connecting a front and back room. The front room looked out across Boylston Street into the Public Garden through a great bank of floor-to-ceiling windows. Bertha planned to have the picture books there and, to make it safe for the small children who would be using it, suggested to Mr. Abbott a window treatment similar to those in H. Willebeek Le Mair's illustrations for the Moffat children's song books. Iron grillwork — forged by Frank Koralewsky, a master smith of the time — small potted trees, cornices, and soft drapes reduced the window hazard and effectively framed the Garden view.

An afternoon reception was held to mark the opening of the Bookshop for Boys and Girls — With Books on Many Subjects for Grown-Ups. So clever had Mr. Abbott been in his renovations that the whole inviting scene lay before the guests when they stepped in from the street.

The relocated and expanded shop was a financial success from the start. After two years at the new address, the Bookshop's profits exceeded the accumulated deficits of all its years at the hard-to-find location. In 1920-1921, the last year there, the sale of children's books had amounted to $24,000; ten years later the gross income of the general bookstore was $161,000.

The latter figure included the profits from two lending libraries: the adult one, and a Junior Lending Library which, after being established in 1926, proceeded to do as brisk a business as the parent activity. Besides supporting the slower sale of books, the lending libraries provided the merchandise for the Bookshop's regular used-book sales, so helpful to institutions with restricted budgets and to patrons, especially children, of limited means. One such sale, held on Halloween, was advertised by a small orange folder decorated with Arthur Rackham's spidery illustrations. "Bring your broomsticks," the leaflet advised gaily, "and make a clean sweep!"

A Special Order Desk was established in the new Bookshop under the direction of Frances Darling. In 1927 it alone did as much business as the entire Bookshop had done in its first year of existence.

Bertha made two other major changes in the Bookshop's facilities over the years. To provide high school students with the special services they required, she established in 1924 a Young People's Section. A year later she opened "The New Room," a quiet retreat above the Bookshop reached by stairs or elevator from the balcony level, where parents, teachers, social workers, churchmen and students might examine "books on the care of children and their education with other books which make for increased understanding of human behavior and the possibilities for growth."[40] Over the years other kinds of adult books that required thoughtful examination before purchase found their way to the room: art books, collectors' guides, books on antiques, gardening books and plays. All the books could be read at window or fireside, bought or borrowed, as the patron desired. In 1935 "The New Room" became "The Study," which name reflected more precisely its content and purpose.

* * *

The cheerful stir in the Bookshop proper was due to the normal business of the day, to the openness of the shop, and to the traffic brought in by the Gallery Exhibitions. There had been some showings of local artists and illustrators of children's books in the first Bookshop, but the limited wall space there discouraged any real gallery plans. The walls of the new Bookshop could accommodate the largest hangings; they were light in color and bright from the shop's northern exposure. When the Bookshop opened at 270 Boylston Street, originals of Maud and Miska Petersham's book illustrations were on display, along with children's portraits by a Boston artist.

The works of New England artists were generally featured through the years, but there were also posters from France, woodblock prints from Japan, and etchings from England. Almost all of the artists who were illustrating children's books in the twenties and thirties had their works exhibited on the Bookshop walls: N. C. Wyeth, Leslie Brooke, Beatrix Potter, Wanda Gág, Helen Sewell, Thomas Handforth, Elizabeth McKinstry, the d'Aulaires, Pamela Bianco, Dorothy Lathrop — the complete list would be a catalog of genius, a review of children's book illustration of the time. Thomas Todd printed handsome brochures for each exhibit which listed the items shown with their prices, for most were for sale.

Each exhibit hung for a month. Bertha and her staff could not handle the details of such an ambitious program without help. A committee of Bookshop friends assumed the responsibility with Marguerite MacKellar Mitchell of Sunny Fields, Weston, Massachusetts, in charge. Genevieve Washburn had introduced Mrs. Mitchell, a Wellesley classmate, to Bertha, thereby striking up a friendship that Mrs. Miller later called "one of the rare treasures"[41] of her life. Mrs. Mitchell was an artist herself and a patron of the arts, sometimes opening her own studio to creative friends and neighbors. She spent several years in France studying, painting, and forming a deep affection for all things French. Her sketches of the Amboise countryside once hung in the Bookshop with those of her young protégée, Beverly Watson.

Mrs. Mitchell brought to the chairmanship of the Gallery Exhibition her first-hand knowledge of art, and judging by the meticulously assembled schedules of the yearly exhibitions, a highly organized mind with a gift for detail. She must also have had Bertha's own capacity for hard work to cope with the physical effort involved in hanging the materials.

Sometimes she was helped with the task by Julius Baldi, who had been the Bookshop's efficient stock-room boy from the day it opened in 1916. He went to school at night and, when he was qualified, became a draftsman in the offices of a Boston architect. It was his pleasure to return to the Bookshop occasionally in the evenings to place the Gallery exhibitions.

Some of the artists preferred to hang their own pictures: Pamela Bianco and her father arranged her exhibition of oils, drawings and lithographs; N. C. Wyeth placed his originals alone. Mrs. Miller recalled the latter occasion:

> One evening about 8 o'clock, Mr. N. C. Wyeth appeared by appointment to hang the exhibition of a number of his originals for Scribner's Childrens Classics. What an absolutely quiet time that was! I am sure we said "Good evening." Then he went quietly to work. His large oils looked wonderfully on the walls of the Bookshop and soon they were all in place and he departed.[42]

Two of the Bookshop's most unusual exhibitions came from France under the aegis of Esther Averill, a creative young American who lived in Paris from 1925 to 1934 where she had her own publishing house, The Domino Press. In the late twenties Bertha had occasion to write to Miss Averill about the contemporary illustrators of French children's books; the letter began a firm friendship that continued through the years. The Bookshop acted as the American distributor of some of The Domino Press publications, including the original edition of *Daniel Boone* with Feodor Rojankovsky's illustrations.

Miss Averill, in turn, acted as a kind of French agent for the Bookshop, sending material for two of its most memorable exhibitions: "Street Murals: The Modern French Poster and the Artists Who Have Made Its History in the Past Ten Years" and "The History of French Children's Books: 1750-1900." The material for the latter was from the collection of J.-G. Deschamps, a famous Parisian rare-book dealer. The catalog of the poster exhibit was bound in the February 1932 *Horn Book*; that of the children's books was too large for such distribution. As late as 1959 a letter was received in The Horn Book offices asking where the Bookshop was that had had French children's books on sale years ago. A young mother had seen the exhibit in 1934 and in 1959, as a grandmother, wished to buy some of the books for her grandchildren.

With her background of the Cape Ann out-of-doors, Bertha saw that there was a garden exhibit each spring in the Bookshop. The exhibit was not just a table of gardening books, but included also an attractive listing of such titles, a Gallery Exhibition of flower prints, a display of garden tools and plants from a local nursery, and a landscape architect to lecture and to advise individually on gardening problems. Once the children had a comparable exhibit of "Supplies and Field Tools for the Young Naturalist," with a follow-up showing in the fall of "Outdoor Collections and Nature Note Books." Thirty-four items were submitted by the boys and girls and Bertha found room to exhibit them all.

There was another kind of exhibit that appealed strongly to the children: that of their own art work. The first Children's Art Show was held in 1922 and was such an instantaneous and overwhelming success that it became an annual institution. The material for the shows was at first drawn from the public and private schools of Greater Boston; later exhibitions came from experimental schools in Chicago, Toledo, New York City, and even England. The showings were of enormous interest to educators involved in the Progressive Education Movement; the general public found the material fresh and original; but it was the children who took pure delight in the whole thing — particularly if their own work was on display.

In 1925 Bertha rashly opened the Art Show to all the boys and girls of the Boston area, inviting them to send in whatever creations they chose; a committee would select the best for the Show. The free-wheeling invitation inspired six hundred children to send in almost a thousand entries. Fifty-eight were shown in the Bookshop — there was no room for any more. Bertha's public relations instincts were too well-developed to repeat the exhibition-contest.

* * *

As the exhibitions flourished in the new quarters of the Bookshop, so did the programs. Those for children were generally given during Children's Book Week in November. That national recognition of children's literature had begun in 1919, organized by a committee of the American Booksellers Association with Mr. Melcher as the chairman.

The Book Week programs of the Bookshop, held in Perkins Hall, usually revolved around an author or an illustrator who had made a recent and distinctive contribution to children's books. When Arthur Bowie Chrisman's *Shen of the Sea* was published in 1925, Mr. Chrisman told stories from it to Bookshop children. Dhan Gopal Mukerji described the boyhood experiences in the jungles of India out of which he wrote his books for boys and girls. The celebration went nautical one year when young David Binney Putnam and Cap'n Bob Bartlett described their Greenland adventures. In 1930 a number of fine children's books appeared interpreting the Mexican scene to American boys and girls; to mark the occasion Bertha gave a gala Mexican Dinner in Perkins Hall. Among the writers and artists honored at the dinner were Rene d'Harnoncourt, the illustrator of Elizabeth Morrow's *The Painted Pig;* Susan Smith, the author of *Made in Mexico* and *Tranquilina's Paradise;* and Thomas Handforth, the illustrator of Miss Smith's fantasy about a toy angel.

Bertha also planned programs for the Bookshop's junior patrons who were more do-it-yourself enthusiasts than readers. One such meeting was concerned with "Home Radio Stations"; another, with "Home Aquaria." The eager child who had once tried unsuccessfully to get an aquarium installed in every classroom of her Rockport school just never gave up!

Recalling the success of the Poetry Afternoons held for high school students in 1918, Bertha arranged a similar series for them in 1930. The Amy Lowell Memorial Poetry Series it was called, established and endowed in honor and in memory of the New England poet who had been a patron of the Bookshop until her death in 1925. "A Venture in Poetry," Milton Byron called the series in a *Saturday Review of Literature* article. "The whole idea," he reported, "was to give a group of serious children of high school age an opportunity to hear good poets and talk to them and draw from them whatever they could."[43]

So many applied for admission to the series that Bertha had to ask the English Departments of the area high schools to provide the Bookshop with invitational lists. To her delight the initial series was so well received that the young people asked for its continuation for another year, but with permission to direct the program themselves with the help of a Bookshop committee. The series ran through 1935 and in those years presented to its youthful audiences such "good poets" as Carl Sandburg, Robert Frost, James Weldon Johnson, T. S. Eliot, Archibald MacLeish, and Grace Hazard Conkling.

Mr. Byron's article concluded with Bertha Mahony's reaction to the whole splendid endeavor: " 'I don't think I was ever so gratified by anything before in my life.' "[44]

Bertha reached out into the community for the teen-age patron when, in 1929-1930, the Bookshop sent John Cronan into eight of the city's junior and senior high schools to tell stories. She wrote about it in *The Horn Book*:

> This service was given without charge [a group of publishers supported it] as a demonstration of the character and value of storytelling. We chose the high schools because it is with those years that the break comes in reading interest. These were the results: public library circulation mounted and applications for the introduced books were dramatically numerous. . . . One master said, "In the beginning I was lukewarm myself though ready to be shown. Every one of my teachers was opposed to the plan. Before Mr. Cronan's series was finished, there was enthusiastic unanimity for it. . . . Moreover, it has vitalized our English department and made a new and freer relation between teachers and students."[45]

The series was so popular that Bertha persuaded the publishers to continue their support of it for a second year.

There were programs for the grown-ups in the relocated Bookshop, as well as "books on many subjects." A year after The New Room opened, its special patrons were invited to attend a series of lectures by a Viennese psychologist on "Individual Psychology and Education." In the thirties a play-production course was offered, directed by an actress who had been with the company of E. H. Sothern for a part of her professional career. Puppet workshops were also held in the thirties, conducted by Jean Mardin of the Bookshop staff. Miss Mardin's own puppets, all literary in origin, were available through the Bookshop for performances in the community.

For five months in 1925-1926 Bertha scheduled what she termed "A Pleasure Course" for those mothers wanting to know more about the rapidly growing number of books available to their children. One of the speakers, Louise Seaman, had had much to do with the expanding field. In 1918 The Macmillan Company decided to set up a separate Children's Department, the first in the United States, to supervise its publications for boys and girls. Miss Seaman, a Vassar graduate with some teaching experience, was working at the time in the advertising department of the company. Her teaching background and her familiarity with the firm's ways persuaded George Brett, the president of the company, to appoint her as head of the new department. With the appointment, Miss Seaman became the first editor of children's books in the country.

Presently Bertha began receiving occasional letters about Macmillan's juvenile publications signed: Louise Seaman. Intrigued by the liveliness of the material, Bertha determined to call upon its writer the next time she was in New York. She reported her visit in *The Horn Book:*

> We . . . found a young woman of candor and charm who saw books for boys and girls as we saw them; who had ideals, vision, enthusiasm, and at the same time the background, experience, judgment and personality to make the first qualities dynamic. Here was a real and very vivid person — a dynamic person — working at a source of our own profession.[46]

Bertha was proud to present the young editor — by then her good friend — to the audiences of "A Pleasure Course." With equal pride she introduced May Massee to the Union's membership at one of the Conference of Committees programs. The friendship of the two women had begun back in 1916 when Mr. Melcher had introduced them at the Chicago Booksellers Convention. "I . . . remember just how she looked the first time I saw her. She came to the podium to speak, wearing a navy blue silk dress and broad-brimmed sailor of the same color, both very becoming with her fair hair. She was a lovely-looking woman."[47] In 1927 Miss Massee had left her position with the American Library Association's *Booklist* to become the second children's editor in America, heading the juvenile department established by Doubleday, Page.

* * *

It would be difficult to say who most enjoyed two very special occasions in the Bookshop: the children, the adults, or the staff. One was the Dolls' Convention which convened in February 1929; the other, the Puppet Parade that marched through the shop four years later.

The Dolls' Convention began appropriately on Valentine's Day and lasted the rest of the month. Elinor Whitney was the chairman of the Convention, but she kept well in the background, allowing Pinocchio to wield the gavel in public. Pinocchio was also the guest of honor and chief speaker, with other dolls of literary heritage chairing the various Round Table meetings.

The Convention was inspired by an idea Eliza Orne White had suggested in her children's book, *Tony*. In token of their gratitude to Miss White, the dollegates sent her from their opening session a bouquet of spring flowers. In acknowledging the gift Miss White mourned, "I wish I could have sent my own doll, Sally, to the convention, but alas! she had a sad accident, for her body was eaten by mice in our attic."[48]

The theme of the Convention was: "Are Animals Replacing Dolls in Home, School and Playground?" The worrisome question had arisen because of the popularity of Winnie-the-Pooh and the other nursery animal friends of Christopher Robin as created by A. A. Milne. No animals were permitted at the Convention but one Teddy Bear managed to sneak in. He was promptly incarcerated, but contrived to bear up in his prison until a vote by the dollegates of "166 eyes and 84 nose" brought about his release. Later Teddy described his experience at a meeting of the New York Society for Promoting Bears. His fine paper — puns and all — was carried by *The Horn Book*.[49]

Announcement of the Dolls' Convention was made in November so that young mothers could procure the necessary entry blanks and prepare their children for the occasion. Some of the mothers were not so young: Louise Seaman sent from Macmillan Pinocchio and a wooden friend, Maria Poppet, the sturdy heroine of *Memoirs of a London Doll*; the entry card for the Empress Eugenie stated that "I belong to — at present — Rachel Field"; and Ethel Calvert Phillips dispatched a model of her peanut hero, Johnny Ping Wing.

The eighty-four dollegates arrived in good repair for the most part and a Doll Hospital conveniently around the corner from the Bookshop was able to cope with all injuries. The Hospital could not, however, help one doll whose eyes had fallen in her head — that was why the vote on Teddy's imprisonment was not mathematically correct. The doll, Jane by name, considered the matter one of inconvenience only and "should be an example to all tired women at grown-up conferences, for she . . . maintained her expression of delight and pleasure to be among so many of her kind, and apparently was determined not to let a little thing like having her eyes pushed in spoil her fun. Of course had they been pushed out, she might have made a fuss, but pushed in, at least she knew where they were."[50]

Jane's distressing story appeared in a playful account of the Dolls' Convention in the Boston *Sunday Post*; equally gay notices ran in the magazines of the book trade. Indeed, the Convention put out its own publication: *Dolls' Convention News.* The sheet told the stay-at-home mamas about the various dollegates attending, the meetings in progress, the prizes awarded for this and that kind of doll, the availability of an official Convention group photograph, and the glass-eye view of Boston the dollegates were being shown by the Bookshop staff. The *News* was subscribed to by department stores in Cleveland and Atlanta, by a children's shop in St. Paul, and the State Historical Society of Des Moines — all of which contemplated similar festivities in their own institutions. In addition, two teachers' colleges requested copies of the paper, although it was not readily clear how they proposed to use it in their curricula.

The dolls were highly gratified at being sped on their way home by Miss Mahony. She had missed the entire Convention because of a severe attack of bronchitis, but had returned from recuperating at Genevieve Washburn's home in Tryon in time to bid the dolls a hearty hail and farewell.

There may have been other Dolls' Conventions patterned after the Bookshop's, but it is doubtful if any could have been as delightful as the one Elinor Whitney directed with such wit and good humor. Her touch was light and sure, neither offending the children with adult whimsy nor the adults with childish sentimentality.

Her imaginative genius made the Puppet Parade of 1933 an equally gay occasion when, according to the advertising flyer, "mirth, music & marionettes" were at home in the Bookshop and Perkins Hall for the month of February. The thirties saw an increased interest in puppetry: unemployed artists and actors found work in the miniature field; books about puppets, including those of Tony Sarg, poured from the presses; a national association of puppeteers was founded. Bertha, always alert to current developments and trends, recognized the interest and celebrated it with the Puppet Parade.

Entries came from far and near and the ages of the performers ranged from seven (hand puppets: "The Boy Hero of Haarlem") to seventeen (marionettes: "Aladdin"). During the week the puppets paraded around the balcony of the Bookshop. On the weekends they joined their creators to perform in Perkins Hall which, for those occasions, changed

> . . . from a long room with bare walls into a gay

> "Marionette Village." There was a stage at one end for hand puppets and one at the other for marionettes, and in between were gaily decorated booths, in each of which a puppeteer displayed his creations and talked of his marionette enthusiasms. Visitors (one day alone there were four hundred) congregated around the booths. . . . Frequently the lights would go out, one of the stages would become illuminated and for fifteen or twenty minutes a play would engross the older people who drew around, oblivious of the fact that there was a depression in the outside world, and the children who had to be forcibly restrained from resting their noses on the stage floor in their eager interest.[51]

The Puppet Parade gave Bertha much satisfaction, for she respected equally the creativity of hand and spirit and saw a relationship of the one with the other. Once she wrote: "There is undoubtedly more importance than we know in the rhythmic circle which links hand and spirit. Perhaps we shall find sometime that natural way once more to show our children the making of beautiful things day by day."[52]

* * *

There was in the Bookshop another exhibition that knew no special calendar but drew its young audiences throughout the year. That was Greenaway House, the home of Alice-Heidi, the Bookshop's own doll. According to a story in the December 1916 *Little Folks Magazine*, Alice-Heidi had fallen out of Santa's pack as he flew over the Garden and was fortunate enough to land in the Bookshop.[53] She was named by the children who attended Miss Sayward's first storyhours and in the old Bookshop she had made her home comfortably, if somewhat publicly, on the mantel near the picture-book shelves.

After the Bookshop moved to its larger quarters, Jeanne Schoonmaker, a steady balcony patron, suggested to Miss Mahony that the doll be provided with a home of her own. Accordingly, Mr. Burleigh of the Toy Furniture Shop of Providence was requested to make a house for Alice-Heidi. It had to fit her as well as the shelves in the picture-book room where it would sit flat against the wall. The side facing the room had to be entirely open so that Alice-Heidi could admire the Garden view and the children could play with her and her furnishings. It should be called

Greenaway House after Kate Greenaway, the famous nineteenth-century illustrator of English picture books.

When the house was completed and installed in its shelves to Alice-Heidi's satisfaction, the doll was "at home" to Bookshop visitors throughout Children's Book Week of 1924. On Saturday of the week Jeanne helped the doll receive and show off her new home. *The Horn Book* carried an open invitation to the affair:

> But in case you cannot come, we are printing a photograph of Alice-Heidi in her house. . . . You can see the wing chair where she rests by the fire on cold winter nights. You can see the stairs leading up to her bedroom. And when you come to visit the Bookshop, you may open the drawers in the bureau in her bedroom and see how neatly she keeps her clothes.
>
> Notice the landscape paper which Mr. Burleigh has painted on the walls of her living-room and notice the little old-fashioned latches on her doors. Perhaps years and years ago right on Boylston Street there were rooms like Alice-Heidi's.[54]

Because the dollhouse had hard usage, it had to be refurbished from time to time — once Marguerite Mitchell and Beverly Watson carried it off to Sunny Fields for a complete redecorating job — but the essential look of an old Boston home was carefully preserved.

Alice-Heidi, however, was completely changed from year to year, for Bertha was never satisfied with the starey-eyed doll in Greenaway House. She wanted a doll that looked like a small person. In 1928 she finally got her wish. On Monhegan Island she met Laura Mackay who made miniature scale models of people for museum exhibits. The Alice-Heidi that Miss Mackay made lived in Greenaway House forever after. She also made a sister, Wendy, to share the dollhouse with Alice-Heidi, and Brownie, to keep them both company.

The little children loved Greenaway House. Lee Kingman Natti spoke for them all when she recalled for *The Horn Book* her own pleasure in the dollhouse and the small people who lived in it.

> It was a large dollhouse, big enough to put your head inside each room, and the game that must be well remembered by many boys and girls was to find the Brownie. . . . He led a busy life, for each child who came to call on

the dolls could search for him, find him, and pluck him out of his hiding place with a discreet cry of triumph. Then the brow-puckering decision — where to hide him so he would be very hard for the next child to find. Once my mother and I made a tiny stamp album with the littlest foreign stamps we could find and gave it to the dolls. But Alice-Heidi and Wendy were more than dolls; they were friends that I went to visit where they were lucky enough to live — in a bookshop.[55]

* * *

When Mary Whitney, Elinor's sister, joined the Bookshop staff in 1922 as Assistant Director in charge of the balcony level, a new kind of service was launched with Bertha's enthusiastic blessing: the sending out from the Bookshop of book collections for exhibit in community institutions.

The service began simply with the exhibits, consisting of new books, going to the schools in the spring months so that the children might select their summer reading from books rather than lists. The exhibits were so successful that the service was almost immediately expanded: a choice of subject matter was offered, the collections were available on a year-round basis, and any organization or institution concerned with children might request them.

Summer camps subscribed to the service heavily, using the exhibits more as libraries correlated by subject matter to their camp activities. Classrooms used them in the same way, as library supplements to their curriculum. Libraries asked for the new book exhibits for Children's Book Week programs in November. Women's clubs were interested in the exhibit of books suggested for the child's own library. There was, of course, a fee for the exhibit service, but by selling the books, at a generous discount, the exhibitor could almost realize its rental and shipping charges.

The exhibits were sent out in sturdy wooden chests with thick rope handles and padlocked hasps. They became very much a part of the Bookshop scene as they were packed for shipping all over the country, even as far away as Honolulu. One year the chests were decorated by Elinor Whitney with the wondrous ships drawn by curlews from Arthur Mason's *The Wee Men of Ballywooden.* Two of those chests are with Mrs. Miller's papers, filled with scrapbooks about themselves, and the ships and curlews can still be seen dimmed only slightly by use and the passage of the years.

The exhibits almost got out of hand during the Depression years when Bertha was using every means at her command to hold her patrons for the survival of the Bookshop as well as the Union. She even tried a whole series of competitions to stimulate reader interest, using *The Horn Book* to publicize the contests: Book Week reading contests, quotation treasure hunts, local history essay contests, literary puzzles, picture treasure hunts, and — with sponsoring groups — playwriting competitions for adults, and art contests for children. Of them all, the playwriting competition produced the most tangible result: a book of plays, *The Jester's Purse,* edited by Elinor Whitney and published by Harcourt, Brace. The annual Book Week reading contests were the most loved by the children who, year after year, sent in their reviews of books, ever hopeful of a prize from the shelves of the Bookshop and the printing of their essay in *The Horn Book.*

* * *

There was one other extracurricular activity that the Bookshop staff engaged in: the making of book lists to accompany exhibits, to complement seasons, or to support current interests. The vacation reading lists continued to appear regularly and after *The Horn Book* came into being were usually reproduced in the annual May issues. One of the most attractive was included in the May 1931 number. Called "Pepper and Salt," the list had the titles of eight Howard Pyle books — including *Pepper and Salt* — as the headings of its various divisions. Mr. Pyle's illustrations, reduced in size, decorated the list.

Two subject lists were outstanding: one, printed in blue on an enormous square sheet feeling somewhat like oilskin, grouped by compass point books about "Boys and Girls Around the World"; the other, a panoramic booklist of the United States, was arranged according to the states' entries into the Union, and opened out sidewise to resemble the train in its title, "All Aboard on the Old 44." The world list carried a portrait of Maud and Miska Petersham's young hero, Miki, whose Hungarian adventures were drawn from Miska's boyhood; the United States list had reproductions of the pictures Berta and Elmer Hader had made for *The Wonderful Locomotive,* Cornelia Meigs' story about old Number 44's record run from coast to coast with a boy at the throttle. The details of the lists indicate the imagination, research, good humor, and book knowledge that went into their making.

No list reflected those qualities more clearly than *The New England Courant*, a newspaper-booklist which Elinor Whitney prepared in 1930 to commemorate the 1630 founding of the Massachusetts Bay Colony. The sheet was named and patterned after the early Boston newspaper with which Benjamin Franklin had been associated. Its eight pages recorded chronologically colonial historical events, with quotations about them from contemporary sources and brief explanatory notes. Because the notes were so clear and concise, and because the apt quotations illuminated the spirit as well as the facts of history, *The Courant* was much more than just a booklist-newspaper: it was a history in miniature.

In 1929 a group of booksellers, all women, became dissatisfied with the Christmas booklists available from the American Booksellers Association. Too small in number to effect a change in the lists within the organization, the women joined forces and produced their own more selective and highly literate list, *Company of Books*. The Bookshop was one of the cooperating bookstores: Bertha prepared the lists of children's books for the annual issues; Frances Darling and her good friend Theodora Perry, also on the Bookshop staff, reviewed adult books. The content of the lists was a pleasant and informal mixture of essay, quotation, book reviews, lists, and illustrative matter from current publications.

The format of *Company of Books* changed from time to time, but the good fellowship of the company of women who produced it remained steadfast through the years: the three representatives from the Bookshop; Marion Dodd of The Hampshire Bookshop, Incorporated, of Northampton; Geraldine Gordon of the Hathaway House Bookshop in Wellesley; and Marion Bacon of the Vassar Coöperative Bookshop in Poughkeepsie.

Realms of Gold

THE MOST BEGUILING LIST to come out of the Bookshop was *Realms of Gold in Children's Books,* compiled by Bertha Mahony and Elinor Whitney and published by Doubleday, Doran in 1929 under the editorship of May Massee. The book purported to be the fifth edition of the original purchase list; but there was little resemblance between the slim, sober 1916 pamphlet of one hundred-odd pages and the splendid chunk of a book that ran just short of eight hundred.

The difference in paging indicated why *Realms of Gold* was compiled: the burgeoning number of children's books had made the old buying guide completely inadequate, even with its revised editions and the 1924 supplement. After that year *The Horn Book* provided guidance to current publications, but an up-to date listing of old and new books in one convenient place was needed. In *Realms of Gold,* the compilers proposed to effect such a combination with enough textual linkage to make the volume not only a list, but also a book on children's reading. Elinor described it as such in a *Horn Book* article, and then continued:

> We wanted to do more than just list titles with annotations. We wanted to tell the story of children's books from the first one, the hornbook, to the glorious present day, with biographies of authors and illustrators and favorite quotations from prose and poetry thrown in in the nature of fireworks.[56]

To make a selective list of books in the English language

available to American boys and girls in 1928 and to trace the development of children's literature back five centuries was a monumental task. It never fazed the stout compilers of *Realms of Gold.* Nor were they shaken by their decision to re-examine every title put into the list, in the interest of a fresh and unhackneyed approach. The earlier buying guides and *The Horn Book* numbers would be used only to direct their reading.

The work was begun in July 1927, and the book was published early in 1929, a remarkable schedule considering the detail and the quantity of material involved. Except for brief, and very human, periods when ideals seemed hopelessly lost in particulars, the compilers worked at their task with unflagging enthusiasm. Indeed there were times when the one or the other would become so engrossed in a book that the list was forgotten. But, as Elinor wrote in *The Horn Book* before *Realms of Gold* was published, that only proved

> . . . that the making of the book list was not a continuous, laborious thumbing of slips and alphabetizing of authors, but a truly delightful revivifying of our whole contact with our stock in trade.[57]

When the manuscript reached Doubleday its great bulk, mass of detail, and combination of list and text almost wore out the imperturbability of Miss Massee "who said she never had such a book to see through the press."[58] Yet, sensing that the book's unorthodox approach would be its most disarming feature, she printed the manuscript as it came to her, except for the removal of one entire section to insure manageability.

The book *did* have form after its own fashion, but the form was never restrictive: the compelling interest of the compilers in the subject matter at hand was of first consideration. The ancient history section, "Roads to the Past," was preceded by lengthy excerpts from Geoffrey Parson's *The Stream of History.* Bertha and Elinor happened to be reading it at the time they wrote the section and it had stirred them profoundly. One collaborator, according to Elinor, "developed a Maria Edgeworth complex and showed every inclination to devote unlimited pages to her!"[59] Alice-Heidi and Wendy edited the doll stories list, and anecdotes from Bookshop experiences enlivened many of the book notes.

All of this gave *Realms of Gold* an intimacy and immediacy that carried it far, far beyond the boundaries of a mere book list. Although the list was based solidly on real knowledge of books and first-hand experiences with children, it was the compilers' delight in both that made *Realms of Gold* take off gaily on its own, once the amenities of bibliography had been duly observed.

The book was hailed immediately upon publication by the literary, library and educational worlds: nothing like it had ever been attempted before, let alone accomplished with such distinction and joie de vivre. Miss Jordan said it was "so plainly a creation that we count the authors unduly modest in classing themselves as compilers."[60] Miss Moore advised: "This fine book is one to own. There is nothing just like it for inclusiveness and scope. . . . For besides all its wealth of information about books and the people who make them, it has the power of stirring the imagination in no small measure."[61] May Lamberton Becker, herself an authority on children's books, called *Realms of Gold* "a sort of affectionate *catalogue raisonée*" in her review of it for *The Horn Book*.[62] To Padraic Colum, writing for the *Saturday Review of Literature*, it was "a Baedeker to the country of children's books. Like a good Baedeker it gives us a sense of competence and completeness in survey; it gives us, too, that sense of richness and variety that is prompting to travel."[63]

Bertha and Elinor's next Baedeker to the world of children's books was *Contemporary Illustrators of Children's Books* published in 1930 by the Bookshop itself. The material in the book was essentially the section that Miss Massee had removed from *Realms of Gold* to avoid a completely unwieldy publication. The compilers had mentioned the deletion in their "Acknowledgments" in the Doubleday magnum opus and promised to publish it later in pamphlet form. But Bertha Mahony's pamphlet days were over and the material, under the personal supervision of Thomas Todd, came from the Todd press as a beautiful book whose appearance was in complete harmony with its subject matter.

Of all the developments in the publication of children's books in America, the most phenomenal was the mushrooming growth of picture books in the 1930s, brought about largely by less expensive reproductive printing processes. Only a general quickening of the movement was apparent in the late 1920s, but enough to focus attention on the artists contributing to the field. In the Bookshop, collectors of certain illustrators watched for their latest works, and questions were asked about new artists as they entered the book illustration scene. *Contemporary Illustra-*

tors of Children's Books was compiled to illuminate the developing field and to provide a kind of Who's Who for those interested in it.

The book contained essays about those great illustrators of the past whose influence extended into the present, and surveys of the contemporary book illustration scene in America, Germany and France. (The French survey, written by Esther Averill from Paris, began her friendship with Bertha.) The heart of the book, however, consisted of brief autobiographical sketches of the artists illustrating modern children's books. Each sketch was followed by a self-made listing of the artist's works.

The introduction to the book was written in Rockport, Massachusetts. In 1926 Bertha began renting Mount Airy from Sadie Butman for the summer months. The cottage was quickly reached from Boston by excellent train service and with the dear familiar Cape Ann scene about her, it was easy for Bertha to relax after a busy day at the Bookshop. Mount Airy offered sanctuary, too, for group undertakings. The *Company of Books* editors met there during the hot days of summer to prepare their Christmas issues. They spread their paraphernalia of cards, lists, books, and typewriter over the flat rock by the side door — the same rock from which, as a child, Bertha had surveyed her world of sea and town below.

Elinor and Bertha had assembled the material for *Realms of Gold* on the rock, and in 1935 worked from it to prepare the book's supplement, *Five Years of Children's Books*. Doubleday's new children's editor, Margaret Lesser, supervised the publication of the book in 1936; May Massee had moved on to become head of the newly established children's department at The Viking Press.

It was indicative of the general growth of children's books that the supplement, which covered only five years of juvenile publication, 1930-1935, should be almost as large as the parent volume which encompassed five centuries. *Five Years of Children's Books* was significant, too, in that it reflected trends in the publishing field. One such trend was emphasized by having the book begin with an essay on picture books, followed by a list of "notable" ones in the judgment of the compilers. The imminent picture-book explosion that Bertha had sensed when she published the illustrators' volume in 1930, was, five years later, in active operation.

Another trend was pointed up by the inclusion of a separate

listing of books about children's literature. Four writers of such books had been listed in *Realms of Gold*, but their books were run in at the end of the "Literary Biography" division with no special heading. In the supplement the "Children's Literature" list included eleven titles, clear evidence of the beginnings of a body of criticism devoted to the examination, the appraisal, and the recognition of the developing field.

Five Years of Children's Books had a particularly pleasing format with clear type and uncrowded pages. Much illustrative matter was used, beautifully reproduced and well-placed on the pages. There were some introductory essays to the various lists but they were short and restrained. The book notes were largely drawn from the lists in *The Horn Book*.

Both *Five Years of Children's Books* and *Realms of Gold* were intended primarily as buying and reading guides. Of the two the supplement was undoubtedly the easier to use for that purpose, because of its correct form and controlled tone. Both books were to be consulted, but *Realms of Gold* could also be read for pure pleasure. It still can today.

Pollen in the Wind

FIVE YEARS OF CHILDREN'S BOOKS was compiled under less than ideal circumstances. General economic conditions in the 1930s imposed severe strains on the Bookshop's operations. The Director's marriage in 1932, while personally satisfying, gave rise to responsibilities in conflict with an already troubled professional situation. Most important, Bertha was trying to withdraw from the Bookshop scene in order to give her entire time and energies to *The Horn Book* which had become her major concern.

During all of the Depression years the Bookshop never operated at a loss, but Bertha and her staff had to work almost frenetically to hold their individual patrons. There was little they could do about the institutional ones, mostly schools and libraries, whose bulk orders had been built up laboriously over the years with the aid of the suggestive purchase lists. Slashes in book budgets reduced such orders to a trickle and their loss was a financial blow to the shop.

In 1936 Elinor Whitney married, too, and with their marriages both women faced the management of established households, expanded family circles, and additional social obligations. It was Bertha's and Elinor's natural and eager desire to respond freely to their new duties which were of absorbing interest to them; all they lacked was the time to do so.

When Bertha established the Bookshop in 1916 it was her sole concern and remained so until she and Elinor founded *The Horn Book* in 1924. Then, imperceptibly, her concern shifted until, ten years later, the magazine was of primary interest to her. It was a natural development from the provincial to the national —

even international — scene; inevitable, considering the pioneering genius of Bertha Mahony and the challenge of the expanding publication of children's books.

As deeply involved as Bertha had become during the Depression years with the *means* of sustaining the Bookshop, she never lost sight of the *goal* toward which she was directing all her efforts: good reading for all boys and girls. Presently she became convinced that she could better achieve that goal through the medium of *The Horn Book* rather than the Bookshop for Boys and Girls. In 1934 she resigned from the Bookshop, as did Elinor Whitney, to devote herself completely to the editorship of the growing magazine. She did try immediately after her marriage, at the Union's urgent request, to direct the Bookshop on a part-time basis. She found the arrangement only compounded her difficulties by forcing her to do in four hours what she had formerly done in eight.

An almost disastrous experience with another directorship made the Union realize that corrective measures were in order, and quickly so. On June 1, 1936, the Union sold the Bookshop to the Old Corner Book Store, basing the procedure on its custom of passing on into other hands a piece of pioneer work once the undertaking had been established beyond the experimental stage. Although Bertha had not wanted a sale — she had wished the Bookshop closed and so brought to a clean end — she reported the transaction movingly in *The Horn Book.*

> The Bookshop for Boys and Girls Changes Management. On June 1st — after twenty years of life — the Bookshop for Boys and Girls ceased to exist in its original form. In 1916, Mary Morton Kehew and Helen Peirce, President and Treasurer respectively of the Women's Educational and Industrial Union, gave a dream a chance to come into being and from then on accorded it the kind of freedom, encouragement and support which are like sun and rain to plants. During these years a group of fine young people, sharing the shop's ideals, have put their own personalities into its life with joy in the doing. Now under the pressure of hard times, the parent organization has transferred responsibility and management of the Bookshop to an old respected Boston firm. *The Horn Book* presents its best wishes to the Old Corner Book Store. If buildings do store up

any atmosphere of the past, much happiness should be the heritage of the new staff.[64]

Later, because she was human and because the Bookshop had been her life for almost two decades, Bertha expressed a personal, wistful hope in a letter to a friend.

> Surely all that was good in the Bookshop for Boys and Girls must be blowing about the world like pollen in the wind. It will settle and take root wherever the soil is most favorable to it, and so while dispersed will not be lost.[65]

It is impossible to give an exact measure of the legacy the Bookshop left behind it — the pollen blown in the wind. So much of that legacy deals with intangibles. How can the effect of a book on the spirit of a child be put into facts and figures? How reduce to statistics the understanding that a spirit so enlightened lends to thought? How tabulate the actions sprung from the thought? And if the child, when grown, passes his love of reading on to those who come after him, how establish limitations to the ever-lengthening chain of cause-and-effect? In truth, the pollen does blow on forever; dispersed, but never lost.

There were, however, certain tangibles that came from the Bookshop: gifts to the children, to those who produced their books, and to those who administered to their reading needs.

To the individual child the Bookshop had offered a collection of children's books selected with impeccable taste so that in the reading of them his own developing tastes should be nourished, never cheapened or demeaned.

To institutions the Bookshop offered the same carefully selected books as presented in the suggestive purchase lists, including *Realms of Gold.* Many children's rooms, just then being established in public libraries, were thus able to have collections of exceptional merit for their first young patrons. Before Eleanor Estes found her life's work as a writer of distinctive children's books, she was the Head of Children's Work in the New Haven Free Public Library. Terrified, at twenty-one, of the responsibility, she managed to survive

> . . . thanks in great part to *Realms of Gold in Children's Books* and to *The Horn Book* and the predecessor of both of these, the pale, blue, well-worn paper back annotated *Books for Boys and Girls — a Suggestive Purchase*

> *List*. . . .These were the golden nuggets upon which, along with probably countless librarians and teachers, I gratefully leaned.[66]

Teachers *were* helped for they could supplement their classroom texts, according to the tenets of the Progressive Education Movement, with additional reading of outstanding quality.

The Bookshop also gave its support and encouragement to those creating children's books. To the children's editors, lately come to the publishing scene, it gave knowledgeable understanding and critical evaluation of their efforts to produce better and more diversified reading for boys and girls. Authors and illustrators of children's books were equally cherished by the Bookshop for their creative genius.

The selection and sale of children's books in other bookstores was influenced by the Bookshop operation. The effect was not confined to the Boston area, but extended to stores in New York City, Philadelphia, Washington, D.C., Cleveland, Pittsburgh, Seattle and Spokane. Several stores were established according to the pattern of the Bookshop, and any number of older bookstores and department stores created children's sections within, yet separate from, their general book area. The stock of the shops, new or re-organized, was based on that of the Bookshop, either by using the purchase lists or from personal examination of the books in the Boston store. Sales persons in the shops were well-educated men and women, many of them from graduate library schools. In short, because of the Bookshop, the whole approach to the sale of children's books was revolutionized, from the purely commercial selling of anything by anybody to the more responsible policy of selling carefully selected books by qualified personnel.

Several of the Bookshop staff went on to establish shops of their own, or to assume management of stores already in operation. Genevieve Washburn founded a shop in Tryon and Pauline S. Langley, another Caravaner, became head of a bookstore in New York City. When the Bookshop was sold in 1936, Frances Darling and Theodora Perry left it to set up a bookstore of their own on nearby Newbury Street. They were later joined by Lillian Gillig, another member of the Bookshop staff. Their Bay Colony Bookshop had a long and honorable life and was very much a part of the Back Bay scene until 1968, when a fire gutted irreparably both shop and stock.

The accomplishments of the Bookshop, tangible and intangible, had their roots in the spirit of Bertha Mahony. Nowhere is that spirit more clearly revealed than in those articles in "Chapters from *Horn Book* History" written for the magazine in the 1960s by former Bookshop associates, that "group of fine young people" who "sharing the shop's ideals . . . put their own personalities into its life with joy in the doing." The Bookshop's ideals were, of course, Bertha's and the joy her colleagues took in their work reflected her own deep satisfaction in laboring for children and their reading pleasure.

> To work with a person who is creative to her very fingertips, ready for new ideas, and determined to carry them out if they prove advantageous is a wonderful experience. . . .
>
> The Bookshop was humming, and the tunes were called by Bertha Mahony, who was tirelessly energetic and constantly making new friends for the Bookshop. *Elinor Whitney*[67]
>
> On whatever problem Bertha Mahony worked her gift of imaginative insight seemed always to lend an unusual touch to its solution. *Margaret Sayward*[68]
>
> The staff at the Bookshop were a "starry-eyed" group, each one indefatigable in learning her part of the thrilling activity. Enthusiasm for their work rose to unbelievable heights. *Mary Adeline Whitney*[69]
>
> Miss Bertha Mahony . . . had a real talent for communicating her love, enthusiasm, and knowledge of books, particularly children's books. This accounted for the excellence of her staff. It is impossible to describe the excitement of all that creative activity. . . . I know that I received my real education at the Bookshop for Boys and Girls, and I am eternally grateful. *Lillian Gillig*[70]
>
> The Bookshop for Boys and Girls . . . was itself a book, and we were the characters of the story. . . .
>
> First came the heroine of the story, Bertha Mahony herself: diminutive, swift, darting here, there, and yonder, a superb business woman, but chiefly a magic person, a charmer, who granted us, her retainers, the boon of working in her Shop. . . .

> Miss Mahony was thorough! We knew our product far better than most salesladies. We read — morning, noon, and night — and we shared our enthusiasms. *Greta Wood Snider*[71]
>
> . . . Many books I lived with have been loved by my own children and grandchildren, perhaps the finest tribute to the Bookshop's founder, Mrs. Bertha Mahony Miller. *Ethel Ranney Crawford.*[72]

When the Union sold the Bookshop, it announced a change in management without a change in policy. The first was easily effected, the latter not so easily done; in fact, it was clearly impossible for anyone else to conduct the Bookshop as Bertha had, since her policy was the very warp and woof of her rich personality, her personal philosophy, her way of life. When Alice Jordan wrote an article for *The Atlantic Bookshelf* about her friend's bookstore, she called it "The Bookshop That Is Bertha Mahony."[73] It was precisely so and when Bertha Mahony withdrew from the scene, the Bookshop for Boys and Girls as she had conceived and directed it for twenty years ceased to be.

The Horn Book: Years of Growth, 1924-1935

We chose this title —*The Horn Book* — because of its early and honorable place in the history of children's literature, but in our use of it we are giving it a lighter meaning, as Mr. Caldecott's three jovial huntsmen on the cover suggest. Just as they are so full of exuberant joy for the hunt that they cannot blow hard enough, so we are so full of enthusiasm for the Bookshop as a hunting-ground, and so keen on the trail of you lovers of books, that we must blow a horn — even our own horn — a little.

First of all, however, we are publishing this sheet to blow the horn for fine books for boys and girls — their authors, their illustrators, and their publishers. Small and inconspicuous space in the welter of present-day printing is given to the description and criticism of these books, and yet the finest type of writing, illustrating, and printing goes into them.

We hope to make our book notes and lists interesting to boys and girls themselves, to parents, to librarians, and to teachers. . . . We also hope to give book news not covered elsewhere, including occasional short sketches of people who have done most for children's literature and who should be remembered. . . .

We find, too, that some of our friends live far away from Boston and come to see us only once a year. To them we want *The Horn Book* to carry greetings and news of the Bookshop and the Bookshop staff. . . .

—Bertha Mahony Miller. From the first issue of *The Horn Book*[1]

A Fresh Perspective

THE HORN BOOK was the first magazine published anywhere that concerned itself exclusively with children's books and reading. When Bertha Mahony and Elinor Whitney founded the periodical in 1924, they sought to put into words some of the joyful noise being made in the Bookshop in celebration of children's books by writers, artists, editors, librarians, educators, and boys and girls. Today, almost fifty years after the magazine's founding, and indeed the most potent of the Bookshop's "pollen in the wind," *The Horn Book* continues its vigorous exploration of literature for children.

The longevity of the magazine has surely been due in part to the blithe circumstances of its beginnings. Early in 1924 Bertha and Elinor mulled over the idea of a magazine that would serve primarily as a publicity vehicle for the Bookshop but would include, along with news of the shop, information about children's books. Somehow the two women, though eager and anxious, were not able to get their magazine down on paper. The truth was, they were involved in so many Bookshop activities that they could not find the time nor summon the energy for a fresh, creative effort. They were fearful, too, of starting something which they might not be able to continue.

Bertha was fond of saying that when a problem made her feel all bound round with a woolen string, a change of scene would not only loosen the tension but also resolve the difficulty that had caused it. It was with that restorative power in mind that two weary Boston bookwomen went aboard *The Orduna* during the last week of April, 1924, for a long summer holiday in France,

England, Wales, and Scotland. Neither had been abroad before. Elinor later wrote of the journey with disarming frankness, though she was perhaps a little hard on herself and Bertha as travellers. They were better travellers than they knew, finding their greatest satisfaction in getting to know something of the people of a country and the land in which they lived.

> We weren't sophisticated travellers, or even proper kind of sightseers. Probably what we missed was infinitely more important than what we saw. I think the English robin and the little English daisy made more impression on me, at least, than Canterbury Cathedral, and I am sure the Luxembourg Gardens and the French children playing there intrigued us more than our tour of the Louvre. A walk in the Lake Country or on Dartmoor was more satisfying than a guided bus trip to Kenilworth or Warwick Castles, and sitting on a stone bridge over a rushing stream in Wales looking at blossoming rhododendron made a more lasting impression than the long trek through Hampton Court and its famous maze. . . .
>
> We chose our inns from the Women's Rest Tour book, but I can remember more than one place where, after our baggage had been deposited, Bertha decided it was not to her liking. The baggage was sullenly picked up by a bellboy and we departed unceremoniously.[2]

The Women's Rest Tour Association, an affiliate of the Union, still publishes two lists of hostelries and restaurants to assist women travelling in the United States and abroad. The Foreign Lodging List was the one referred to by Elinor, and it could not be faulted for Bertha's dissatisfaction with the rooms she and Elinor booked through it. Bertha was destined to be an uneasy, nervous traveller all her life, who, by her own admission, enjoyed any trip more in retrospect than in actuality. She was not comfortable in the role of tourist and found stopping places most congenial when they approximated the atmosphere of the home she was missing.

A precipitate departure such as Elinor described marked the close of the travellers' first day in France. Bertha wrote about it later:

> Within half an hour after landing we were driving down through Normandy with the apple trees all in blossom. We must have left Cherbourg close to nine o'clock

> in the morning. At noon we were at Coutances and at three o'clock in the afternoon were mounting up the steep hill to Mont-Saint-Michel. The day, which had been beautifully sunshiny, had changed when we came down from Mont-Saint-Michel to our hotel on the Mont. There was a chill wind blowing and both water and sky were overcast. Our chauffeur seemed our one friend in a lonely land. So what did we do but have our baggage all carried down the hill again to our automobile. I shall never forget the heart-sinking feeling I had as we looked back at that wonderful place where we had intended to stay overnight, and might not see again, but were leaving after a two-hour stay. It was a mistake, of course, but as a result of the mistake we discovered the Norman hill town of Avranches, bade our Cherbourg car and chauffeur goodbye and stayed in Avranches for three days.[3]

That three-day stay in a small town was the kind of travelling experience that Bertha found most appealing: she liked to settle down in one place and get a little acquainted with it. Elinor, too, enjoyed their stays at Avranches in France, Chagford and Rosthwaite in England, and Beddgelert in Wales. Even rain could not dampen their pleasure in such bucolic days, as an entry from their joint diary indicated.

> Elinor and I started out with a lunch and our rubber capes for a day's walk. It was raining. We went out of the village by Holy Street and over Teigh Bridge where rhododendron were blooming by the stream. The wayside hedgerows were lovely with quantities of stitchworth and pink campion. The foxgloves were just in bud. It all seemed very strange and lovely to us. We climbed to the top of a high bank by the roadside for lunch. After lunch we walked on roads toward Drewsteignton and Gidleigh, finally having a great desire to get to Gidleigh but we couldn't manage it. We finally reached home very wet and very weary and had the nicest tea before the sitting-room fire: tea and bread-and-butter and jam and such a wonderful nut and fruit cake — "currant bun."[4]

The delectable tea was served Bertha and Elinor at "The Three Crowns" at Chagford in Devon. Bertha had disliked both the village and inn on sight and had been sure the food would be impossible. Instead the inn proved to be most comfortable and the food the best they had yet had in England; moreover, after being introduced to Devonshire cider, their outlook on life brightened and they began to feel that Chagford might be pleasant after all. It was so pleasant that the travellers stayed there a week, revelling in the long walks they took each day on the moors, over the hills, and along the river.

Bertha sent home to her sister Ruth postcards of the paths she and Elinor followed in Chagford and, later, in Rosthwaite in the Lake Country, and in Beddgelert. Almost every card spoke of continuously renewed health and refreshed spirits, of a real zest for work once again, of having a wonderful time, and of a longing to be home. One card ended: "You know I've said I'd like to feel at home in the world. Well, I do. I shall never feel nervous about going anywhere from now on."[5] The last was either wishful thinking or sheer bravado, for, although Bertha may well have felt at home in the world, she never managed completely to enjoy travelling around in it.

In the cities — Paris, London, Edinburgh and Glasgow — the two friends did the things tourists are expected to do, as Elinor indicated in the diary, but their hearts were not too gay in the doing of them. In Paris the hotel where they had reservations could not take care of them, nor could they find a really satisfactory restaurant until they discovered, after a walk through the Luxembourg Gardens, a tea room in Montparnasse kept by a woman from Maine. Their introduction to London was a little happier.

> There entered [the train compartment] a middle-aged Englishman. He sat down opposite Elinor and me and soon offered us the *Daily Mail.* Then asked if this was our first visit and proceeded to tell us about the places we passed. . . . He finally told us about his work. He was a water finder. An altogether delightful journey. He made us all interested and happy. Helped us get a porter at Victoria Station. Arrived American Women's Club beautiful sunshiny afternoon at three o'clock. Went out at once and bought a coat.[6]

According to the diary, Bertha bought another coat in Scotland six weeks later; in fact, in that land of thrift, she and Elinor went on a regular shopping orgy, wrecking their joint expense account in the process.

> The expense account was more erratic even than the diary and how, when in Edinburgh, we managed to indulge ourselves in so many purchases at Romanes and Patterson's is more than I can now understand. I remember a wrassle with the accounts the night after, when Bertha took to writing lb./s./p. in her effort to clarify the dubious situation. We gave it up in the end, and she began reading aloud "The Lady of the Lake."[7]

In all of their journeying there was one constant that delighted both women whether in city or village, town or country: the children. The French boys and girls at play in the Luxembourg Gardens had their English counterparts sailing boats on the Round Pond of London's Kensington Gardens. They shared the Close of Canterbury Cathedral with a class of fine-looking boys visiting it with their Masters, and strolled along the Thames with the tophatted scholars of Eton. An enchanting baby distracted them from the Welsh Highland Railroad's thumpy, bumpy ride to Beddgelert from Whitney-on-the-Wye, the home of Elinor's ancestors. From Rosthwaite they carried away a charming picture:

> As we approached [Thorneythwaite Farm] two little girls about seven or eight, with the sun shining on their fair hair and rosy faces, were coming in from the fields with flowers. They looked so shining in their Sunday-clean dresses.[8]

On July 4, after a two-day trip through the Caledonian Canal, Bertha and Elinor sailed for home from Glasgow. Ten days later they were back among their own children at the Bookshop for Boys and Girls.

The long holiday had accomplished its purpose: it had renewed them physically and refreshed them mentally. More important, it had released them from the woolen strings of doubt and fear that had made them hesitate in April about undertaking their much-discussed magazine project. In July they were full of zest and courage for the new endeavor, eager to launch it and confident that they would be able to carry it forward once it was begun. In later years Mrs. Miller often said that without the fresh perspective gained from the trip, *The Horn Book* might not have come into existence at all. It was an auspicious beginning.

From Sheet to Magazine

BERTHA PLUNGED AT ONCE into one of her characteristic periods of concentrated intensity; out of it *The Horn Book* was born. Paced in energy and enthusiasm by Elinor, she was able in short order to draw up a prospectus for the magazine, elicit Union approval of it, gather together the material for the first issue and deliver it to Mr. Todd for printing. On October 1, 1924, scarcely ten weeks after its founders' return from abroad, Volume I, Number 1 of *The Horn Book* was published.

The only difficulty in all of the preparations had been with the name of the magazine: the absolutely right one simply eluded the editors. Then one noon, while sitting on a park bench near the Union, deep in a discussion of early children's books, they suddenly turned to each other and "like spontaneous combustion" shouted together, "The Horn Book!"[9]

The name came, of course, from the device English monks began to make in the sixteenth century to teach their pupils the mechanics of reading. A hornbook consisted of a lesson-sheet pasted on a thin wooden paddle and then prudently covered with a protective piece of transparent horn. The whole looked not unlike a square-cornered table tennis paddle only smaller, more the size of a large playing card. The hornbook was the first book actually made for the child to take in his own hands and use freely. He was encouraged to do so by a hole in the paddle's handle which permitted him to attach the hornbook to his belt for frequent easy study.

Bertha and Elinor were delighted with the mutually-inspired name for their periodical; it seemed perfect to them that the first magazine concerned with children's books should be named after the first paddle-primer book for children. They dashed back to the Union to tell the good news to Mrs. Peirce. She agreed with them. " 'That is just right,' said she, 'and far more important than you realize today.' "[10] Her prophecy was not without foundation, given Bertha's demonstrated ability to make a small thing "grow into something of almost miraculous proportions."[11]

Lest the name of their magazine indicate too didactic an approach to children's literature, its editors chose a gay picture-pun for their cover design: three scarlet-coated huntsmen who, with horns a-tilt, hunted and hollo'd in pursuit of good books for boys and girls. The exuberant drawing was adapted from an illustration by Randolph Caldecott for his nineteenth-century English picture book, *The Three Jovial Huntsmen.* Except for a few rare instances, the drawing, in one form or another, has been used on the cover of every *Horn Book* so that it has become a kind of motif for the magazine.

The huntsmen led a colorful life during *The Horn Book's* first experimental years. Bertha changed their cheerful red coats for green ones for several issues. Unfortunately the green washed over their faces, too, transforming outdoor ruddiness to indoor biliousness. Another time she tried a soft blue, but that was no more successful than the more robust green for it gave huntsmen and horses alike a wan, declining air. After a return to the original Caldecott scarlet, Bertha was content and no more color changes were tried, although during the Depression either the paper or the ink used, possibly both, made riders and their mounts look as if they suffered severe sunburn.

Over the years Bertha and Elinor altered the cover on which the huntsmen pranced. On the first issues they put a great quantity of printed matter: the names of the magazine, the Bookshop and the Union; the address of the latter; the schedule of issuance; volume and number; month and year of publication; and the source of the cover illustration. Then in May 1932 they added to the already over-burdened cover a banner line, "Books and Reading for Young People" and the qualifying phrase of the Bookshop's name, "With Books on Many Subjects for Grown-Ups." It was more than the six-by-nine-inch cover could decently bear. Bertha saw it at once and in the next issue she and Elinor began to clean up the disorder. First they removed the considerable grass patch that had been provided for the comfort of the horses; then, after some experimental re-grouping, they relegated much of the printed matter to the inside of the magazine. The result was a fresh, uncluttered cover which emphasized dramatically the name of the magazine, its banner line and its motif.

The Caldecott cover drawing influenced Bertha's choice of paper for *The Horn Book:* an ivory-tinted stock similar to that used for the artist's picture books. Bertha selected Garamond for printing the magazine, a popular typeface designed by Claude Garamond in sixteenth-century France. She chose it because of its easy readability, its unobtrusive punctuation marks, and its most attractive italic including a bold italic. For a magazine running booklists as well as articles a typeface with a variety of styles was essential for clarity in printing.

Bertha had had considerable experience with matters of typeface, paper and design as she worked with the Todd establishment on Union and Bookshop printing jobs. Neither she nor Elinor knew anything whatsoever about preparing magazine copy for the printer — an art in itself — but they quickly learned by doing, with Mr. Todd and Otto H. Miller, his plant superintendent, guiding and advising them with unfailing kindness, patience and forbearance. Before too long a paste-up of each issue — a kind of dummy magazine prepared from printed copy to show the printer just how each page should look — was an everyday chore for Elinor. She was engaged with a paste-up when Lillian Gillig met her in the Bookshop.

> Nothing I had learned in business courses at school prepared me for my first glimpse of the office of the Bookshop for Boys and Girls. It was incredibly small, crowded, and noisy. To add to my bewilderment, sitting imperturbable and serene in the midst of confusion was Miss Elinor Whitney, busy with paste pot and scissors, working on something called *The Horn Book.*[12]

The editors' inexperience with paste-up techniques accounted for the unused space in their earlier numbers, particularly the first one. In acknowledging his copy of that issue, Mr. Melcher offered Bertha his congratulations on her "interesting house organ" and then took her to task, as he had when she published her 1916 purchasing list — and for the same reason: "You must not be so extravagant again as to have three blank pages and a back cover with nothing on it."[13]

The last was not quite true for in the middle of the outside back cover was a very small picture of a schoolgirl with hornbook in hand. Two issues later the maid was moved to make room for an ad for the magazine, shaped like a hornbook and covering almost the entire page. Bertha learned quickly. Thereafter, until 1930, she regularly used the back cover for Bookshop or *Horn Book* announcements and advertisements. In 1928, she deviated from the policy when Wanda Gág's *Millions of Cats* appeared, one of the first picture books published in the United States that told a story by means of words and pictures and was illustrated by an American artist. Bertha recognized the book for the milestone it was in American publishing, as well as a highly original piece of writing and illustrating; in salute she put illustrations from it on three back covers of *The Horn Book*. It was a tribute to her judgment that the book became a classic in her time.

In 1930 publishers' advertisements became a regular and important part of each *Horn Book*, and there were no more blank pages or back covers to worry Mr. Melcher. Until then, no outside advertisements of any kind had appeared in the magazine except in the November issues beginning in 1926. Twenty-seven publishers responded to Bertha's invitation to take space in the 1926 issue. The ads were grouped together at the back of the magazine and introduced by a statement from *The Horn Book* editors.

> The Editors of *The Horn Book* wish to give expression on this page to their enthusiastic appreciation of book publishers. Whether your joy in books be that of scholar, collector, general reader, or bookseller, you obtain that joy thanks to the vision, faith, enthusiasm, and skill of Publishers, and we recommend to our readers the following pages written specially for this number of *The Horn Book*.
>
> As Booksellers as well as Editors we extend to Book Publishers our thanks and our support for their fine books and fine book making, cordial co-operation, fair business treatment, courteous, considerate, and honest wholesale selling.[14]

Bertha urged the publishers to compose their ads so that they would be in keeping with the general tone and appearance of her magazine. Because of that, the advertisements in the early *Horn Books* have historical value today: they not only record what books were being published in a yeasty pioneer time, but they also reflect the publishers' remarkably serious and responsible approach to the whole business of producing good books for children.

Neither Mr. Melcher nor anyone else could have subscribed to *The Horn Book* after examining his complimentary copy of the first number, for the innocents making it forgot to list the subscription price. They rectified the matter in the next issue: fifty cents a year, fifteen cents a single copy. Miss Seaman promptly sent a check to cover gift subscriptions for eight of her "most delightful friends," as she put it, whom she expected to be as enchanted with the magazine as she was. Miss Moore subscribed at once and then, after the March 1926 number — the first one that really satisfied its editors — advised all of her colleagues to subscribe also, even if institutional copies were available to them. In 1927 Leslie Brooke sent in a subscription from England to the Secretary of the Women's Educational and Industrial Union claiming that he, too, had "great need to be Industriously Educated." The current rate of exchange troubled him; in the end "I have just to make a shot and hope for the best. The best, of course, being *The Horn Book*."[15]

The first modest rate held through June of 1926. Then, to put the magazine on a paying basis, Bertha was forced to double the subscription price, with single issues costing twenty cents. She had expected the magazine to support itself in large part by stimulating a fresh flow of Bookshop orders. Ironically, the immediate success of *The Horn Book* defeated that expectation. The subscribers were scattered all over the United States and in nine foreign countries. They welcomed the magazine's recommendations for book purchases, but they found it easier to place their orders for the books with local outlets, rather than with the far-distant Bookshop.

The rate continued to increase gradually through the years until November 1933 when Bertha announced it as $2.50 the year; single copies, fifty cents. Incredibly, that rate was sustained until January 1947, through the Depression and war years. In Mrs. Miller's files there is poignant evidence of those lean times: handmade cardboard charts listing day-by-day expirations, renewals, and new subscriptions. Red stars were pasted on the charts to mark the occasional days of rejoicing when, for instance, forty-two new subscriptions came in or sixty-eight renewals were received. An ad on the inside back cover of the August 1932 issue echoed the poignancy of the star-spangled charts, as the editors asked for support through new and renewed subscriptions. "Do you value *The Horn Book*?" they asked hopefully. "Do you want to see it survive these days of testing?"

The doubling of the subscription rate in 1926 had coincided with Bertha's determination to put the magazine on a regular quarterly publication schedule: February, May, August, and November. The cover of the October 1924 *Horn Book* had announced such a quarterly intent, but the first two years followed more closely Bertha's editorial statement in the same issue: "Lest this horn-blowing become tiresome to you or to us, we shall publish *The Horn Book* only when we have something of real interest to say, not oftener than four times a year."[16] That had a certain grand ring to it, but it was not exactly reassuring to subscribers, especially institutional ones. Good business practice demanded a regular publication calendar and Bertha responded to the need.

Other production and business matters were resolved in 1926. That March issue which pleased the editors and Miss Moore was the first to be dignified with a complete table of contents. With the same issue the Union began to copyright the material in the magazine, and the Post Office granted the editors a second class mailing permit — after they had agreed to add the word "magazine" to the name of their publication. With the addition of a five volume index in 1929 and an annual one thereafter, *The Horn Book* had acquired all the proper furnishings of a magazine.

That Bertha and Elinor were able to get their magazine in order in ten years was little short of a miracle, given their inexperience, their complete responsibility for all aspects of its publication, their deep involvement with Bookshop matters, their editorship of two major reference books about children's literature, and Bertha's marriage in 1932. The wonder is not that it took them a decade to accomplish the miracle, but that it was effected at all.

In 1934 two events occurred that made the following years easier on the editors and allowed them to concentrate on being just that: editors. The first was, of course, their withdrawal from the Bookshop scene to devote all of their time and energies to *The Horn Book.* The second was announced in the January 1934 issue of the magazine:

> On January 1, Miss Beulah Folmsbee joined the staff of the Bookshop for Boys and Girls as Circulation and Business Editor of *The Horn Book* and Promotion Assistant for the Bookshop. She comes to *The Horn Book* from fifteen years of work with the *Atlantic Monthly* and

> *House Beautiful*. Some *Horn Book* readers will also recognize Miss Folmsbee as author of a volume of plays, *Guki and the Moon Boy and Other Plays* (Harcourt).
>
> In November, when the Bookshop gave a play reading to assist those who must select plays for Christmas, Miss Folmsbee read the plays. It will mean much both to the Bookshop and to *The Horn Book* that Miss Folmsbee combines this genuinely creative side with her thorough knowledge of magazine-making and development.[17]

Miss Folmsbee had joined The Atlantic Monthly Company directly after graduation from Emerson College in Boston and served there in various capacities. When the company took on the expiring *Youth's Companion*, she assisted in preparing its weekly issues for the printer. As assistant to Henry Beston and Victor Clark, she was responsible for the make-up and proofreading of *The Living Age*. She was the assistant editor of *House Beautiful* when the Atlantic sold it to the Hearst Publications. Miss Folmsbee then decided it would be an advantageous time for her to leave the company and seek work more compatible with her interest in writing for children.

At about the same time, word of the separation of the Bookshop and *The Horn Book* had spread through Boston's book community. Beulah heard the rumor and sought an interview with Bertha to see if there might be a position for her on the staff of the magazine. She and Bertha were known to each other, though they had not met; indeed, it was Bertha who had secured the publication by Harcourt of Miss Folmsbee's book of plays. The interview was held on a Saturday morning. Bertha spent the weekend considering the qualifications of the applicant; Miss Folmsbee devoted it to an examination of the back issues of *The Horn Book*. On Monday, editor and applicant were of one mind: Beulah Folmsbee should join the staff of the magazine.

With the promise of release from Bookshop responsibilities and from the business and circulation details of *The Horn Book*, Bertha and Elinor were emboldened to change the magazine from a quarterly to a bimonthly, with six issues each year beginning with the January 1934 number.

The Horn Books for that year were of unusual merit, both in content and appearance. Bertha and Elinor swung into their stride as editors, and Miss Folmsbee took the material they gave her and made it into issues of real distinction. Bertha could never call her publication a "sheet" again, nor could Mr. Melcher refer to it as a "house organ." *The Horn Book* in ten years had grown from a slim, eighteen-page publicity vehicle for a Boston bookstore into a distinguished magazine of substance, influence, and international repute.

B. E. M.— Editor

ATTRACTIVE FORMAT AND honest business arrangements cannot by themselves make a magazine great; they can only support and enhance its content. It is the content that holds the seed of greatness. While Bertha and Elinor were learning how to put *The Horn Book* together and get its circulation details in order, they were also acquiring — again by doing — the editorial proficiency that enabled them to produce issues of increasingly significant content and appeal.

In the doing, Bertha discovered that the role of editor was even more congenial to her experience and temperament than that of bookwoman. As Bertha Mahony *was* the Bookshop, so was B. E. M. — her editorial signature — destined to be *The Horn Book* for the twenty-five years of her editorship. Elinor wrote to the point in an introduction to the Twentieth Anniversary Number, the only personal piece Bertha allowed in the magazine in her time:

> To anyone who has followed *The Horn Book* from its beginning . . . it is apparent that the magazine's vision and vigor have had their source in the personality of its editor. . . .
>
> At twenty years [it] stands a mature magazine with the depth of understanding, the breadth of vision, and the heights of the spirit. To Bertha Mahony goes the credit, for she has the gift of rare sensibility.[18]

Vision and vigor — the vigor Bertha had from the time of the magazine's active planning; the vision needed time for complete clarification. The heart of it was in the statement of purpose and policy that Bertha wrote for the first *Horn Book*.

> Just as [the three jovial huntsmen] are so full of exuberant joy for the hunt that they cannot blow hard enough, so we are full of enthusiasm for the Bookshop as a hunting ground. . . .
>
> First of all, however, we are publishing this sheet to blow the horn for fine books for boys and girls — their authors, their illustrators and their publishers.[19]

There was little in that first number to indicate the eventual universality of the magazine: between a listing of the Bookshop's personnel in the front and a section of friendly chit-chat about shop and staff in the back was a series of articles about the bookstore, including one by Miss Jordan. A brief booklist was the only item not specifically related to either the Bookshop or the Boston scene.

For almost two years that was the general pattern of *The Horn Book*'s contents and in following it the editors were doing exactly what they intended: putting the Bookshop on paper. "We were not attempting then anything of great depth or scope," Elinor wrote. "We were deeply absorbed with our own environment and our own enterprise. . . . We were enjoying ourselves; we were enthusiastic about good books for boys and girls and eager to spread the gospel of their importance."[20]

However, as Bertha worked with the magazine over the years, its potential became increasingly clear to her — the vision acquired breadth and depth. She indicated as much in a late 1926 statement, "*The Horn Book's* Future":

> The material to draw upon is unusually rich and delightful, so that the magazine is worth doing well for its own sake, and not simply as a publicity vehicle for the Bookshop.[21]

Yet while she was still associated with the Bookshop, Bertha found it difficult to cast off local and regional ties. Indeed, she did not accomplish the feat entirely until the shop was sold in 1936. Until then she gave much space in the magazine to matters relating to the Bookshop's activities, to Boston, to New England in general. She also attempted to follow the bookstore's dual appeal to children and grown-ups which, in a magazine, is rarely successful.

Some of the restrictive regionalism was evident in the listings of bulletins prepared for local teachers by a group of Massachusetts educators and the Bookshop staff. Of wider appeal was an extra issue that grew out of an exhibit in the Bookshop of children's art work from six experimental schools in England. In 1925 Bertha prepared a special "Visitors' Number" for summer vacationers in Boston and New England; but five years later, when Massachusetts celebrated its tercentenary, only an ad for Elinor's *New England Courant* marked the event in *The Horn Book*.

For the children, Alice-Heidi explained her various pre-Mackay transformations and reviewed books with doll-appeal. Her articles were printed in the large type juvenile magazines use for material intended for their youngest readers. Elinor's firm hand on the doll's pen kept her contributions light and amusing, even to adults. In a number of issues Bertha ran hobby papers sent in by older boys and girls, and for them a Harvard professor wrote three articles about the causes of the Depression. There were also reports on Bookshop affairs and notices about the innumerable Bookshop-*Horn Book* art, literary, and playwriting contests for children and grown-ups.

Bertha gave such material, limited in appeal by locale and age, less and less prominence in *The Horn Book*, as she came to a full understanding of the magazine's role and responsibility in the expanding children's book field. She put the completely realized vision in a 1933 editorial. It was the first editorial she wrote that was not in part a book review, the first to reveal the seasoned editor she had become, the first to flow confidently from the richness of her own inner resources.

> A magazine devoted to books must always consider ways of keeping its character vital and fresh. It is dealing with records of life — for that is what books are. It is an appreciative critic with a vision which concerns itself very much with the present, but looks, too, both backward and forward. This vision should be clear and informed upon what it is which gives meaning, significance and beauty to living, for only by such vision can books be judged. It should realize also that truth has many forms to be gleaned constantly but never completely from books.
>
> To reach and maintain a place of vigor and excellence, every journal must have its boundaries. A journal for books sets itself a boundary inherent in its character. Its salvation then will be if it recognizes the three arts

which meet in a book and permits the three some flow through its pages: — the art of words, of illustration and of typography.

The book journal must have a real point of view on the nature of criticism. The basis of criticism is an understanding and an appreciation of real creative ability and a recognition of the fact that the critic is less important than the artist. It is the latter who gives the critic his reason for being. But the artist wants and needs the resistance of the intelligent, appreciative, but honest and salty judge of his work. Commendation without this resistance of critical judgment pats an author's work softly and puts it to sleep. Genuine criticism helps to keep it alive indefinitely.[22]

* * *

"What magnificence is yours!" a librarian once wrote to Bertha in a spontaneous salute to *The Horn Book*'s record of excellence.[23] The praise of Bertha's genius as an editor is not to be denied; only clarified perhaps by a consideration of the circumstances which contributed to it aside from her own personality and her "gift of rare sensibility."

They were, briefly, four: she had the wisdom to place her magazine on a philosophical basis that would hold firm for all seasons, yet be flexible enough to respond to the inevitable seasonal changes; from her Bookshop associations she was able to secure as contributors to *The Horn Book* almost everyone working with children's books; she had an instinct for the needed article, the right person to do it, and its placement in the magazine for maximum effectiveness; a self-taught editorial pen enabled her to put the spirit of the magazine — that is to say, the spirit of its editor — into compelling and timeless words.

The basic philosophy on which Bertha established her magazine is still serving it well today as *The Horn Book* approaches its fiftieth anniversay. It derived from her own commitment to reading as a joy in itself, an illumination of life, and an extension of the spirit. In terms of children's reading, Bertha's philosophy had two concerns: the immediate effect of reading on the child, and the later effect childhood reading exercised on the adult. She saw books as a source of delight to the child, if he were granted the grace to read them for their own sake, on his terms, in his good time. She saw books also as adding to the child's understanding of life, since the revelation of life was their essence.

When the child matured, the reading taste he had acquired would help to give his spirit "the invincibility of a house founded on a rock,"[24] and the understanding he had of life would enable him to become an intelligent and contributing member of society.

The major function of *The Horn Book*, as Bertha came to recognize it, was to celebrate those children's books that offered delight to the young reader as well as nourishment of mind and spirit. As books were records of life, so must a magazine devoted to books interpret that life; those best qualified to offer such interpretations were the writers and illustrators who, out of their unique genius with words and lines, had created the living records. No child, Bertha believed, read a book in a vacuum; the life pattern of the scene in which he had his being influenced his understanding of what he read. Therefore the child's life scene must have its acknowledged place in a magazine concerned with his reading. And, since that scene was constantly changing as man struggled toward the ultimate realization of his humanity, so must the pages of *The Horn Book* change to reflect his labors. In that way, and in that way only, could the magazine remain vital and self-renewing.

* * *

Such an editorial policy — simple, strong, allowing for change, and seeing books as a part of life — could not fail to attract contributors to *The Horn Book*. They came at Bertha's bidding like bees to a honeypot, much as writers and artists had gravitated to *St. Nicholas* when Mrs. Dodge was its editor, and as creative talent would be drawn to *The New Yorker* by Harold Ross' inspired editorship.

Many of the contributors were the authors and illustrators of children's books who already had a heady taste of Bertha's appreciation of their work from Bookshop associations. The appreciation was a reverence really, a reverence for one manifestation of life that she, like Albert Schweitzer, revered in its entirety. It would be more correct to say that she had a reverence for the power of creative genius rather for what it always produced, for when the genius was shoddily used she could be salty in her criticism — as the 1933 editorial, quoted earlier in this chapter, suggested.

Yet in their struggles to use their talents well, many writers and artists had come to depend upon Bertha's almost intuitive understanding of their purposes and motivations, and on her encouragement in moments of self-doubt. In 1930 Bertha said confidently to a floundering young writer, "Someday you'll write"; when, in 1962 Elizabeth Yates wrote a book to aid would-be authors, she used for its title the phrase that had sustained her through the years: *Someday You'll Write.* Dutton published the book. When Annis Duff momentarily lost confidence in her ability to write, Bertha helped her regain it; she gently insisted that Mrs. Duff could produce a certain paper for the magazine, knowing, in her wisdom, that the writing of it, though painful at the time, would in the end effect the needed restoration of faith in self and talent. Out of the talent came two volumes about the Duff family's pleasures with books, both published by Viking: *Bequest of Wings* and *Longer Flight.* Some of the chapters of the former first appeared in *The Horn Book.* When Viking published *Reading with Children*, by Anne Eaton, the author wrote to Bertha: "I expect the book would never have been written if it had not been for you — and I hope, as you have time to meditate on it, you won't regret the responsibility."[25] The book had grown out of a talk Miss Eaton had given at the Bookshop while she was the Librarian at the Lincoln School of Teachers College, Columbia University.

No writer knew Bertha's encouragement more than Elinor when she began to write children's books in 1925. Bertha took the greatest pleasure and pride in all the literary efforts of her colleague and friend, particularly in *Tod of the Fens*, which she heard read aloud twice before the manuscript went off to Miss Seaman for publication by Macmillan, and *Try All Ports*, a re-creation of Boston's stirring days as a shipping center, with Elinor's great-grandfather one of the leading characters.

A letter from Cornelia Meigs is representative of the hundreds in Mrs. Miller's files from the creators of children's books who had been encouraged by her cheerful reassurance and strengthened by her honest criticism.

> You have renewed what was always the wonderful thing I got from you, a knowledge that here was somebody who really understood what I was trying to do and who came to meet me in all my efforts . . . your paper has to the full that beautiful quality of yours of generous understanding and stimulation that has been the basis of your immense service to the growth of children's literature.[26]

The editors of children's books were also early contributors to *The Horn Book;* after all, they had all grown up in the field with Bertha, so to speak. After Macmillan and Doubleday had established their separate children's departments, other publishers were quick to follow. Some of Miss Seaman's and Miss Massee's earliest editorial colleagues were Bertha Gunterman at Longmans, Green — the publisher of Elinor's *Tod of the Fens;* Helen Dean Fish at Stokes, later Lippincott Stokes; and Virginia Kirkus at Harper. Bertha read manuscripts for almost all of them at one time or another and advised on other publishing matters as the occasion arose.

A letter from Houghton, Mifflin asked her opinion about publishing J. R. R. Tolkien's *The Hobbit* in the United States as a book for adults or for children. When Doris Patee, Louise Seaman Bechtel's successor at Macmillan, arranged consultant meetings before the publication of *A Critical History of Children's Literature,* she included Bertha in the Boston group. Bertha had known of the book from the time of its inception and had encouraged Cornelia Meigs in her plans to edit the long-needed volume. Bertha's decision not to review a Stokes book brought no rancor from Miss Fish, only a hopeful letter that she and her author might please *The Horn Book* editor the next time.

In 1953 Miss Massee had occasion to prepare a summary of children's books published in America from 1923 to 1953. She wrote to Bertha about her research for the paper.

> Of course, I used *The Horn Books* from the beginning, and I haven't had such a good time in years — you just gave point to all that the children's books were meant to be — there's wisdom and high morality and beauty and gayety of spirit and they still shine out today as they did twenty-five years ago — and *what* a good time we had and how lucky we were to be in at the beginning![27]

Librarians in school and public libraries were also willing contributors to *The Horn Book.* There was a special rapport, based on shared philosophies and similar goals, between Bertha and the library pioneers in children's work. They were the movers and shakers in the children's book world and it has not seen their like since. Working together — and with the makers of children's books — they willed a literature for the young into being by creating it, publishing it, evaluating it, and spreading the glad tidings of its existence far and wide.

Once *The Horn Book* was fairly launched, contributors came from its subscription list: readers who shared the editors' convictions about books and gave fresh expression to them by describing reading experiences of their own in school, library and at home. Bertha rejoiced in those self-generated articles — particularly from parents — for they often brought a bright new point of view that was lively and exhilarating to the magazine.

* * *

Bertha's task in acquiring articles for *The Horn Book* was primarily one of selection: who, among her friends in the children's book world, was particularly and uniquely qualified to produce the paper she wished to publish? And, if no name came to mind, then which friend might best direct her to a competent authority on the subject to be covered? Like Pirandello's six characters in search of an author, Bertha pursued her contributors: a determined editor on the trail of an article. The constant search became in time a habit of mind, a kind of subconscious preoccupation with article and writer that went on independently of conscious considerations. The right pairing might come at any time, from any experience: during office hours or at social occasions; while on journeys or quietly at home; from casual conversations or lengthy correspondence; out of books, newspapers or magazines.

To hold fast to such inspirations when they came, Bertha kept small notebooks about her, of the size to fit comfortably into a woman's handbag and with stiff covers to support a scribbling pencil. She filled the notebooks with quotations from the books she was reading; with bits and pieces of her own thoughts which would emerge later, in more polished form, on the editorial pages of *The Horn Book*; and with suggestions to herself about possible articles for the magazine and who might best write them.

"Get an article on silhouette artists," she directed herself in one notation. "Would Anne Casserley [a writer of Irish stories for children] do a short article on Ireland's history for young people?" she wondered in another. "Write William H. Carr (*Stir of Nature*), American Museum of Natural History, about some nature articles"; "Article on photographic picture books"; "Write Maxwell Reed [author of science books] about articles"; "Article by someone who knows the history of the Pueblo region"; "Perhaps Eloise Davison to review the Mirza books [about Persia] or books in which Constantinople occurs" — all were jottings in one of the notebooks of an editor-in-search-of-an-article.[28]

Bertha's voluminous correspondence with almost everyone in the children's book world was a major source of help in matching articles with writers. She knew who was writing or illustrating what, what was being published when, when a new children's editor came upon the scene, which librarians working with children were involved in original programs, and which teachers were using books with their students in new and exciting ways. Moreover, because she was a warmly human correspondent who could never write a purely business letter, Bertha came to know about experiences that produced articles richly personal in content and tone. No incident, no detail was too small to catch her attention if it derived from or related back to books and reading. The book world was her oyster and by way of correspondence primarily, she found the pearls in it and presented them in the pages of her magazine.

After a holiday in England, Miss Fish described for *Horn Book* readers her two-day walk over the Sussex Downs with Eleanor Farjeon and her visit with Beatrix Potter in the Lake Country. Miss Eaton wrote about the extraordinarily vital operation of the Lincoln School library, an operation that anticipated by a good twenty-five years the concept of the school library as the heart of an educational institution. Who better to review Louis Untermeyer's *The Donkey of God* than Mary Gould Davis? Out of her experience as the Supervisor of Storytelling in The New York Public Library and extensive travels in Italy, Miss Davis had edited a similar collection of Italian folktales, *The Truce of the Wolf*. Harcourt published both books. The article Bertha wanted on silhouettes may have materialized when Miss Gunterman wrote about her Longmans, Green author-artist, John Bennett, whose merry way with words and deft grace with silhouette illustrating distinguished *The Pigtail of Ah Lee Ben Loo*. Somehow Bertha discovered that Virginia Kirkus had been for one enchanted winter in her childhood among a group of children to whom Howard Pyle read aloud each afternoon in his studio. A charming article presently appeared in *The Horn Book* capturing an intimate experience for all time. In one of her notebooks Bertha admonished herself to get an article by Margaret Taft about the imaginative way she was using children's books about the craft guilds to teach a course in Medieval History at The Thomas School in Connecticut; the article ran in the March 1934 issue.

It would require a second volume to this biography to discuss adequately all the splendid articles contributed to *The Horn Book* by the writers and illustrators of children's books: articles about their childhoods, the backgrounds out of which their work came into being, their reasons for writing or drawing for children, the ways in which they pursued their crafts, their comments on fellow-artists in the field. The following is offered only to give some indication of the scope and the variety of their contributions.

In 1929 Eric Kelly did a moving article, "The City That Sings," about the setting for his *Trumpeter of Krakow*; Bertha ran the article again after the rape of Poland in 1939. What had been moving ten years earlier, by tragic circumstances became then a salute to the spirit of a heroic people. Mr. Kelly also did a series of articles for Bertha on writing as a craft; W. Maxwell Reed did a similar series on scientific research in the world of natural phenomena. Miss Meigs, in one of her almost regular contributions, described her seafaring ancestors, particularly the great-grandfather whose sea chest had come to hold her manuscripts — many of them stories about the sea. Eleanor Lattimore, the sister of Owen Lattimore, wrote of her childhood in China and illustrated her article with two sketches made expressly for *The Horn Book*. Lida Siboni Hanson, in writing of her early years in Denmark, recalled the sanctuary her grandfather had given in his Copenhagen home to a gangling boy of fifteen who wanted to be an opera singer. The boy was Hans Christian Andersen. Rachel Field and Dorothy Lathrop described their writing and illustrating experiences with the six-and-a-half-inch carved, pegged, and painted ash-wood heroine of *Hitty*.

After she had found the right person to do an article for her magazine, Bertha discovered she had still another task before her: getting the article out of the contributor. Willingness and eagerness to write, she found, were not necessarily equated with productivity nor an awareness of the adamant deadlines of magazine publication. Yet, perhaps because she herself was a reluctant formal writer, she found the right words to encourage others in their creative efforts. She rapidly became adept at the gentle art of hounding — or maybe one should say of her, the art of gently hounding; in any case, how to persist and insist until the contributor, to get rid of his determined gadfly, produced the article — often to his own surprised delight and always to her satisfaction. As a result, each article published in *The Horn Book* during

Bertha's editorship, left behind it a fat correspondence folder in her files. The articles in the magazine bespeak the spirit of its editor; the files attest to the prodigious labor it sometimes took to give that spirit expression and suitable format.

* * *

If the selectivity of writers and the acquisition of articles presented occasional problems to Bertha, there was no difficulty in determining what articles were needed. *What* she needed Bertha knew precisely, for she made each issue of *The Horn Book* to please herself first of all. She explained her reasons for doing so to other workers on the staff of the magazine.

> I feel sure that a magazine cannot be made to please any individual or group. To be really valuable it must be made as one person sees it, a person who is doing her level best to make a fine magazine within the established boundaries.[29]
>
> A magazine should have a clear editorial vision of its own and be guided by that, not try to make a magazine to suit its readers. A magazine like ours should bring to its readers things they have not thought of. It should be a leader, not a follower.[30]

So long as Bertha edited *The Horn Book,* then, its articles presented one point of view — hers — with conviction and integrity and the magazine led, even inspired, because of that singleness of purpose.

After pleasing herself, Bertha's aim was to appeal to the parents among her subscribers. She believed strongly in the importance of the home environment on the development of the child; moreover, she felt that articles directed to those creating that environment would present a fresh and stimulating point of view to the professional workers in the field of children's books.

* * *

No matter who the reader of the early *Horn Books* was, he could not help but be instantly aware that the magazine was as deeply involved with life as with books. Bertha was ever alert for articles that reflected the currents and the temper of the time. The series that explained the Depression to young people was a case in point. The surge of interest in aviation after Lindbergh's Atlantic crossing in 1927 brought into the magazine a spate of articles and book lists about flying. Comparable articles and lists marked the beginnings of the twentieth century's preoccupation with science — Mr. Reed's were among the first.

America's awakened interest in the world around it after World War I brought forth an unprecedented number of children's books about other cultures than ours: stories, biographies, histories, and collections of folktales. Bertha, an ardent supporter of the League of Nations, willingly gave space to the reviewing of such books that were introducing to boys and girls the ideas of brotherhood and the universality of life. She supplemented many of the reviews with articles about the way children lived in other lands, including the books they read. The most comprehensive of the book articles were those Esther Averill sent from Paris about French children's books, but all the pieces were written from personal knowledge and personal experience.

A special phase of the contemporary children's book scene in the United States was noted by Bertha in *The Horn Book:* the increasing number of volumes being published about literature for the young. All were duly, and usually enthusiastically, reviewed by Bertha herself; one, however, did not fare so well under the "caustic humor" of her critical pen.

> When a great Foundation contributes money and a group of busy librarians and teachers devote time to the making of such a book as *The Right Book for the Right Child*, there should be those in lay circles who would express themselves with caustic humor upon this earnest testing of the reading ability of children, and the analyzing of books. It is possible, we are told, to send any book to the Research Department of a far-famed school system and have it analyzed "at cost."
>
> Who can say what is the right book for the right child? That, thank God, is the child's own adventure. And part of the adventure lies in *in*complete knowledge of words — and life. Always the road leads away, always the horizon widens. That is the wonder and joy of books.[31]

* * *

Bertha's absorption with the content of *The Horn Book* had two facets: first, the acquisition of material for the magazine; then, its placement in the various issues. Before too many numbers had come from the Todd presses, she had learned that if the placement was judiciously done it could add immeasurably to the general effectiveness of an issue, with the articles reinforcing each other to produce an overall excellence beyond that of the individual pieces. She also discovered that the putting together of the lively stuff was almost as fascinating as its acquisition had been.

The basics she learned rapidly: the strongest article was best placed first in the magazine to set the tone of the number and lead the reader into it. Another forceful piece was needed at the end lest the issue dribble away into nothingness. Short and long articles gave balance to the content as well as variety. Book lists separating the articles offered a welcome change for the reading eye. Illustrations or poems reproduced from the books reviewed broke up the solidity of the textual pages and avoided monotony in the book lists.

Within the framework she established for maximum readability and inviting format, Bertha was free to combine her articles in any way she chose. She did try to have in each number one paper on the writing and one on the illustrating of children's books and, if possible, one in a humorous vein to lighten the overall content — although she learned early that humor was not an easily ordered commodity. She generally followed three patterns in making up an issue: the first had no apparent plan except the celebration of excellent books by good articles and dependable lists; the second combined two or three articles which supported each other in subject matter; the third consisted of an entire issue being given over to one particular theme, sometimes stated, more often simply implied.

The March 1926 issue, the one that pleased equally Miss Moore and the editors, had two double-articles: an appreciation of Caroline Dale Snedeker's books about Ancient Greece, and an article by Mrs. Snedeker telling how she came to write them; a review, by Elinor, of Juliana Horatia Ewing's old-fashioned stories and a companion article about the charm of such stories in general. With the Howard Pyle "Pepper and Salt" summer book list, Bertha used a paper about the author-artist written by one of his pupils in the famous Wilmington, Delaware, studio.

The content of a June number had to do with children out-of-doors in summertime; one February issue focused on the sea; another ranged all over the world: Poland, England, Arabia, France, Long Island — a truly international number and one with writers, artists, publishers and librarians all represented as contributors.

The issue prepared for Boston's summer visitors in 1925 was the first of the consciously planned thematic *Horn Books.* It was followed in 1928 by a number that paid tribute to the editorial acumen of Louise Seaman. The number is historically invaluable today as a chapter in the publishing of American children's books, particularly because one article in it dealt with other pioneer editors in the field as well. Bertha had intended to present entire issues about those editors from time to time, but was discouraged from doing so by the suggestion that she had been paid to do the Seaman number — possibly because she had included in it much of the handsome Macmillan catalog as a dramatic way of pointing up Miss Seaman's accomplishments. "A memorable blow" Bertha termed the unjust accusation. "We did think that we had made the aims and purposes of the magazine so clear that such a question would never occur to any one." Bertha's unworldliness made her especially vulnerable to the attack and it was six years before she could bring herself to reply to it in the pages of the magazine.[32]

Fortunately, she revived her plan to "render praise where praise is due" and devoted a 1936 issue to May Massee and her work at Doubleday and The Viking Press.[33] The number is today a part of The May Massee Collection in the William Allen White Library of the Kansas State Teachers College. It is a real tragedy for the children's book world that the legacy of such historically rich *Horn Books* is limited to two.

The most distinguished of the early thematic issues was the one prepared in 1934 as an eightieth birthday tribute to Marie Shedlock. Miss Moore, as Miss Shedlock's good friend, acted as consulting editor for the number and wrote the lead article. It was Miss Moore's third paper for the magazine, but two years later she became a regular contributor discussing children's books from her own point of view in "The Three Owls' Notebook."

All of the 1934 issues were distinctive in format and content and all carried within them the seeds of future *Horn Book* policies and enterprises. The first marked the beginning of a series of articles by Miss Jordan about early American children's books. Later the papers were gathered together, entitled *From Rollo to Tom Sawyer,* and published by Bertha's own company, The Horn Book, Incorporated.

The July issue of that memorable year contained the speech Cornelia Meigs gave in accepting the John Newbery Medal for her biography of Louisa Alcott. In honoring *Invincible Louisa* with the Award, the Children's Librarians Section of the American Library Association named it the most distinguished contribution to American literature for children published during the previous year. Mr. Melcher, the donor of the Medal, had conceived of it in 1921 — the same year he read poetry from the steps of the Book Caravan to delegates attending the Association's Swampscott Conference — as a means of recognizing and encouraging excellence in the writing of children's books. The Medal was named, of course, after the same eighteenth-century English bookseller whose Juvenile Library had been described in Bertha's 1916 purchasing list for the Bookshop. It had been a source of pride to Bertha that in 1929 Elinor's *Tod of the Fens* had been a Newbery honor book, a candidate for the Award.

Acceptance speeches were not a regular part of the Award ceremonies in the beginning. When they did become established as such, Bertha felt the need to make them more widely available than permitted by the restrictive printing in the Conference Proceedings of the Association. After arrangements were completed with the Association in 1937, the acceptance papers became a regular feature of the mid-summer *Horn Book*. When the Randolph Caldecott Medal was established by Mr. Melcher in 1938 to recognize distinction in the American picture-book scene, the speeches of the artists awarded the Medal were also run in *The Horn Book*.

In the 1934 issues of *The Horn Book* Miss Folmsbee worked to achieve for The Booklist section a formal, regular and attractive format more in keeping with its increased importance in the magazine. There had always been lists of new books, briefly reviewed, in the various issues, each list having its own format and arrangement; but many of the books had been considered in longer, essay reviews, either as individual titles or grouped together by subject matter. It had become increasingly clear to Bertha that the essay kind of review, which she really preferred, was not going to be possible much longer in the face of the greatly increased numbers of books to be evaluated in each issue. Therefore, in 1934, The Booklist was formalized in appearance to carry the burden of the new book reviewing; the essay review was reserved after that for the outstanding title that merited individual treatment. The space formerly taken by the lengthy review articles was then available to Bertha for papers more generally informative or critical in nature.

Because of the hundreds of children's books being published each year, Bertha felt it necessary to clarify the book review policy of her magazine in the last issue of 1934.

> Until recently it has been *The Horn Book* policy to give space in general only to those books we wished to recommend. Now we feel that that is not enough. We have not the space to list and comment upon every book published for children, even if we had the time to read them all. We are endeavoring to comment upon those books likely to be given widest prominence. We ask our readers to write us when they disagree with us, or when they wish to comment in any way upon our pages. Often we shall wish to present a point of view opposed to our own, for while there are certain constants in judging books there is a wide area for diverging tastes and reactions. . . . We endeavor in *The Horn Book* to record our reaction to books honestly and sincerely, but we do not claim that ours is the only opinion worth having. Moreover, the more chance we have to quote other opinions, the livelier *The Horn Book* will be.[34]

In the issue that carried the policy statement, Bertha precipitated just such an expression of dissenting views by reviewing adversely a picture book that attempted to interpret God to the small child. Reaction ran high — all through 1935 in fact. In commenting on a similar picture book, Bertha expressed her feelings about crystalizing in pictures what she felt should be a purely visionary and individual experience for the child.

> Since in the realm of the spirit even the wisest grope, only a Blake seeing visions should try to set down his vision in pictures, and then for mankind, not for babies.
>
> The meaning of the Lord's Prayer cannot be brought within a child's grasp. Why make an infant's picture book of it? A little child is so close to the world of nature, and reverence and wonder come to him so naturally, that it would seem better to let him learn the words of the prayer by rote and leave him free of images other than those everchanging ones of his expanding mind and heart.[35]

Bertha published the subscribers' letters of opposition or exception in the revised and revitalized Hunt Breakfast. The section had appeared irregularly in the early *Horn Books*, usually at the back, and consisted primarily of letters from authors and illustrators about some phase of their work or their lives. Then, John A. Holmes, a young Massachusetts poet who reviewed other poets' works for Bertha, suggested that she give each issue of *The Horn Book* "a front section which would form a kind of portico or entrance" and lead the reader into the body of the magazine. He saw his proposed "portico" as having two levels: the first would consist of brief, newsy items about the children's book world; the second would be an editorial derived from the subject matter of the issue and bespeaking its spirit as well.[36]

The hospitable idea appealed to Bertha and when the bimonthly publication schedule gave her more room in 1934, she began the first level of Mr. Holmes' "portico" under an appropriate Caldecott drawing and captioned "The Hunt Breakfast." Before the year was out she had established the pattern of its content: notes identifying the contributors in the issue, informal comment on matters relating to children's books, announcements of *Horn Book* news, and letters from subscribers in praise of the magazine or opposing an opinion expressed in it. The early Hunt Breakfasts hold treasure for anyone doing research on American children's books; his labors will be lightened by items concerning the books Bertha was reading, the plays she was seeing, seasonal vignettes, and occasional flashes of humor, for it was almost impossible for Bertha to keep the human, personal touch out of anything she ever wrote. The following illustrated the point.

> *The Horn Book* Editor was interrupted at this point by the news that her younger, gay black-and-white cow had gone UPSTAIRS in the barn. While these notes are being finished the cow is being persuaded to come downstairs and the Editor cannot be there to see! An editorial life is not a happy one — at times. This is a household where Mrs. Bianco's *The Good Friends* has afforded the jolliest evening we've had this summer.[37]
>
> The white-breasted nuthatch. There was a positive, clear, new bird-note in the maple. A leap out of bed to the window showed that it came from a small bird very like the chickadee — but long where the chickadee is round, and with a long bill. Call and bill seemed to go together. . . . And now in spite of cold winds the arbutus is blooming and May is here![38]

> *The Sowers* by Jean Giono was presented by The Appprentice Theatre at the Repertory Theatre in Boston on the evening of April 10. May Sarton, who directed the apprentices for Eva Le Gallienne at the Civic Repertory, is the leading spirit in this genuine hard-working group. . . . The Apprentice Theatre is only one of those fresh springs in which the river of a new theatre is rising.[39]

* * *

Young John Holmes made his suggestion of front introductory matter in *The Horn Book* in 1931. The Hunt Breakfast had to wait upon space to be started, but the editorials were begun at once. That took courage, for formal writing of any kind was sheer labor for Bertha.

Letters seemed to have presented no difficulties at all: they were written with apparent ease, were organized and to the point, and conveyed great personal charm. Each letter, after dealing efficiently with the reason for its writing, moved on to a more leisurely consideration of other matters. Intimation of *Horn Book* writings can be traced in some of the letters as Bertha tried out her thoughts on her friends for clarity and smoothness of expression. Some contained vivid pictures of her Cape Ann childhood; others, gropings to put into words her deepest spiritual convictions. Almost every letter, no matter how short or to whom sent, mentioned at least one book being read; and in many Bertha spoke of her concern about national and world affairs. The paragraphs of quite a few fairly march down the pages; when she typed those bits of indignation, Bertha must have been feeling like the Irish shillelagh which she said she turned into in moments of righteous wrath. Since she typed almost all of her letters herself, making the proper carbon for even the most personal, it is small wonder that she suffered almost constantly with painfully split fingertips — especially after a shillelagh mood had been upon her.

When faced with formal composition of any kind Bertha froze, her spontaneous, natural style lost in a struggle to cope with grammar, syntax, and logic. To a friend she once mourned her lack of training in the art of writing, particularly in the organization of material for a lengthy effort and the making of an outline to guide such writing. Plagued by her own self-consciousness and urged by Ruth, Bertha went so far as to submit a sample of her writing for criticism to a professor in the English and History Department of the Massachusetts Institute of Technology. Professor R. E. Rogers' reply was kindly and astute:

> I really haven't anything to criticize about this. I think your sister must be hard to please. *Hidden Shops* strikes me as a very nice idea, simple and unpretentious in management and phrasing, and rather charmingly written. So much of it is quotation that there is very little of yours for the critic to comment upon. But the quotations are all full of flavor and picture-making, which nicely matches your own opening description, which, so far as I can see, is not perceptibly inferior to those you quote. If you try longer things, I should suggest trying your own wings more and not lean quite so hard on quotations. Your own descriptive writing is pleasant and personal enough to please for its own sake . . . and too many quotations in a short paper give rather the effect of drowning originality. You need practice in a rather more sustained piece of work. I have no opportunity yet to judge of your capacity for architectonics, composing an article so that it jells. But these bits I have seen are excellent practice, and I am sure that you have in your shop and in your own reading, many possibilities for charmingly personal articles with a touch of the bookish in them.[40]

The quotations Bertha could never entirely drop — both Mrs. Mitchell and Miss Folmsbee took her to task on the same score years later. But she did learn, in time, to have more confidence in her own expressions which were, as Mr. Rogers so aptly said, "not perceptibly inferior to those you quote." Twice Mr. Rogers used the word "personal" to describe Bertha's writing and that is perhaps the key to its effectiveness. Her writing of all kinds — letters, reviews, articles, editorials, Hunt Breakfast items — always expressed her own personal beliefs and her own personal experiences, and did so with warmth and deep feeling.

The (London) *Times Literary Supplement* summed up Bertha's struggle with words and her triumph over them in a tribute written in the year of her death.

> This great woman . . . was not the easiest of writers, seeming often to be locked in battle with words rather than directing them firmly to her purpose, but there

was never a doubt about the strength of her convictions or of the profound thought that went into forming them.[41]

Except for book reviewing, Bertha had very little time in the early years of *The Horn Book* to write general articles. Three of her book review essays, however, were also richly autobiographical. "Children and Solitude" (June 1926) was a revelation of her childhood years happily alone in the woods and wild pastures of Rockport. *"Long Island's Story* — Why Not Other Regional Books?" (February 1930) was one part Long Island and three parts Cape Ann as Bertha recalled the history and the geological formation of the Cape. *"Not a word of any of this ever came into one of the school rooms I sat in."* The impassioned italics are Bertha's who continued, "Would not a natural process of education which was based upon a complete knowledge of the section of earth one trod lead naturally to interested, vital citizenship and intelligent politics?"[42]

"A View Halloo" (May 1929) contained some of Bertha's gayest, least restrained writing; indeed, the galloping of the fox-hunters in the books reviewed was echoed in her headlong prose. It all began in Boston where she read Siegfried Sassoon's *Memoirs of a Fox-Hunting Man,* and continued when she went to Genevieve Washburn's home to recuperate from the bronchitis that had kept her from the Dolls' Convention at the Bookshop.

She had carried many books, but scorned them all and ranged the house for ones just to her liking. Nothing suited, nothing suited, until she found a volume by Somerville and Ross . . . she remembered there was hunting in these books, and fell upon *All on the Irish Shore*. . . .
The fit being on her in Tryon, she tore through *All on the Irish Shore* and *Dan Russel the Fox,* and paused perforce for breath. Even when in Boston again, [and] life took on a serious and laborious cast, she must, notwithstanding, spend all her nights with wild riders in Ireland. And she raced through *In Mr. Knox's Country,* and not content to ride alone she thought of a lad down the state who read and re-read Surtees. So while pursuing a first English edition of the *Memoirs of a Fox-Hunting Man* for him, she started him off on the same mad orgy and now, after three Somerville and Ross volumes have gone down to him, all the rest have to go.

> As for the Editor herself, she still rode on and on — through *Some Experiences of an Irish R.M.* AGAIN, and through *The Further Experiences.* Important spring books stood about her rooms in piles waiting to be read. An article for an educational journal on new spring books glowered to be written. But the Editor could stop only to find out more about the authors of these rushing tales which give such perfect pleasure . . . and go off like spiral rockets.[43]

Bertha's first editorial appeared in the August 1931 *Horn Book*, taking the place of the poem she usually placed opposite the table of contents to set the mood of the issue. The editorial was a salute to Elizabeth Coatsworth who had just been awarded the Newbery Medal for *The Cat Who Went to Heaven.* It was not signed, but all the editorials that came after it, written by Bertha, bore the now famous initials: B.E.M.

Most of the early editorials followed the pattern of the first one: that is, they were salutes to outstanding books in the field. Yet even those book-review editorials gave promise of the moving, forceful ones that would appear in time, for in each Bertha went from specific comments on the book in hand to more general remarks on all books, or on life itself.

Editorial writing presents its own peculiar problems, not the least of which is the restriction of space, but Bertha mastered the art, again learning by doing. Later she passed on the wisdom she had acquired through experience to other staff members of *The Horn Book.* "Have a central theme and hew to it," she advised Ruth Hill Viguers. "Don't admit a bit of repetition, and try to have each short and memorable. It is important to have the editorial short enough to look well on the page."[44] "The more you make it express something urgent in your own interest, the better it will be," she told Norma Fryatt.[45]

It was the compelling urgency in her own editorials that drew the reader right into them to experience Bertha's concerns and share her views. The views were honest and expressed in forthright terms, but saved from authoritarianism by the warmth of her humanity. One striking characteristic of Bertha's editorial writing is more apparent today than when it first appeared: its timelessness. That is as it should be, for Bertha, a deeply thoughtful person, wrote not so much of current issues but of the changeless fundamentals underlying them.

It took Bertha a little more than two years to get her editorial pen in complete control. Then in January 1934 she wrote an editorial whose form and content indicated that she had mastered the art of editorial composition. From then on, so long as she was the editor of the magazine, her editorial was the heart of each *Horn Book* giving it "the depth of understanding, the breadth of vision, and the height of the spirit."

The January 1934 editorial had been inspired by two books rooted in Irish folk lore: Lord Dunsany's *The Curse of the Wise Woman*, and *The Big Tree of Bunlahy*, by Padraic Colum. Bertha reviewed the books in the same issue, calling her essay-review "Tir-Nan-Oge and Tir Tairngire." She used the same words to begin her editorial.

> Tir-Nan-Oge, Tir Tairngire — Land of Youth, Land of Wonders — these were two very real worlds in ancient Gaelic folk lore, and they live in the hearts of some people today as shown in the two books reviewed on page 31. There is an instinctive wisdom that has nothing to do with schools. The American Indian had this wisdom. He recognized himself as a part of the universe. He was sensitive to his rhythmic brotherhood with animals and his sharing of life with the plants and trees. He knew, too, that as he stood upon the earth and was in every way a part of the universe, drawing his life breath from it, so he could draw his spiritual energy from it, too.
>
> The spiritual power was there. He must discover the way to let it flow deeply and freely into his own personality and express itself anew through him. He developed a special kind of communion with the great spiritual forces, a way of opening his soul to the power he needed. Did he understand the forces? No. Nor does any one today. But he was filled with wonder and reverence before them. Wonder and reverence are rights of childhood. And prayer, too, because it is this last which is the soul's communion with the spirit of the universe, and it is by means of this that each works out for himself the way to spiritual power.
>
> That is why it is so foolish to say "we ought only to give the child conceptions it can understand." His soul grows by its wonder over things it cannot understand.

It is the spirit which guides the personality. If the spirit has never had a chance to find itself, and has had no nourishment or exercise, then we have just the kind of people we do have now in such numbers. Homesick people longing for they know not what. Real vision comes from the spirit. And human life is like a plant. The future is within itself. If we can only find the way to help young human beings to develop themselves fully — body, mind and spirit — in far simpler, more genuine ways than at present pursued! Then we shall have a true sense of values. Then we shall insist upon an adventurous, creative life; recognize superiority in its essence and choose for ourselves leaders who have it. B.E.M.[46]

The Early Years at Ashburnham

You and William are creating a masterpiece. It is great fun to see you mixing and putting on the colors — there is a great deal of light in the picture — the brush strokes are sure — the harmony of the composition is full of promise — it is not nearly finished.

-- Marguerite Mitchell. From a letter to Mrs. Miller[1]

In the Latter End of the Harvest

TO WRITE EDITORIALS like "Tir-Nan-Oge, Tir Tairngire," Bertha needed the time to think them through and the privacy to work with them on paper until they conformed to the standards she had established for herself. She gained the time when she withdrew from the Bookshop, when Miss Folmsbee joined *The Horn Book* staff, and — most important — when marriage endowed her with a well-established household that functioned with a minimum of direction. The grace of privacy came from an appreciative and understanding husband and a quietly peaceful study-with-a-view to work in.

Bertha had known William Miller for fourteen years when she married him in 1932. She had met him and his first wife, Celena Whitney Miller, on Monhegan Island, as her Diary for July 3, 1918 recorded:

> Was sitting on the Millers' piazza today — very comfortably ensconced — when the Lord of the Mansion arrived. He was very nice indeed. Persuaded me to stay & showed me over [the] house. At lunch I met Mrs. Miller. She said Miss Jones of the Commission had just recently spoken of me to her.[2]

The association, begun under such happily relaxed circumstances, moved quickly into friendship as similar New England backgrounds were discovered and mutual interests explored. The friendship continued when the vacationers left Monhegan, for the Millers' Boston apartment proved to be just around the corner from the Beacon Hill address shared by Bertha and Ruth.

The apartments were so near in fact that it was easy for Bertha to step around daily with friendly notes for Celena, when she was house-bound by her heart condition. Bertha wrote one series of notes on British Museum cards representing some of Celena's interests: Persian prints and reproductions of Persian book illustration, Chinese vases, and rare English china. The greetings were gay bits of Bookshop anecdote and gossip. Those, too, had special meaning for Celena, as Bertha lost no time in interesting her new friend in the Bookshop activities, asking her to serve on the Advisory Board, to make reading lists of adult books for patrons requesting them, and to review books for the shop and, later, for *The Horn Book.* Celena brought the children of the family to the Bookshop, too, especially book-loving Jeanne Schoonmaker, the daughter of her younger sister. It was Jeanne who had suggested Alice-Heidi's apartment to Bertha and co-hosted its "at home" party.

Indeed, the Millers were so involved in the Bookshop that it was natural for them to give a dinner party in their apartment in honor of Ella Young, after the Irish poet and folklorist spoke for Bertha at a Union Department Conference. In later years Bertha recalled two aspects of the occasion: the beauty of Miss Young's head in the candlelight and William's reaction to the fairy music the Celtic mystic purported to hear.

> I wondered how he would regard the fairy music for he is a realistic person and considers himself lacking in imagination and mystical sense. He only said, however, that some people were so finely attuned they could pick up sounds in the air as wireless does.[3]

Bertha came to know the Millers' Ashburnham home, too: a Massachusetts farmhouse which managed to retain its simplicity of line outside and its graciously proportioned rooms inside in spite of the many additions and changes made over a hundred year period. The rooms reflected the tastes and interests of their occupants: glowing Oriental rugs on the floors; cherished pieces of family furniture; silver gleaming on server and sideboard in the bay-windowed dining room; Celena's objets d'art everywhere, brought back from many journeys abroad; William's fine collection of Graeco-Roman glass in its specially made cases; books in hand-tooled bindings; Persian prints, Japanese hanging scrolls, and Claude René Martin oils on the walls.

William had lived with the Martin family for two years while studying French literature and the French language at the Sorbonne. When he returned to his home in Haverhill, Massachusetts, he had in his possession his *Certificat D'Etudes Françaises* from the Sorbonne and a contract to teach French at Annapolis. The contract was never signed; instead, William joined the W. F. Whitney Company, a furniture concern which specialized in colonial reproductions and maintained its factories in South Ashburnham. Mr. Whitney had the enthusiastic aid of his eldest daughter in persuading William not to leave the New England scene he loved so and to enter the business, rather than the academic, world. Celena's argumentative powers, Wellesley trained, were considerable; even more effective was her dark-eyed, wide-browed beauty. Celena and William were married in 1904 and soon after acquired the century-old farmhouse in Ashburnham as their home.

The setting of the Miller home delighted Bertha: a hillside that swept up from the heart of the town and continued, beyond the house and barns, to a high-meadow crest. The east view was down and across the rooftops of the village; west, from the highest point of the meadow, Mt. Monadnock could be seen across the New Hampshire border, deep blue on the horizon. The views were balm to eyes trained to distance by the landscapes and seascapes of Cape Ann.

Of equal pleasure to Bertha was the beautifully landscaped setting the Millers gave the old house under the direction of Nellie B. Allen, a prominent Boston landscape architect of the time. The pictures of the grounds which appeared in the May 1930 *Home & Field* did not convey to the full the way Miss Allen had used the natural slope of the property to create terraced effects, nor the contrast of flowering borders with dark evergreens to mark the various levels and boundaries.

Celena took great joy in her Ashburnham garden and when her heart condition would not permit her to visit its terraced heights, she rode to them on a small donkey. She kept notebooks of her garden, recording the seeds ordered each year, the peak blooming time of each flower, the look of flower with flower, the results of experimental plantings, and the visitors to her flowering hillside. In one such book, Celena recorded that Bertha E. Mahony visited the garden on August 14, 1930.

Celena noted in the same book that hollyhocks, larkspurs, snapdragons, and zinnias were at their height of bloom in the garden on July 25, 1931. Five days later she died at the age of fifty-eight. The next entry in the notebook, dated August 1933, was in the handwriting of Bertha Mahony Miller.

After Celena's death it was natural for her husband and her friend to be brought closer together in their mutual grief. In good time William left off his black tie of mourning for a gay blue one that matched his eyes, eyes bright again with his habitual zest for life. The tie began to flash in and out of the Bookshop with disarming regularity, so it was no real surprise to her staff when Bertha announced her engagement to William at a lobster dinner party at Mount Airy.

It was at Mount Airy, too, that Bertha and William asked the Reverend Ben Roberts, pastor of the Newton Highlands Congregational Church, to officiate at their September wedding. Ben Roberts had begun his ministry in Ashburnham and, although William had not been of his congregation, it was inevitable the two should meet in the small community. They argued themselves zestfully into a firm and lasting friendship, with the unorthodox New Englander pricking neatly the theories of the fresh, young seminarian.

In 1931 the friendship had broadened to include Bertha. In the Ashburnham music room the three formed a trio: "a sorry trio," Ben Roberts termed it, "but we enjoyed ourselves and we did not perpetrate our efforts ever on anyone else. She was a pianist of sorts, I a violinist of very poor sorts, William a cellist (self-taught, I believe) of a villainous sort."[4] At Mount Airy the men sailed during the day and in the evening Bertha took them up to "some boulder-strewn wasteland" and introduced them to Duck on a Rock, the childhood game she and her brothers had played in the same place. "She had us hopping from one monstrous relic of the Ice Age to another in a most undignified, perilous, but exciting manner."[5]

Bertha Everett Mahony and William Davis Miller were married by the Reverend Ben Roberts on September 7, 1932. The ceremony took place under the grape arbor in Marguerite Mitchell's garden in Weston, Massachusetts — "such a . . . garden as is beloved of the fairies" Bertha called it.[6] The bride wore a soft summer print dress with a lacy picture hat and carried a bouquet of garden flowers. In the pictures of the wedding party she looked quietly happy beside her sturdy Yankee husband.

Miss Jordan was at the wedding; Miss Moore could not attend, but sent a greeting: "I'm prepared to like Mr. Miller sight unseen and wish him, as well as you, great happiness."[7] The entire Bookshop staff was there. Mary Fitzgerald, Bertha's devoted secretary, was especially moved by the occasion. "I shall never forget it," she wrote to Bertha. "The whole setting was so serene and beautiful and it seemed symbolic of the future happiness of you and Mr. Miller."[8]

The staff's wedding gift to Bertha was a copy of Rosenbach's *Early American Children's Books*. In thanking them for the beautiful volume, Bertha wrote: "Most of my own books I keep in my study upstairs, but I find that I like to have this book of yours where I can really see it in the landscape even when I'm not actually using it."[9] The book came to rest on a large table in the library, the room that was the heart of the Miller establishment.

The table was placed in a corner of the room, with wall bookshelves on two sides of it and William's easy chair at one end. From the chair he could admire the terraced hillside through a west window, keep an attentive eye on the hearth on the east wall when a fire burned there in season, or look directly across the room where Bertha was "very comfortably ensconced" on a sofa or in one of its flanking wing chairs.

Additional chairs, easily moved, invited guests to become a part of the scene — for tea, for cocktails, for after-dinner conversation, or for late reading-aloud hours. The library was a friendly room that could accommodate a number of small conversational groups or one large listening circle. William's dry wit and Bertha's sense of fun sparked any gathering in the room, and their unfailing courtesy and thoughtfulness made each guest feel welcomed and cherished. Occasionally the Lord of the Mansion and the new Mistress of the House were most happily alone in the library, enjoying the pleasure of each other's company.

The Mistress of the House

THE ASHBURNHAM HOME was undeniably and unquestionably Celena's — her forceful presence was everywhere. Bertha felt it to be so when she came into the house as a bride, and the passing years did not diminish the feeling. Indeed, in 1960 she confessed to a grandniece that even after living in the house for twenty-eight years she still thought of it as Celena's. Yet the presence of the first wife did not distress Bertha: instead, it carried a measure of comfort and reassurance. She once wrote to Annis Duff: "I have never understood the feeling some people have of not wanting to be in the place where the loved one had been. That is where I have always wanted to be. Rockport is filled with my mother and father. And this house with Celena."[10]

Then, too, the pattern of life as established by Celena was congenial to Bertha and she continued it quite naturally when she assumed her new role as wife, mistress of a house, and member of a small community. Consciously she adapted it to accommodate her peculiar needs as a professional woman; unconsciously she modified it by the gentleness of her personality.

In directing her husband's household with a minimum of disturbing changes, Bertha had the help of Hanna Kovanen, the Finnish cook, and Duncan Munro, the Scottish gardener. Hanna had come to the Miller kitchens in 1926 after the death of Celena's mother, for whom she had worked for twenty-five years. She stayed with the Millers until her own death in 1953. She was a gifted cook with special skills in baking. The family members who visited the house in Hanna's time as children and young people remember the fragrance of her freshly-made bread, when she removed it from the oven of the great old wood-burning stove she favored for baking purposes.

Bertha's cooking was limited and usually disastrous. She was glad enough to leave the management of the kitchen to Hanna's competency. The only change mistress and cook effected together was to introduce greater variety into the menus, restricted before by Celena's special requirements. William's preferences were of major consideration, as they were in every other household arrangement. Bertha and Hanna, of the same age, were at ease with each other, often gossiping companionably over the evening dishes, occasionally sharing the tri-weekly chore of butter churning.

Although the Miller property was no longer operated as a farm in Bertha's time, the barn across the road from the house held chickens, cows, and horses well into the 1940s. That was the barn where Bertha's youngest cow went UPSTAIRS. Although she resisted the temptation to watch the bovine descent, she did at times join the household in getting the perverse cows back in the barn of an evening, leaving *Horn Book* affairs to do so and laughing to herself at the contrasts in her new way of life.

Near the barn was Duncan Munro's greenhouse, where he raised each spring the plants for the flower borders and the cutting and vegetable gardens. After graduating from Scotland's famed Dumfries Academy, where he studied gardening, landscaping and greenhouse operation, Duncan had used his educated green thumb as a ticket to world adventure. He was working for Miss Allen in Boston when she designed the Miller garden and was sent to Ashburnham by her to translate a paper garden into a green and growing one. Duncan never left the Massachusetts hill-town, remaining there, at Mr. Miller's invitation, as gardener of the estate and, presently, as the husband of pretty Esther Ryan Munro.

One of the pleasantest tasks of Bertha's new life was working with Duncan over the garden arrangements. The work began right after the Christmas holidays with the ordering of seeds for the greenhouse trays. The orders were properly recorded in the garden notebooks, reading like a poet's colorful and fragrant litany: canary bird and polar bear pure white zinnias; early yellow globe onions and American Flag leeks; flaming violet, ballerina and Comanche petunias; tennis-ball lettuce and snowball cauliflower; coral moon scabiosa and trillium grandiflorum.

In April Duncan fired the boiler in the greenhouse and planted the seeds in their trays. If Bertha was absent from home for any length of time in the spring, immediately upon her return she walked across the road to inspect Duncan's seedlings. Later, she sometimes helped set out the plants in the garden that supplied the cut flowers for her vases. The fresh earth pleased her fingers and nose; the routine, repetitive task allowed her mind to busy itself with other matters as she set out plant after plant, row upon row.

Perhaps it was Bertha's satisfaction with Duncan's beautifully kept garden that prompted her to choose for her study a small second-floor room whose one window looked out over the hillside panorama. An adjoining sleeping porch repeated the view and added, through a bank of north windows, one of thick woods of birch, oak, pine and hemlock. Bertha created The Study, as it came to be called, so that she might work on *Horn Book* affairs at home, going into Boston only a few days each week to confer with Miss Folmsbee and to visit Ruth in the apartment she continued to maintain with her.

Given the distracting view from its window, it was a small miracle that Bertha ever accomplished the business for which her study had been established. Occasionally eye and typewriter conspired against her and seasonal vignettes got into her *Horn Book* writing as a result. Even The Three Owls could not resist the garden's beauty; Miss Moore wrote about it frequently, finding in it the bright memory of her mother's Old World garden at the Limerick, Maine, home.

> After the balloons, the snow crystals, the snow man and the magical bouquet of the Newbery-Caldecott Awards dinner at Atlantic City, I found myself under the pine trees of Bertha Miller's hillside garden. Believe it or not, the very roses, delphiniums and starlike white flowers of the cherished bouquet were blooming all over again in that New England garden.
>
> It is an enchanting spot in which to dream, to read or to watch a group of children playing at hide-and-seek among the trees. It is a garden beloved by birds and butterflies and children playing with their dolls. Between two rows of tall pine trees a path leads up to the sunny hilltop where the blueberries grow. To walk up that path is to go far away; to walk down is to come home again.[11]

The children to whom Miss Moore referred were the grandchildren, grandnieces and grandnephews Bertha happily acquired when she became Mrs. William Miller — happily, because she loved all children and because there were none at all in her own immediate family. The grandchildren were the sons and daughters of Alice Rice Miller Dean, whom William and Celena had adopted in her adolescent years, and Stuart Dean, an educator in the private school field. The three older Dean children — Celena, Eric and Bill — called the new Mrs. Miller, affectionately, "Bertha." To the youngest Dean, Nancy, born just a year before Bertha's marriage, she was more simply, "Gran." She was "Aunt Bertha" to Arnold and Billy Manthorne, the sons of Mary Arnold and Gordon Manthorne, William's nephew and the only child in his family. She was also "Aunt Bertha" to Kit and David Jarmon, the children of Celena's niece, Jeanne Schoonmaker, and Oscar Jarmon; and to Reta, Jean and Sally, the daughters of Celena's nephew, David Schoonmaker, and Anne Palmer.

The Manthornes, the Jarmons, and the Schoonmakers all lived on nearby Ashburnham hills, so that the children were in and out of the Miller house on a daily basis. Nancy spent so many vacations and holidays in her grandparents' home as to have a room there designated as her own. The children enjoyed the freedom of the rambling old farmhouse with its many rooms, maze of hallways, and numerous stairs. There was rarely a problem of discipline, for Bertha had her father's talent for controlling the children by her gentle presence alone. Even the occasional wilfulness of Nancy was understood, for wilfulness had plagued Bertha herself as a child and even in her adult years was not always to be denied.

For the children's pleasure Bertha gathered together a special collection of books: picture books for the younger ones including those of Randolph Caldecott, Leslie Brooke, and Beatrix Potter; Kipling and "funny" books for the boys; and for sensitive and imaginative Nancy the fantasies of Anne Parrish, Kenneth Grahame and Paul Fenimore Cooper. The permanent collection was supplemented by the new books as they arrived for *Horn Book* consideration. Many of Bertha's reviews for the magazine contained the children's reactions to the books as she read them aloud.

For the little girls Bertha arranged in a corner of the music room a family of dolls, complete with furnishings and wardrobes. The bureaus, beds, and tables were turned in the Whitney shops and the clothes were elegant enough to please the most particular child and varied enough to suit any occasion. Bertha meant the dolls to be loved and played with, not just admired and looked at;

their appearances in the late 1960s suggested that her intentions had been completely realized. One of the dolls, Anne Whitney, went all the way to China to keep Kit Jarmon company and remind her of the home from which her father's naval duties were temporarily taking her.

For the boys of the family Bertha amassed over the years an extensive collection of small toys with which they could work and play. Most of them were related to farming, a familiar occupation in that rural area: buildings, equipment, stock, and farm workers. The toys were kept in the front hall closet, not too far from the dolls' corner in the music room, where they could easily be brought out for the amusement of the occasional visitor as well as the family regulars.

Bertha delighted in having the children around all the time but especially during the December holidays when they made for her, as she said, "the peak of my Christmas." Sometimes on Christmas Eve the children decorated a tree for the dolls, and sometimes a living one out-of-doors for the birds and the squirrels. Occasionally William was prevailed upon to read a Christmas story to them. After refreshments, which always included ice cream, the children sang carols until their parents called for them. The 1943 festivities were particularly gay.

> The day before Christmas we had a neighborhood party here with all the children I come closest to — sixteen, including Nancy Dean and a friend of hers. The two twelve-year-olds were a wonderful help, helping the small children off with their wraps in Nancy's room, presiding at their supper table — sandwiches, ice cream (as much as they wanted within reason) and two large cakes, one for the children and one for the grown-ups. We had carol singing. Then Mrs. Evans, the minister from South Ashburnham, read "Christmas in Norway" from *The Horn Book.* After that her eight-year-old son told in his own words the story of the Nativity and as he told it, Mrs. Evans set out the characters on a low table. When the story was done the crêche was before the children. Then there was a hand-in-hand skipping dance through the house followed by refreshments and, just before they left, things which Santa had left under our tree, knowing of our party, were given out by Nancy. This was the peak of my Christmas.[12]

Bertha established herself with the young people and the adults of her new family with the same sensitivity that marked her relationship with the children. The first evening alone with Celena, Alice Dean's older daughter and a sophomore at Wellesley, had its anxious moments, but awkwardness and self-consciousness were swept away in shared laughter when Bertha began to read aloud Margery Bianco's funny story about a New England farm, *The Good Friends.* With Alice Dean there was no difficulty whatsoever, for Bertha was immediately appreciative of the younger woman's creative talents and encouraged her to train and develop them. As a mark of her affectionate regard, Alice modeled the head of the infant Nancy and had it cast in bronze for Bertha's first Christmas in the Ashburnham home.

The nieces of the family were equally at ease with Bertha. They sensed her interest in their concerns as women, wives and mothers from the way she listened, really listened, when they talked to her. Sometimes just the listening alone clarified a problem; sometimes Bertha's unhurried and gentle questions brought fresh insight to a troublesome matter. Although Carolyn Norris was not a relative, she called Bertha "Aunt" and came to depend on her wise counsel in relation to the small private boys' school she and her husband established in Ashburnham in the mid-thirties. In an appreciation Mrs. Norris wrote when Mrs. Miller died, she spoke unwittingly for all the nieces:

> In the fall . . . the long years of her quiet and sustained interest, affection, and encouragement began. It is looking back that I realize that the delightful experiences, the sharing of books, peoples and ideas, the thoughtful comments and quiet humor came from a master educator.[13]

Mrs. William Davis Miller

Bertha's interest and influence in Ashburnham went beyond the family circle. As Mrs. William Davis Miller, the wife of one of the town's prominent citizens, she was obliged to become involved in its educational and social service activities. In doing so she was following her own instincts, a credo nurtured by association with the Union, and the pattern established by the Whitney and Miller families.

Mr. Whitney had been for years the Vice-President of the Board of Trustees of Cushing Academy. From its founding in 1865 the Academy had been the heart of the town. William Miller served a lengthy term as Chairman of the Stevens Public Library Board of Trustees. The wing of the library that is now used by the children was made possible by a gift from Celena Miller and her mother, Emeline Jewell Whitney. Three bequests by Celena benefit the library's building fund, make possible the presentation of speakers and special exhibits at the library, and supplement the librarian's salary. This last fund, the largest of the three and quadrupled over the years by William's prudent management, is administered by the Massachusetts Library Aid Association. It was also the inspiration of a similar endowment fund by Alice M. Chandler of Boston which provides general financial aid to small libraries in the Commonwealth.

Bertha's interest quite naturally focused on the library with special emphasis on its books and services for children. She gave many of her own children's books to the institution, so that it acquired over the years an excellent and discriminating collection rarely found in a library of its size.

To make the collection better known and to increase its use,

Bertha launched two programs. One, directed primarily to the mothers and teachers of the town, consisted of talks by personalities from the children's book world about the mushrooming publication of juvenile literature and the value to the child of reading such heady stuff. The program was not a formal one, no series of lectures; but whenever Bertha was responsible for the speaker at a club, school, library or church meeting, she took the opportunity to forward her plan.

Occasionally the speakers brought in for the adults were also used by Bertha in her second program, which was organized for the town's children and had for its goal the revelation to them of "the joy and the endless adventure, the ever-widening, deepening and heightening of life which books offer to them."[14] A Book Week festival, as reported in *The Horn Book*, demonstrated the spirit and the quality of Bertha's duo-programs on behalf of the reading of Ashburnham's children.

> Book Week in Northern Massachusetts. The Library Book Committee of the Stevens Public Library, Ashburnham, arranged in a vacant store, next door to the post office, a gay book room of children's books, with a few of the recent books for grown-ups. The room was furnished with homelike pieces of maple, India prints were hung on the walls, Christmas trees were placed where needed, with small ones in the show windows. Jeanette Eaton, author of *Leader by Destiny*, and Marguerite de Angeli, author and illustrator of *Copper-Toed Boots* and *Henner's Lydia* . . . were guests of honor on Friday, meeting the children in the book store during the morning and speaking in a hall to grown-ups and children in the afternoon. Apparently most of the children who had been in the book store in the morning were present at the hall in the afternoon. Many people visited the exhibition. A surprising number of books were sold. More than a hundred persons were present at the book talk, a large number for a small country town.[15]

Bertha's program for the children had a second, more formal, part: a series of regular storyhours given in the classrooms of the local schools to lead children from the oral to the written word. Bertha tried to get funds for the demonstration program from the Department of Education in Washington, but was refused. Undaunted, she organized a local committee which sponsored all manner of festivities for the benefit of the Library Storyhours in the Schools Fund. One year a Town Hall Cabaret was held with Cushing students headlining the bill; another time Fairbanks Memorial Hall rang to the calls of a country-dance master of ceremonies; once the Millers gave a silver tea in their garden on behalf of the Fund.

The first storytellers sent into the schools were recruited from the children's librarians of the Boston Public Library. Then Helen Cowell, the daughter of one of Cushing's most beloved headmasters, took on the task. She was well qualified to do so by her experience in conducting a small, private kindergarten in the town. For two years the storytelling was done by Jennie Lindquist, the children's librarian of the City Library in Manchester, New Hampshire. In concluding a *Horn Book* article about the Ashburnham storytelling experiment, Bertha wrote:

> To make treasure-seekers of our children in books and in life . . . that is the purpose of our Storyteller's work. In the belief that nothing will do more to enrich the life of our children and, eventually, the life of the town itself, we shall do our best to support and maintain it.[16]

Bertha was vitally interested in two organizations in the town: the Clio Woman's Club and the Ashburnham Visiting Nurse Association. The Clio Woman's Club, as its name would indicate, began as a musical society, but largely due to Bertha's influence expanded its interests to include all the arts. It was for the Club's meetings primarily that Bertha secured speakers from the children's book world.

The Ashburnham Visiting Nurse Association lists Bertha as one of its founders. Functioning at first on its own, the Association later came under the direction of the Clio Woman's Club. Today it stands again independently, a vigorous community service organization.

Bertha also supported the Women's Auxiliary of the Ashburnham Community Church where she worshipped. The simple white New England meetinghouse, set in a grove of arching maples, was just down the hill from the Miller home. As an adult Bertha responded to the mysticism of a church service with the same intensity that had characterized her church experiences as a child. Credos and patterns of worship were important to her, but important, too, was her own personal understanding of God as a source of spiritual power. In one of her memoirs she wrote of the revelation that crystalized her faith.

> One warm sunny day in the summer of 1930, a small woman nearing fifty was walking in the Public Gardens in Boston. She was thinking of a simple spiritual exercise she had tried every Sunday of the preceding winter while walking in the woods of Cape Ann.
>
> Suddenly, like a revelation, she found herself thinking, "Why, of course, whatever else God may be, He is an element of spiritual power like air, and just as accessible." At the same time came a realization that this wonder about God had been the preoccupation of a lifetime, albeit an unconscious one. It was suddenly seen to have taken its place at a very early age in a secret chamber of the mind, and there like a dynamo to have turned endlessly and finally to have resulted in this day's revelation. Along with this realization there flashed pictures of particular places where a child had sat on a hill raised above and back of the town and had wondered and wondered as she looked off to the sea.[17]

The hill, of course, was Squam Hill and one of the "particular places" was that flat rock just outside the door of Sadie Butman's cottage, Mount Airy. In 1937 the rock and the cottage became Bertha's, as well as six acres of surrounding woodland scrub, a gift from William on his wife's fifty-fifth birthday.

After Mount Airy was her own, Bertha delighted in offering it to relatives and friends, to writers and artists — to all who had need of the special restorative powers its solitude and view had for the distressed or weary spirit. She continued to use the little aerie herself, too, but after her marriage she enjoyed it most when she and William were there together. In Boston also she stayed with Ruth "a little home-sickly, for William is at home and it is beautiful there."[18]

William was not content away from Bertha either, his uneasiness sharpened by not knowing precisely where she was in his absence: at home in Ashburnham, in the Boston apartment, or at Mount Airy. Once, from a lumber journey into Michigan, he wrote a letter to Bertha that ended pensively: "Where are you, I wonder? Wherever you are — I love you."[19] In 1939 William was persuaded by friends to take a freighter cruise alone for his health. It did him little good, for he hated every lonesome minute of it away from Bertha. His new shoes were burdensomely heavy; the weather excessively hot; the sea disobligingly calm — he liked some movement to a boat deck; the cruise members were noodle-heads whose chief pleasure was sitting around in a circle and listening to the radio. "I have been wishing we were to land in Philadelphia today instead of Barrios," he wrote to Bertha as his ship lay in the Guatemalan port. "Possibly I'm missing you and feeling badly you aren't here."[20] It was the last journey he took alone.

When William travelled by car in the eastern states in search of material for the Whitney factories, he delighted in having Bertha with him. Often she was at the wheel of the large cars he favored, for she had learned to drive shortly after her marriage. Duncan had undertaken to teach her, but a professional instructor was engaged after the first lesson: Bertha had frozen at the wheel with her foot firmly pressed on the gas pedal — the car shot off the road, climbed a bank, leaped a low stone wall, and came to rest in the middle of a neighbor's lawn. The heavy foot on the accelerator was prophetic, for Bertha proved to be a vigorous jehu at the wheel. She was often stopped for speeding but rarely ticketed. The officers probably could not reconcile what their eyes saw and what their speedometers recorded: a gentle-voiced lady of years, so small that she had to be cushioned and propped to see through the windshield, cruising along at a good eighty-miles-an-hour clip. In spite of the penchant for speeding, Bertha was a good driver with no major accidents over the years as she whipped in and out of Boston in the blue Chevrolet William bought her, negotiated the icy hills of Ashburnham in the winter, and coped with the tourist traffic of Rockport in the summer.

The sorties into New England and eastern New York after lumber combined William's business with Bertha's pleasure. All along the way they stopped to visit with her friends who wrote, illustrated, and published children's books: Ethel Parton in Newburyport, Massachusetts, from whose garden Bertha brought back to Duncan a bulb of the Egyptian onion; Elizabeth Coatsworth and Henry Beston at Chimney Farm, their Maine home; Dorothy and Gertrude Lathrop in Albany, New York, where the illustrator and sculptor maintained their separate studios; Ned and Louise Seaman Bechtel in their beautiful home in Mt. Kisco, New York, famed for Ned's prize-winning rose garden; Cornelia Meigs or

Elizabeth Gray Vining, when they were vacationing in Vermont or New Hampshire.

Visits to Elinor and Will Field at their homes in Milton, Massachusetts, or Alstead Centre, New Hampshire, did not wait upon business trips. When Bertha married her Will in 1932, the friendship between herself and Elinor was in no wise impaired; instead its boundaries extended easily to include William Miller. In 1936 the friendship expanded once again to encompass Elinor's husband, William Field. The marriage was announced in *The Horn Book:*

> Personals. On April 29, Elinor Whitney, *The Horn Book's* Assistant Editor, was married to William L. W. Field, Head Master of Milton Academy. Mr. Field is a naturalist and an enthusiastic gardener of plants as well as of youth.[21]

A firm friendship was established between the Millers and the Fields, one that was to endure throughout their lives. The two Wills engaged in spring rivalry to see who could first serve the other with fresh vegetables from his garden. In the winter they exchanged rhymed greetings in the name of Cat, who, on occasion, stalked mice in the Ashburnham woodshed when master and mistress were visitors there.

One of the greatest joys the four friends shared was the reading aloud that usually closed every day they spent together whether at Milton, Ashburnham, or Alstead Centre. They read old and new books to suit the mood, to lighten the spirit, to deepen their understanding of the complicated world man had created. Although both husbands did the reading aloud, Will Field carried the burden of the task. He had the gift of illuminating what he read by the way he read it, but so skilfully as never to thrust his own personality between the writer and the listener. While the men read, Bertha stitched away at some plain sewing — the plainer the better — and Elinor counted stitches for a complicated knitting pattern.

A day spent with the Henry Greenes at Green Top also ended with a reading-aloud hour. Henry Jewett Greene, a friend of William's, was an extraordinary man. As a boy he had observed two things: the beauty of the natural world and the little time the average man had to enjoy it. He therefore determined when quite young to work hard, live frugally, make a fortune quickly, and then retire and enjoy life. He did exactly as he planned —

with the help of Bertha Auerbach Greene, who shared her husband's love of the out-of-doors and was as creatively gifted as he.

They climbed mountains all over the world, skied in Switzerland long before it was the *in* thing to do, and fished for salmon in New Brunswick. Bertha was a champion archer; Henry had a gun collection. Together they grew flowers, vegetables, herbs and ferns and studied the stars through lenses Henry ground. Bertha was skilled in needlecraft; Henry had a carpentry shop — many of the birdfeeders at Ashburnham came from that shop. They studied pottery with two of Japan's leading folk-artists, Kanjirō Kawai and Shōji Hamada, and then produced on their own wheel pieces that became museum items.

Green Top was in Petersham, Massachusetts, an easy hour's drive from Ashburnham. The Millers and the Greenes were in constant communication, either by visits or through Henry's letters. The letters revealed the man: typewriter-size paper with no more than twenty-five or thirty words scrawled on a sheet in bright green ink. They were usually sent to Bertha, hailing her with "Hello, Sweetheart," or "Hello, Sweet One" and sending her "Lots of SMAKKERS," or "Lots of LUFF." Henry Greene was a hustler for life and his contagious enthusiasm and good-humor were boundless.

Of all the adventures the Millers and Greenes shared, the most extraordinary for Bertha to become involved in, given her background and interests, were the annual fall fishing expeditions they made to the Laurentides National Park in Canada. Bertha was no sportswoman at all: she never learned to swim; she abandoned skiing after one lesson which she and Elinor gave themselves on the sloped terraces at Ashburnham; she did not sail with William. Even spectator sports baffled her. "Well, where *were* the men?" she once asked William indignantly, when he complained of two home runs made in a baseball game — with no one on base.

Bertha had not intended to fish at all when the first trip was discussed in 1939; she would read and knit and walk, while her three companions went their angling ways. Henry could not tolerate such a plan: she would fish; he would teach her how. Strangely enough Bertha became a good fisherman and found the sport exhilarating, even though she prepared for the initial experience under less than ideal circumstances. The new fall children's books were pouring in to be read and evaluated; the material for the September-October *Horn Book* had to be in Miss

Folmsbee's hands before Labor Day; Ruth and Miss Moore were both house guests; appropriate clothing in her size was not to be found in Ashburnham; and daily letters from Henry prodded her about certain minor equipment like rods and reels, lines and flies.

He took care of ordering them all, after he saw the rod Bertha proposed to use and the line she expected to buy from the great spool of twine in Leslie Nims' grocery store. He also gave her the promised lessons in fly-casting, two books to read on the subject, and a bombardment of postcard admonitions to PRACTICE EVERY DAY!!! On the way to Canada the party stopped at the L. L. Bean store in Freeport, Maine, and Bertha's wardrobe of knickerbockers and boy's shirts was supplemented by the coats, sweaters, hats and rain gear Henry deemed essential.

A letter written by Bertha to Elinor, but never mailed, gave some indication of the dimensions of the fishing expedition.

> We are on the shores of a lake in the Laurentians. To reach it we came one hundred miles north of Quebec; spent a night at Camp Le Gite on another lake; drove 28 miles through the woods along a river to a fire warden's station; were met there by a motor boat on which we traveled for a half hour or more; then by canoes, each of us in his own canoe with his guide, making three carries through these wonderful Laurentian woods; then at last we were met by the motor boat from this Camp des Ecorces. We were traveling all the time up the Rivière aux Ecorces and this is the Lac aux Ecorces, entirely surrounded by mountains.[22]

Bertha responded completely to the grandeur of the mountains, to the beauty and deep solitude of the Canadian woods, and the unexpectedly exciting sport of fishing. Several years later the Millers and the Greenes took a two-week canoe trip on the Metabetchouan River in the Park. Afterwards Bertha tried to put into words the essence of the whole wonder-filled adventure. She called her exercise "Rain on Metabetchouan."

> There was drought in the spring. All day from Kiskisink to the Camp, a haze had lain against the distant mountains from forest fires burning forty miles away. At times the breeze brought the smell of smoke. The river was so low seven carries had to be made.
>
> Now after four nights at Camp and four days of sunshine, the longed-for rains had come. The sound of it

made a beautiful background for sleep on Saturday night. . . . But weather is a part of life in the Laurentians and one must be out in it. The Indian guide, Onesime, led us out on the one path that followed the Camp telephone wire; a wire that served the Fire Wardens as well as the Camp. This trail was an old one. How old no one could say. Once Indians travelled it and caribou were seen on its way. Now moose often broke the wire with their antlers and beaver with their vast lumbering.

New spinulose ferns were growing beside the path. The bunchberry, star flower and gold thread were blossoming and the red elder tree held up its flowering cones. The snowberry vine lay softly over the rocks and there was even the vine of the rare, delicate twin flower. Spruce, balsam, hemlock and birches, gray and white, large and small, made the forest. . . .

By mid-afternoon between showers, with rubber boots, coats and hats — and fly rods — we took to our canoes and were off up the river to fish. The muskrat was out, too, steering himself swiftly with his long rudder tail. The air was clear. The verdure wonderfully fresh. The river was up two inches, a thick slate blue, and no longer clear. . . . The hook brought in grasses more often than fish. . . .

The fisherman — the greenhorn fisherman, strong in persistence, but weak in fishing aptitude — cast her line with a black gnat fly, and when the occasional rise came, strove to "strike" according to instruction and, at last, with some success. Strangely enough the effort — and the success — seemed to make the union with the natural world more complete.

The sky grew black, down came a pelting rain which raised nubbly glass balls on the stream. The rain ceased, and was followed by wind that roughened the water. The fisherman sought a sheltered bay and there came a hawk to take up his watch from the top of a dead tree.

Now the river was less rough. The fly was cast in still another place, this time a silver doctor. Hours had passed like the wind. Dark was coming on. There was a sense of a deep and big experience — a feeling of something steadfast in nature and in man. The canoe came home against the wind and was beached.

> The fisherman mounted the bank with her six fish — and her feeling of re-creation. And there, across on a distant point in the lake stood a moose clear in the evening light, like a living expression of nature's strength. . . .[23]

In another paper Bertha wrote about the Laurentides' fishing adventures, she commented on the quiet rhythm of everything that the Greenes did together. "Not that there weren't arguments at times, and plain speaking, but this was the surface sounds of the deep-flowing brook of their closely knit life together."[24] She might just as well have been writing about herself and William Miller.

The Horn Book: Years of Maturity, 1936-1950

In 1924 she launched *The Horn Book,* beloved guide and counselor from then to now to all who serve the reading interests of children, a magazine without parallel or precedent, a magazine which carries the distilled, potent spirit of Bertha Mahony Miller.

— From the Citation, written by Frederic Melcher, which accompanied The Constance Lindsay Skinner Award for 1955 when it was presented to Mrs. Miller by The Women's National Book Association[1]

November Spring in London

FROM 1932 THROUGH 1936 Bertha moved steadily from one change to another in her personal and professional lives. The changes culminated in 1936 with her sister Ruth's marriage to Harry Burnham, the childhood friend from Gloucester and *The Horn Book's* legal counselor, and with Elinor and herself founding their own company to publish *The Horn Book*. The November issue of that year carried the announcement of their brave new venture.

> The Horn Book, Inc. — On October 1, 1936 *The Horn Book* Editors in friendly agreement with their parent organization, the Women's Educational and Industrial Union, took over the ownership and publishing of the magazine which they started in 1924 and have since edited. With Thomas Todd, their printer, and their husbands, William D. Miller and William L. W. Field, they have formed a close corporation now solely responsible for the magazine.[2]

To help Bertha and Ruth gain the perspective they would need to discharge their new responsibilities adequately and with some sense of joy, William Miller sent the sisters to London for a November holiday. Bertha expected while there to call upon persons connected with the children's book world and Ruth planned to attend lectures in her field of social work. The visit was not to be entirely a busman's holiday, however; there would be time for a modicum of sightseeing and a very real indulgence in the sisters' shared taste for gallery exhibits, concerts and plays.

When Bertha returned home from the London vacation, she filed away the catalogs and programs she had gathered and then, while the adventure was fresh in her mind, wrote a paper about it in one of her composition books, working carefully from an outline. The paper, though never published in its entirety, yielded a number of Hunt Breakfast items over the years as well as editorial material. This chapter, too, derives from Bertha's literary exercise and the quotations that follow are largely from it.

There was a strange enchantment about the winter holiday, so that in spite of November rains, fogs, and bone-chilling cold it seemed like spring to Bertha and Ruth. The London arrival, however, gave little indication of the delightful month that was to come. Sophisticated travellers though they both were — Ruth went abroad frequently, perhaps less self-conscious of her tremor among strangers — they spent their first afternoon in the city taxiing in the rain from one hotel to another in search of a satisfactory hostelry. Once that was secured, they left it almost at once for the St. James's Theatre to see the Max Gordon-Gilbert Miller-Rex Whistler production of Jane Austen's classic.

> And on that first cold, rainy night we had our first touch of spring in London for we went to see *Pride and Prejudice.* I did not see the Theatre Guild performance here in America but I cannot imagine that any cast or performance could have excelled the one we saw in London. . . . Elizabeth Bennet (Celia Johnson) and her father (Athole Stewart) have left a long echoing reminder of the dear, cool meaning of strong, reasoning and salty character with its roots in virtue, in this chaotic world.[3]

The sisters spent the first week of their holiday walking about London during the day and going to concerts or plays in the evening.

> It happened that almost everything we saw at the theatre pointed up our daily strolls about London. *Charles the King* brought to life our visit to the Tower of London, gave additional background and life to an evening spent at the House of Commons, and made the procession on Lord Mayor's Day an historical pageant as well as a picture-book procession. . . .
>
> Later it happened that we saw T. S. Eliot's *Murder in the Cathedral* just before going down to Canterbury so

> that Thomas à Becket became a real figure, and we went about Canterbury full of wonder about him.[4]

One play, unexpectedly, had a more personal association for the Mahony sisters — so much so that they saw it three times.

> Then, because we hoped to see Eleanor Farjeon, we made a point of seeing *The Two Bouquets,* a comedy with music which [she] wrote with her actor-brother, Herbert. . . .
>
> Now my sister and I in our teens were always singing, and one of our songs was "Twickenham Ferry". . . . And lo! the scene for the Farjeon comedy was the Twickenham of our old song and Twickenham was an easy coach drive, or better still, a ferry ride from London. And there at the Regatta on the Thames there was an amusing mixture of lovers' bouquets, gay romance, and old songs. . . . And again it was spring![5]

After a week's refreshment from the sights and sounds of London, Bertha sent out notes to people connected with children's books and was presently engaged in visits with them.

> One Sunday afternoon when rain was falling I found my way to Rose Fyleman's apartment for tea. She lives not far from Madame Tussaud's at the top of a comfortable apartment house, overlooking a large park and with a wide view out over London. The room gave a sense of having dark wainscotting and the dark oak furniture seemed to complete the atmosphere properly. We sat before the fire and Miss Fyleman toasted English muffins and poured tea. We talked about books, book fairs, the state of the world, and enjoyed ourselves.[6]

Bertha and Miss Fyleman were not strangers: the Bookshop had been the unofficial booking agent for the English poet during a 1928-1929 lecture tour of the United States. The book fair that prompted the discussion over the London tea had been held in London earlier in the month, sponsored by the *Sunday Times.* Bertha had attended several of the programs and was disenchanted with the whole experience.

> It was impressive, of course, to be one of five hundred unable to get in to hear Aldous Huxley speak. And still more impressive to sit for an hour and a half waiting to

> hear the young poet, Stephen Spender. . . . When Mr. Spender finished nearly half his audience stayed on to hear Miss Delafield speak on children's books. . . .
>
> Miss Delafield quoted one of her friends as saying that she ought not to speak on children's books, because she knew none of the modern ones. This seemed to one listener a reasonable point of view and her lecture could not fail to be disappointing when it left entirely out of account such people as Leslie Brooke, Kenneth Grahame, Walter de la Mare, A. A. Milne, Arthur Ransome and P. L. Travers.[7]

It was Rose Fyleman who secured a ticket for Bertha to attend a Poetry Dinner at the Lyceum Club.

> A little late and somewhat breathless [after the day at Canterbury] I ran up the stairs and straight in to the dinner table to find myself sitting between W. H. Auden and Rose Fyleman. Mr. Auden is a tall, reddish-blonde young man, direct and genuine in manner and with a running humor of perception and expression which makes me think he would not take anything except his work too seriously, not even himself.[8]

Mr. Auden, Ruth Pitter and William Empson read exquisitely phrased papers about their poetry after the dinner and Bertha was distressed because "I have to confess humbly that I did not understand what any one of those young poets said." Later she did some research to sharpen her appreciation of their work but with only fair success. Even Mr. Empson's Notes explaining "incidental difficulties" did not clarify his more abstruse lines. "Although the Notes are a help the difficulties are more than incidental to this reader. One does not want a poem to be too clear. There must be some wonder about it. But one must be caught and held and *wish* to wonder."[9]

Then the day came when Bertha was to see Eleanor Farjeon. She knew well Miss Farjeon's books for children and earlier in the year had reviewed for *The Horn Book* the delightful account of her childhood, *Portrait of a Family*. *The Two Bouquets* had sharpened Bertha's anticipation of the meeting.

> We met for luncheon and spent most of the afternoon talking in the library at 47 Grosvenor Street. She told me how Martin Pippin had grown out of the letters written to

> and received from a young soldier in the War. He had written first in comment upon a story of Sussex, his own country, and had written in the tone of Martin Pippin. She told me of Edward Thomas, the Poet who died in the War, and of how she had herself typed his first poems after Robert Frost had pointed out that his prose writing was of a subject matter better adapted to poetry. She spoke of the pleasure she had had in writing *Ten Saints* and was so eager to see the finished volume.[10]

After Miss Farjeon left at four, Bertha could not let the fine high day come to a flat close, so she decided to visit the Banks Sisters bookshop in Kensington. She had expected to walk through Kensington Gardens to the shop, but when she tried to enter the Gardens through the Alexandra Gate, she found it closed and locked. She also found, on the other side of the gate, an elderly gentleman quite obviously locked in and just as obviously wanting to get out. With brisk efficiency Bertha attempted his rescue but, after urgent appeals to policemen, tradesmen, and even lavatory attendants, she was forced to tell him he would have to rescue himself. The keys to the gates of the Gardens were kept in the various Keeper's Lodges inside the Gardens. Frustrated, and deprived of a promising dramatic rescue, Bertha could only watch helplessly as her elderly gentleman turned back into the Gardens and disappeared in the London fog.

> The day ended brightly though because of the bookshop visit. As I opened the door to the Banks Sisters shop on Holland Street, I saw a scene which will always remain. Several rooms open one out of the other and each one on a somewhat higher level. You have before you, not a garden, but a shop in terraces. On the terrace nearest was a bright fire and beside it a large wise-looking cat, Saturday by name. In a corner, beyond the fire, seated on a stool at a high counter, was an old lady making baskets. . . . The shop makes a specialty of old children's books and books on the theatre.[11]

On another day Bertha had tea with the staff of the Oxford University Press. She had hoped to meet there Grace Allen Hogarth, whose career as a children's editor had begun in the United States, and also to see a copy of Eleanor Farjeon's *Ten Saints*. Unfortunately, Mrs. Hogarth was in New York on business and Miss Farjeon's book was still with the printer. She did see, however, the completely hand-made dummy Edward Ardizzone had put together of *Lucy Brown and Mr. Grimes,* the picture book he had written and illustrated for his own small daughter. Bertha was so moved by the beauty of the "manuscript book," as she called the dummy, and the tender story it told, that she promptly gave the name "Lucy Brown" to the doll she had bought at Liberty's for five-year-old Nancy Dean.

Of all the experiences in London that November, the happiest by far for Bertha was her meeting with Leslie Brooke and his family. There were four meetings really, for the gentle enthusiast from Boston seemed to have captivated the Brookes as much as they had enchanted her. The first meeting came directly after Bertha and Ruth had watched the Lord Mayor's Procession as it moved through Trafalgar Square.

> And then when it was all over I walked up Piccadilly to Berkeley Street, to Berkeley Square, and thence to Charles Street. And there at Dartmouth House I ordered tea and found the quietest, pleasantest place possible to meet and visit with a maker of picture books on a picture-book day.
>
> As Mr. Brooke came up the stairs I knew him instantly and at once I thought, "He's nicer even than I expected." Now, I could not tell you what we talked about that afternoon. I know that there was the happiest kind of friendly converse. But this I knew that I had been with a person so wise, so fine in his perceptions, so humorous and so modest that intercourse became a much more natural and happy process than is usual. . . .
>
> Then there was another interesting thing about this meeting. While my first week in London had been very, very interesting, with spots of spring, I had been constantly homesick. Now I was homesick no longer. Now I began to enjoy London in a new way. And now I felt wholly my best self. It is a strange but actual fact that the effect of some friends upon one is to make one's personality give itself up to its fullest and most complete state, almost a state of bloom; and under other conditions one has a sense of discouragement, of diminution, of disintegration.[12]

The second meeting was a luncheon in the Brookes' Hampstead home at which time Bertha met Mr. Brooke's wife, Sybil, their daughter-in-law, Barbara, and two-year-old Peter, the beloved grandson of the house. It was for Peter that Leslie Brooke had made *Johnny Crow's New Garden* just the year before. In the friendly ambience of the Brooke household, Bertha was completely at ease.

> When I had to start most reluctantly to leave, Mr. Brooke asked if I would like to walk out over the Heath. There followed an enchanted stroll in the late afternoon light over the open part of the Heath, past Jack Straw's Castle and the stretch from which one can look down to the house where Keats lived. Then up through the bracken to see Mrs. Siddon's lovely house and John Galsworthy's. And now with early evening upon us, into the old part of Hampstead with its winding roads, its hidden lanes and courts. It will always remain one of the delightful memories.[13]

There were to be two more such memories. One was a luncheon given by Mrs. Leslie Brooke at her club so that her son, Henry, might also meet the American bookwoman who had won their hearts. At the end of that festive occasion Bertha became the proud possessor of one of Mr. Brooke's drawings. "It is here in my study as I write, and never fails to cheer me. It is a preparatory drawing for *Johnny Crow's New Garden* and shows the penguins on gala occasion, each with a large bouquet and a particularly proud manner."[14]

A final quiet talk with Leslie Brooke in the American Women's Club ended the visits, "but to the pleasure of those visits there is no end. They have become a part of the fabric of life, the bright colored portion. And the spring light they cast then and since is that of sunshine in May."[15]

When Bertha and Ruth sailed for home after their November spring in London, each was ready for the fresh adventure that lay before her. On the day after Christmas Ruth Mahony and Harry Burnham were married by the Reverend Ben Roberts. Bertha moved forward into the editorship and ownership of *The Horn Book* with renewed strength of purpose and clarified vision.

A Magazine without Parallel or Precedent

BERTHA NEEDED COURAGE, as well as vision and strength of purpose to undertake in 1936 the ownership and publication of a highly specialized magazine with a limited readership. The crash of 1929 and the Depression that followed it were within uneasy memory. The present was filled with the noise of demagogues making their first threats to test the temper of a world dedicated to peace. The shadows of World War II held the future in obscurity.

In spite of the times, from 1936 to the end of her editorship in 1950, Bertha carried *The Horn Book* to heights of excellence, influence, and repute. During the same period, from The Horn Book, Incorporated came two of the most significant books about children's literature ever to be published: *Books, Children and Men,* by Paul Hazard, a Member of the French Academy, and *Illustrators of Children's Books: 1744-1945,* compiled in part by Bertha herself.

Perhaps it was *because* of the times that Horn Book affairs achieved such eminence and productivity in the 1930s and the 1940s. Bertha, by nature, responded instinctively to challenge and worked well under pressure, in full command then of her mental and spiritual resources. If righteous anger was a part of the emotional scene, so much the better; and she was in a perpetual state of anger during the war years.

Bertha was wise enough to realize in 1936, however, that no matter how hard they worked, she and Elinor could no longer produce *The Horn Book* by themselves — even with the sturdy help of Beulah Folmsbee to support them. Husbands were to be considered and, in the case of Elinor, a whole schoolful of chil-

Above: Mount Airy in Rockport on Cape Ann
Below: The Bay View home on Cape Ann, built on a hill locally called "Mount Misery."

Bertha Everett Mahony

Elinor Whitney

The Bookshop for Boys and Girls in its first location

Relocated and enlarged Bookshop. Children's Balcony Level

Dollhouse

Above: The Book Caravan. Mary Frank is at the front of the car; Genevieve Washburn, at the rear

Below: Interior and exterior views of the Caravan

Thomas Todd (1878-1956)

Alice M. Jordan

Anne Carroll Moore

Mr. and Mrs. William Davis Miller, with The Reverend Ben Roberts, who officiated at their marriage on September 7, 1932, in the garden of Marguerite Mitchell's home.

Henry and Bertha Greene

Above: Marguerite MacKellar Mitchell. *Below:* William L. W. Field, Headmaster of Milton Academy, whom Elinor Whitney married on April 29, 1936

Above: Mrs. Miller's sofa and chair in the library at Ashburnham

Below: Mr. Miller's favorite chair, at left.

Above: A Claude René Martin oil painting hung above the fireplace in the Ashburnham Library. *Below:* The dolls always ready for a young visitor in the Ashburnham house

Above: Rear view of Ashburnham home. Awning partially raised is at window of the Study. Sleeping porch is to the left. *Below:* Mrs. Miller's Study at Ashburnham. Door at right leads to sleeping porch

Views of the Ashburnham grounds from Mrs. Miller's Study and sleeping porch in summer and winter

The kind of plain sewing Mrs. Miller liked best

Making good use of a spare moment at the South Ashburnham Railroad Station

Above: "Glamor Manor," the Millers' residence in Winter Park, Florida, for a number of years *Below:* The Floridian Mrs. Miller

FOR MERIT IN THE REALM OF BOOKS
Presented by the Women's National
Book Association to
Bertha Mahony Miller 1955

REGINA MEDAL
for Continued Distinguished
Contribution to Children's
Literature presented by
the Catholic Library Association
to Bertha Mahony Miller 1967.

dren. Then, too, the surge in the publishing of children's books was producing more titles than the two of them could cope with adequately alone. In the past, the Bookshop staff had assisted in the reviewing of the books; after the new company was formed, Bertha and Elinor had to carry the full burden of the task. Although the bi-monthly publication schedule begun in 1934 gave them the additional space they sorely needed, it meant planning and preparing two more numbers each year. In brief, *The Horn Book* operation was growing in magnitude and additional persons were needed to keep pace with the increasingly complicated development.

With Bertha, the filling of a need was almost simultaneous with its recognition. She set about at once gathering around the masthead of *The Horn Book* a nucleus of professional women who would contribute regularly to the magazine, sharing particularly in the evaluation of new books. The contributors would also advise on the general content of the journal and on the undertakings of The Horn Book, Incorporated. Then Bertha began to create new departments to broaden the base of *The Horn Book's* appeal and to increase its usefulness. To edit them Bertha also found women of national repute in their professional fields.

The Union had taught Bertha the sound practice of going to the top when help was wanted for any enterprise. It was natural, moreover, for her to appeal first to her two friends of many years: Anne Carroll Moore and Alice Jordan.

From 1924 to 1930 Miss Moore had edited for the New York *Herald Tribune Books* "The Three Owls," an exciting pioneer page of weekly criticism of children's books. It was Bertha's desire that the Owls should venture forth on a second critical flight with the three jovial huntsmen of *The Horn Book* as companions. "Admiration for the integrity of a fine performance during years of depression"[16] made Miss Moore receptive to the idea. In the quiet seclusion of Mount Airy the bookwoman and the librarian made their pact.

> It was in the old-world village of Rockport on the Massachusetts coast one foggy night last June that the Owls felt the stirring of wings and the desire to fly again. On Midsummer Eve in the deep woods above Damariscotta Lake in Maine they made up their threefold mind — author, artist, and critic — to fly for *The Horn Book* in the same quest of reality in children's books on which they

> first set forth in Books for the New York *Herald Tribune*. . . .[17]

In the September-October 1936 *Horn Book*, Bertha proudly announced "The Three Owls' Notebook" as a special feature of the magazine. Its initial appearance in the following number coincided with the first issuance of the magazine by The Horn Book, Incorporated.

Miss Moore brought the prestige of her name to *The Horn Book* and an implied approval of its policy, purpose, and content. Bertha was sensible and appreciative of both. "The value of her page to *The Horn Book* is inestimable," she wrote in 1949.[18] The Notebook, in turn, gave Miss Moore again the opportunity to direct her sharp, discerning eye on children's literature for the benefit of an international readership. When she retired from The New York Public Library in 1941, the Notebook provided Miss Moore with a sustaining, tangible link with the children's book world, a world that had long been, and would continue to be, the core of her life. For almost twenty years after her retirement, until her death really, Miss Moore used The Three Owls' Notebook to present her original point of view about children's books to the fortunate subscribers of *The Horn Book*.

The Notebook's name indicated the variety of its content and the informality of its arrangement. Books were naturally its major concern. Miss Moore discussed them in critical essays, or listed them more conventionally with brief, astute comments. Occasionally she devoted an entire piece to a single title which she judged deserving of special praise or castigation.

She also shared with readers the rare adventures her zest for life both sought and attracted: following a marching Salvation Army band into Salisbury Cathedral for a Good Friday service, or listening to the *Marseillaise* ring out over New York's City Hall Plaza at the Mayor's reception in 1943 for the French sailors from the *Richelieu;* riding the bridges of Manhattan with Arthur Rackham to see the lights go on in the city's skyscrapers, or watching Eleanor Farjeon — in New York for the Broadway opening of *The Two Bouquets* — listen delightedly to the telling of her own Sussex stories at a library storyhour; presiding regally at the celebration of a Queen's birthday in the courtyard of a Dutch inn, or leading the children through the Japanese Chrysanthemum Festival at the Pratt Insitute Library where her career began.

Miss Moore's lively accounts of such experiences caught

Horn Book readers up in her pleasure and inner excitement. As they read, their own horizons expanded, adapting to her wider and fresher view of life. The same expansion of spirit came from the wisdom in the Notebooks. The wisdom knew neither pedantry nor didacticism. It spoke primarily of the need to cherish, in life as well as in books, originality, honesty, and gaiety. The Three Owls' Notebook was in itself a testament to that wisdom: honest, original, and gay.

Three years after Miss Moore began to write informally about children's literature in *The Horn Book*, Bertha was able to persuade Alice Jordan to assume the responsibility for the more formal reviewing of books in the magazine's Booklist. Dramatic announcements were not in character for Alice Jordan. Her first Booklist, in the September-October 1939 *Horn Book*, was introduced by a simple sentence in Bertha's editorial for the same number: "Alice M. Jordan, for many years Supervisor of Work with Children for the Boston Public Library, will edit the book list regularly."[19] The Owls, however, were dedicated celebrants and when Miss Jordan retired from the Library in 1940, they seized the occasion for a joyful tribute to a fellow columnist.

> The New Year sounds a jubilant note for *The Horn Book* since it promises greater freedom to Alice Jordan to write of her own discoveries, past, present and future, in the field of children's books.
>
> For nearly forty years . . . Miss Jordan and I have enjoyed a friendship at once spacious and firmly rooted in mutual recognition of unchanging values in children and in literature. To a fine inheritance of discriminating taste in books Alice Jordan brought wisdom and tolerance to her selection of children's books for the Boston Public Library. . . .
>
> Out of the trial and error of a consistent effort to plant the seeds of a free cultural development in a great cosmopolitan city rewarding buds, blossoms and fruits gradually appear — very often in strange places. Wherever Alice Jordan has walked in Boston . . . wherever story hours have been held at her command, the living stream of literature flows on.[20]

From 1939 to 1950 Bertha made it possible for "the living stream of literature" to flow far beyond the boundaries of Boston in the Booklists which Miss Jordan did for *The Horn Book*. The full extent of her accomplishment is best realized if a few figures are cited. In 1940, her first full year as book editor, she reviewed 117 books; in 1949, her last full year, 294. If she followed the pattern of most reviewers, she examined at least six titles for every book commented upon, and then actually read three of the six in the final separation of the wheat from the chaff. In round numbers, Miss Jordan reviewed some 2,000 books in the 65 Booklists she prepared. That she managed to do that, year after year, with no jaded sensibilities and no diminution of enthusiasm was proven by the freshness of her book notes. She never lost the eagerness with which she opened each new book, hoping *that* book would be the one about which she could joyfully write, "I long to share it with a child."[21]

The full measure of Miss Jordan's contribution to *The Horn Book* is not to be judged solely by the numerical dimensions of her achievements, astonishing though they be. The real significance of her Booklists lay in the selection of titles she chose to comment on, and the crisp notes she wrote about the books. Bertha saluted both her selective and writing genius in a *Horn Book* editorial. "Her editorship marked a real advance in the value of the magazine, for her judgment of books has always been based upon her close association with children and their books. Moreover her notes have had so fine a writing style as to be miniature essays on books."[22]

Readers came to depend on Miss Jordan's recommendations and used her Booklists with complete confidence in selecting books for the home, school, or public library. Frequently, and with some wonderment, those who might have read a book before Miss Jordan reviewed it, found their understanding of it sharpened, even changed, by the perceptive "miniature essay" she wrote about it.

The books which Miss Jordan and Miss Moore discussed were of their own independent choosing. That they repeated each other was of little consequence, for the approach of each was original and individual. They were in agreement about most titles, but for some expressed strongly divergent views. The honest differences of opinions strengthened, rather than weakened, the integrity of their departments. Occasionally, if Miss Jordan knew Miss Moore was particularly keen about a book, she refrained from reviewing it. Instead, the reader was referred to the Notebook where he could meet Miss Moore's enthusiasm without having had the edge taken off his interest by a Booklist comment. Miss Moore returned the compliment.

Miss Jordan and Miss Moore had advised Bertha informally on *Horn Book* matters almost from the first issue. When the Booklist and the Notebook brought them into closer association with the magazine, Bertha proposed to expand their advisory roles and acknowledge their help by designating them as "Associate Editors." She gave the same title to Elinor and to Louise Seaman Bechtel, valuing highly the businesslike approach of the former editor of children's books.

Bertha's associate editors were all colleagues and friends of many years' standing. They were also strong-minded and plain-speaking women, more accustomed to making decisions and issuing directives than participating in group judgments and advisory recommendations. Their positions had trained them in the act of leadership, rather than committee operation. They made no concession to friendship in the advice they gave Bertha. It was honest, direct and uncompromising.

Yet *The Horn Book* flourished under the stimulation of their criticism, for Bertha accepted it with grace, profited by it with gratitude, and seldom allowed it to overwhelm her. On occasion, she could offer steel to the flint of their criticism. Miss Moore's forthright opinions were especially prized. "Probably she has never given to any book sterner criticism than she has given to *The Horn Book*," Bertha wrote. "Even when it was hardest to bear, we have known ourselves blessed to have one person in the world who could and would."[23]

At about the same time that Bertha created her associate editors, she persuaded The Horn Book, Incorporated to expand in order to bring Mrs. Bechtel and Marguerite Mitchell into its governing body. The two women infused new life and vigor into the Board of Directors, just as the associate editors had revitalized its magazine. Supported by the advice of her editors and her enlarged board, Bertha was able to direct Horn Book affairs with strengthened vision and renewed confidence.

Out of that vision came a new department: Hunters Fare. Bertha created it in 1941 for a dual purpose: to answer questions about children's books for those remote from libraries or bookstores, and to give yet another dimension to the discussion of children's literature in the magazine. Bertha planned to have the department edited for two-year periods by working children's librarians with knowledge of and access to both the old and new in children's books The first Hunters Fare editor was Jennie Lindquist, with whom Bertha had worked in connection with the storytelling experiment in the Ashburnham schools.

At the suggestion of her associates, Bertha sought the next editors of the book inquiry department outside of the New England community. Although *The Horn Book,* in content and purpose, had long sloughed off its regionalism, its directors and associates were all drawn from Eastern states. Hunters Fare provided an opportunity to broaden the geography of the editorial base.

The fresh wind of the West Coast blew into the magazine, when, from the School of Librarianship of the University of Washington in Seattle, Siri Andrews became the second Hunters Fare editor. She was followed by two Californians: Gladys English, the distinguished Director of Children's Work at the Los Angeles Public Library, and Leone Garvey who held a comparable position in Berkeley. The Midwest had its first voice in *The Horn Book* when Della McGregor became the fifth Hunters Fare editor, bringing to the task the same imagination with which she supervised the children's work in the St. Paul Public Library. Miss McGregor's direction of the special department coincided with Bertha's last year as editor of the magazine.

In 1948 Bertha introduced still another department and as its editor a young librarian whose career would bring distinction to the journal for which she wrote. The department was Outlook Tower and its editor, Margaret Scoggin. Miss Scoggin was then the librarian of the unique Nathan Straus Branch of The New York Public Library. She had organized the library in 1940; it was unique in that it served only children, and young people under twenty-one.

Outlook Tower had its roots in an article, "Young People in a World at War," which Miss Scoggin had written for the November-December 1943 *Horn Book.* The article, based on Miss Scoggin's observations of her patrons at Nathan Straus, had impressed Bertha by its concern for the adolescent and its understanding of his book needs at a difficult time. She therefore had asked Miss Scoggin to review for the magazine "for the duration" those adult books about the war which would appeal to young people. They had called the column "The War Years."

When the war itself brought the column to an end, Bertha replaced it with Outlook Tower. The purpose of the new department was "to highlight books of interest to high school boys and girls, predominantly current adult books but occasionally [adult] books of other times."[24] The department took its name from the Edinburgh building which housed Patrick Geddes' laboratory of sociological inquiry. "It is the symbolism of his Tower," Bertha wrote, "the wide look over the world in time and space and the close-up look as well, which has made this title seem good for the Department in which Miss Scoggin presents for young people's reading those volumes as varied as are people and places."[25]

Margaret Scoggin edited Outlook Tower for almost twenty years. During that time she left Nathan Straus to supervise the work with young people in all the branches of the library, and to receive innumerable honors in recognition of her devotion and service to young people and their reading. Bertha took great pride in Miss Scoggin's accomplishments, none the least of which was her editorship of Outlook Tower.

After launching Outlook Tower in 1948, Bertha turned to the creation of still another department, the last to be initiated during her editorship and one especially dear to her because it directly concerned the children. Indeed, the department was *by* the children. It was called "The Horn Book League" and, like the St. Nicholas League after which it had been modeled and whose motto it bore, it was made up of art work, poems, and essays sent in by boys and girls. The first column appeared in the March-April 1949 *Horn Book* under a headpiece designed by Hilda van Stockum, an author and illustrator of children's books and one of Bertha's most faithful correspondents.

Since children were not readers of *The Horn Book* in great numbers, Bertha solicited the cooperation of adult subscribers in making the League known to them. Individual entries were encouraged rather than classroom projects. There was no dearth of material once the League became known, for the children, as in the earlier days of the magazine, were eager to see their work reproduced in its pages. The League lasted for almost a quarter century and its contents offered eloquent evidence of what children found to wonder at and be interested in from 1949 to 1972.

While Bertha was imaginatively creating associate editors and new departments, she did not neglect the preparation of the regular content of the magazine. In planning that, she held fast to her oft-repeated dictum: if a periodical was to remain vital, it had to allow some flow of the times through its pages. Consequently, during her editorship, *The Horn Book* was a lively, contemporary magazine that gave its readers articles not only about developments in the world of children's books, but also about those aspects of the educational, social and political scenes which affected children and their reading.

Released in the late 1940s from the printing restrictions of the war years, the publication of picture books in America surged forward. To readers bewildered by the need to judge the illustrations of those books, Bertha offered articles and lists by the artists who were making them: Fritz Eichenberg, Warren Chappell, Marcia Brown, and Lynd Ward. Miss Brown's guidelines for distinction in picture books were particularly helpful. Then Bertha asked Louise Seaman Bechtel and Frances Clarke Sayers to write articles about the intelligent and pleasant use of such books with small children. Mrs. Bechtel wrote out of a special experience she had had with the New York Kindergarten Association; Mrs. Sayers, as a writer of books for little children and as the successor to Miss Moore in The New York Public Library.

Another article by Mrs. Sayers, "Lose Not the Nightingale," was the most forceful piece of writing that Bertha presented in a whole series of editorials, articles, and Hunt Breakfast items about the science of reading versus the art of reading. Parents, librarians, and educators were represented in the series. They wrote about the ways reading was taught in the schools, the use of vocabularized texts in the classroom, the rigid grading of all reading matter for children, and the re-writing of standard titles according to prescribed word lists.

Mrs. Bechtel, in response to Bertha's recognition of the impact of the comic book on the young mind, contributed an unemotional article on the subject — not an easy thing to do in the heated atmosphere that surrounded it. Two illustrators, Virginia Lee Burton and Helen Sewell, described their experimentation with comic-book technique in the making of picture books.

In the second issue of *The Horn Book*, for November 1924, Bertha had listed several adult books "for those of inquiring minds," as she put it. The books had to do with the oppression of the Negro in the United States. Her concern for the minorities never wavered through the years and she searched constantly for competent writers to deal with the subject. Marjorie Hill Allee wrote with sensitivity about a fellow Quaker's experience in presenting books to the black children of a Chicago school. Lois Lenski described a Christmas with the Appalachian Mountain boys and girls she came to know while writing one of her many regional stories. A happy pairing of articles combined one by Arna Bontemps and one about him as a distinguished patron of the Watts Branch of the Los Angeles Public Library.

When the Japanese-American children left their West Coast homes for inland evacuation centers at the beginning of World War II, their bewilderment was recorded for *Horn Book* readers by librarians and writers who witnessed the scene. In the January-February 1945 number Howard Pease reviewed the facts of that tense and confused moment in American history and then assailed those who would deny the interned citizens the right to return to their homes at the end of the war. His courageous article, "Without Evasion," was hailed by Miss Moore in the Notebook as "a contemporary human document of compelling interest."[26]

Throughout the war years Bertha ran many other articles as equally human as that of Mr. Pease, and of the same compelling interest. The impact of the war was titanic, almost more than mind could comprehend or heart endure. *Horn Book* readers were fortunate to have in Bertha an editor with the spiritual stamina and mental vigor equal to the challenge. Most magazines of the times reflected in some way the terror of the war; in *The Horn Book* that terror seemed somehow more appalling because it was seen as affecting the children of the world.

Yet Bertha did not dwell on occupation, bombardment, and devastation. As country after country felt the effect of the Nazi forces, she found some way, in either an editorial or an article, to salute the unconquered spirits of the invaded and the bombed.

Bertha welcomed to the pages of her magazine those artists, writers, and publishers who had fled Hitler's policies and his invading army and were presently enriching American children's books with their talents: Fritz Eichenberg from Germany, Dola de Jong from Holland, Kay Neilsen from Denmark, Feodor Rojankovsky from France, Hanna and Marian Kister from Poland.

She used articles, when she could get them, about the effect of the war on the children in occupied countries or in countries actively engaged in the war. Each article was a revelation of national character and ideology as well as of childhood. She gave space generously to those committees organized to aid children in exile from their homes or in war-ravaged countries. She was in particular sympathy with the Children's Crusade for Children, the Women's Council of Post-War Europe, and Books Across the Sea because their programs involved American boys and girls with children of other countries. To Bertha, that was one step toward brotherhood, toward a one-world community. Throughout the war she never lost her faith in such a concept and transferred her support of the League of Nations to the United Nations with undiminished ardor.

Bertha had her own ways of helping those caught up in the war. In the grim summer after Dunkirk, notices were sent to all English subscribers informing them that they would receive *The Horn Book* regularly "for the duration" regardless of paid renewals. A steady stream of food and CARE packages went out from S. S. Pierce in Boston to Bertha's friends in England. She and William invited the Brooke grandchildren — a second boy had been born since Bertha's London visit in 1936 — to live with them in their Ashburnham home until the war was over. They were prepared to offer the same sanctuary to Grace Allen Hogarth's children, but Mrs. Hogarth brought them to America herself and resumed in Boston her career as a children's book editor.

Mrs. Hogarth returned to England in 1944 and wrote for Bertha a chilling account of a V-2 rocket that took the life of one of her son's schoolfellows as he sat at his tea. Eleanor Farjeon's detailed description of her bomb shelter, though cheerful enough, had the same chilling effect — not because of what it said, but of what it implied. Nora Unwin, an artist and a member of the well-known English publishing family, described for *Horn Book* readers her war years tending evacuated children — very little children — in her country studio. The three articles testified to the steady courage that carried England through its gravest peril.

The same was most eloquently true of those articles based on the letters Beatrix Potter wrote to Bertha during the war years. The *Horn Book* editor and the creator of *The Tale of Peter Rabbit* never met, but became cherished friends through the letters they exchanged over the years.

The initial contact had come from Bertha in 1927 in the form of a questionnaire asking for facts about Miss Potter's life and the roots of her nursery classics. The material was needed for *Realms of Gold*, which Bertha and Elinor were just then compiling. Miss Potter had hesitated about replying: she guarded jealously her privacy as Mrs. William Heelis, she was not given to introspection, and she had no idea who "Miss Bertha E. Mahony" and "Miss Elinor Whitney" were. A selection of *Horn Books*, which Bertha had had the wit to send along as a follow-up to the questionnaire, reassured Miss Potter. Her reply was so rich in background information that Bertha had used it as a *Horn Book* article, after excerpting what was needed for *Realms of Gold.*

Later in the same year Bertha had been able to repay Miss Potter's trust and generosity by selling fifty of her autographed drawings at the Bookshop for Boys and Girls "to raise a fund to save a strip of foreshore woodland and meadow, near Windermere Ferry, from imminent risk of disfigurement by extensive building and town extension."[27] Bertha had placed Miss Potter's illustrated letter of solicitation, in the name of Peter Rabbit, in *The Horn Book,* so there had been no dearth of buyers. The sale had been happily concluded for all concerned, especially for those fortunate enough to buy a signed Beatrix Potter original for five dollars!

The friendship of the two women had flourished after such a mutually satisfying beginning. Their letters at first had been primarily concerned with professional matters, each sensing in the other a natural reserve. There had been more about the sources of Miss Potter's small books, and much about the only long one she wrote, *The Fairy Caravan.* Bertha loved the animal fantasy, rooted so firmly in the English countryside and its creatures. So did Nancy Dean, to whom Bertha read it more than once. Indeed, Nancy's expressed pleasure in the book had made her the proud recipient of a Beatrix Potter letter of her own.

The letters became more personal when a comfortable respect had been established and common interests discovered. After Bertha sent a catalog from William's company about its colonial furniture reproductions, Miss Potter revealed her detailed knowledge of old English cottage furnishings. When William's younger sister and her husband planned to undertake the operation of a sheep ranch, Miss Potter, through Bertha, advised them on the best breed of sheep to stock. She spoke with authority, for on her own farm in the Lake District she, too, raised sheep. There was much in their letters about the countryside of England and New England, as if each wanted to make known to the other the natural scene from which she wrote.

Even during the war years Miss Potter dwelt on the seasonal beauty of the Westmorland country she so loved. The letters sent during those troubled times, however, were mostly filled with her sharp comments on national and world events, and her wry descriptions of coping with farm life as circumscribed by the war. There was no self-pity in the war letters, only a stubborn courage and the dry humor that sustained it. In reading the letters today, it is not only what they say that still has the power to stir the heart, but also the physical evidence of the circumstances of their writing. They were written on all manner of paper scraps: torn-out pages from a composition book, the back of a form from the Wool Control Office, old sheets from a bank book, and the unused part of a letter from the War Agricultural Committee. Some letters were duplicated and mailed several days apart; hopefully, one would escape the U-boats and reach Bertha. All of the letters were slitted and slotted by the censors' tool, so that they looked not unlike player-piano rolls turned sideways.

In 1943 Miss Potter sent the manuscript of *Wag-by-Wall* for publication in the Christmas *Horn Book.* Bertha was so proud to publish an original Beatrix Potter that she asked if it might be held for the May 1944 Anniversary Number. Miss Potter cordially assented. "It leaves time to see proofs, and I would like to make it as nearly word-perfect as I know how, for the credit of your 20th anniversary. The winter's snows will be over by then."[28] In the same letter she thanked Bertha for the latest food package, especially for the chocolate — "It is good!" — and the lemon juice which eased the bronchial cough that was troubling her. Miss Potter never saw the proofs of her story nor the end of the winter's snows, for on December 22, 1943 she died.

To honor the memory of Beatrix Potter, Bertha used *Wag-by-Wall* as planned, and wrote to go with it an article based on her letters from the English writer and illustrator. The letters, Bertha felt, best gave a "clear, direct expression of [Miss Potter's] vigorous and salty personality" and showed "her thorough understanding of the changing world, with its increasingly disturbing events. . . ."[29]

The Twentieth Anniversary Number also marked another step in Beulah Folmsbee's experimentation with the cover design of *The Horn Book.* While Bertha strove to give expression of the times in the magazine, Miss Folmsbee labored to keep the war restrictions from affecting its appearance. There was little she could do about paper stock that had all the life of cold, gray oatmeal, or ink that refused to hold a true color or a sharp line. She concentrated therefore on the continuous improvement of the cover design and the make-up of the text pages.

The Anniversary cover, as Miss Folmsbee rearranged it, established the pattern that is still used today: the name of the magazine across the middle, above it the huntsmen, and below it a partial listing of content. The new design made a beautifully balanced cover: the huntsmen galloped more freely without the weight of the magazine's name over their heads; and the content listing, in increasingly helpful detail, was an invitation to the reading pleasure within.

That pleasure was enhanced by the way Miss Folmsbee placed the printed matter on the page. "What you do with the material after it goes into your hands is always exciting to me," Bertha wrote to her managing editor after a particularly handsome issue had come from the Todd presses.[30]

In addition to the regular numbers, there were many special issues to challenge Miss Folmsbee's talents and ingenuity. Such numbers saluted those persons whose creativity had in some way enriched children's literature. Although special *Horn Books* were usually also memorial ones, Bertha did not allow the finality of death to darken them. She emphasized instead the living spirit that a writer or an illustrator left behind in his work.

The special numbers have grown in significance through the years because they contain invaluable primary source material. Bertha knew intimately most of the persons she honored, and expressed her appreciation of their particular genius in editorials or articles. Her associate editors brought their own extensive friendships in the children's book world to the enrichment of these issues. The articles Bertha secured outside of the Horn Book family were written by relatives, friends, or business associates out of memories still firm and recollections still clear. Bertha chose each contributor as the person best qualified to illuminate a particular aspect of the honored one's life or career.

The authenticity of the articles, their sense of immediacy, and their variety of subject matter combined to create a full-bodied representation of a man and his work. Frequently, the man spoke for himself when a piece he had written for an earlier *Horn Book* was reprinted in the memorial number, or when letters from him to his associates were quoted in their articles about him. Distinguished special issues published during Bertha's editorship, each one a contemporary study in depth, paid tribute to Leslie Brooke, May Massee, Rachel Field and Wanda Gág.

In the Hunt Breakfast of the Wanda Gág number for May-June 1947, Bertha wrote: "*The Horn Book* Editor wishes to extend her thanks to each contributor for his distinguished part in making this issue. To Rose Dobbs [Miss Gág's editor at Coward-McCann] for her help in the planning of the issue. To Anne Carroll Moore for special editorial assistance. . . . And to Beulah Folmsbee . . . who has brought to the designing of these pages particular pains to make this Wanda Gág issue a memorable *Horn Book*."[31]

It *was* a memorable *Horn Book*, inside and out, the first to carry Warren Chappell's striking new cover design, commissioned after the war years' restrictions on paper and ink had been removed. The design rearranged the components of the cover, framed them in a great wide brown border, and printed the whole thing in five colors. It was as if Bertha, released from enforced economies, had cast off all budgetary restraints. Alas, the design proved too costly to be sustained even in peacetime and, after four years, the familiar two-color cover was restored, sans border.

The Wanda Gág issue was memorable in another, and less pleasant way. It was the last *Horn Book* prepared for Mr. Todd by Beulah Folmsbee. Bertha announced the sad news in her July-August 1947 editorial, "A Tribute to Beulah Folmsbee."

> In the resignation of Beulah Folmsbee as Managing Editor to join the Art Department of D. C. Heath, *The Horn Book* has suffered a great loss. Miss Folmsbee came to *The Horn Book* in January 1934 when the magazine was ten years old. Two years later it was taken over by a small newly formed corporation and she brought her unique gifts of typographical skill, craftsmanship and order generously and devotedly to the strengthening and upbuilding of The Horn Book, Inc.
>
> The new Company started with a tiny capital investment and little to spend for promotion, but under Miss Folmsbee's careful and creative management, the subscription list has grown steadily. She had given the magazine's format outstanding distinction with work which is memorable in certain special issues. . . .
>
> Our thanks to Beulah Folmsbee for all she has done for *The Horn Book*. She will be missed — how much it is impossible to say. Our warmest good will and best wishes go with her to her new work.[32]

Miss Folmsbee's resignation marked the beginning of another period of change in Bertha's professional life. It ended when she withdrew from the editorship of *The Horn Book* on December 31, 1950.

In remarking today on the various stages of the four-year transition, they seem uncomplicated enough, almost prearranged as each followed the other in apparently easy and logical sequence.

Such was not the case at all, according to the 1947-1950 files. The difficulties of the personnel situation were aggravated by financial crises and — most of all — by Bertha's anguished realization that her retirement was imminent. The problems seemed so incapable of solution to her that more than once she contemplated bringing her magazine, her company, and her career to an end.

Fortunately, after several persons had been tried in Miss Folmsbee's position, Jennie Lindquist assumed its responsibilities on July 1, 1948. She left her position as Director of Children's Work at the Albany Public Library to become the managing editor of *The Horn Book*. With her appointment, a measure of calm was restored to the magazine's somewhat turbulent affairs.

It was not to last. Alice Jordan asked to be relieved of the Booklist after the July-August 1950 number. To lose Miss Jordan was a real blow, but there was time for Bertha to seek a worthy successor. Her search did not go beyond the Horn Book family. In the September-October 1950 issue Bertha proudly listed as the Booklist's new editors Jennie D. Lindquist and Siri M. Andrews. She had been able to bring her second Hunters Fare editor into closer association with the magazine because Miss Andrews had exchanged the West Coast for the East. After working for a time as the children's editor for Henry Holt & Company in New York City, she had become affiliated with the Concord Public Library in New Hampshire. From Concord it was possible for her to participate actively in Horn Book affairs.

Miss Andrews and Miss Lindquist shared a Swedish heritage, a common professional background as children's librarians and teachers of children's literature, and the editorship of Hunters Fare. Subscribers to *The Horn Book* would sadly miss Alice Jordan's sparkling Booklists, but they could accept with confidence the experienced collaboration of the new editors.

In 1950 Bertha was making reluctant plans for her own retirement. Before leaving *The Horn Book* as editor, however, as if in defiance of the passing years, she brought out one of the magazine's most distinguished issues. It was an extra number — the second only since the magazine's founding — and it bore the date: October 19, 1950. On that day, two years before, Thomas Schofield Handforth had died suddenly and swiftly in Los Angeles at the age of fifty-one. Bertha's extra issue was a memorial to the creative genius of an extraordinary human being who had been at once writer, illustrator and artist. Mr. Handforth's beautiful picture book, *Mei Li*, had won the Caldecott Medal in 1939. Like the other special *Horn Books*, the Handforth Edition is rich in primary source material.

In the next regular issue of the magazine Bertha revealed her retirement from the editorship of *The Horn Book*. She had been prepared in 1950 to name Jennie Lindquist as her successor, but could not make the appointment until a replacement had been found to assume Miss Lindquist's responsibilities as business manager. In the early fall of the year such a replacement became almost miraculously available: a young woman who was personable, qualified, talented, and a Simmons graduate — eminently suited to the work and in harmony with the spirit of the Horn Book organization. Bertha introduced the new staff member in the Hunt Breakfast of the November-December 1950 *Horn Book*.

> The Horn Book's Staff. On October 2, 1950, Miss Norma Fryatt joined the staff of The Horn Book, Inc., as Promotion Manager. She will have charge of all business matters relating to *The Horn Book Magazin*e and to Horn Book publications as well as of promotion and publicity. Miss Fryatt comes to The Horn Book from four years with Young & Rubicam, Inc. After graduating from Simmons College her first work was in the Promotion Department of *The Christian Science Monitor*. Her tastes extend beyond business and advertising to literature, art and music, birds and water-color painting — all matters of importance to The Horn Book.[33]

In the editorial of the same issue Bertha presented the new editor of *The Horn Book* to its readers.

> On January 1, 1951, Jennie D. Lindquist will become Editor of *The Horn Book*. She has been preparing definitely for this step since July 1, 1948, when she became Managing Editor. . . .
>
> Miss Lindquist knows well, and is thoroughly in sympathy with, the goals for which *The Horn Book* strives. The Horn Book, Inc. now starts upon a new chapter in its history with confidence and faith. B.E.M.[34]

With the two announcements Bertha's direct responsibility for *Horn Book* affairs came to an end. That her retirement was implied rather than stated was in character with her personal reticence and a life-long concern with the future rather than the past. "What's past is prelude" she called her editorial for the

Twentieth Anniversary Number, borrowing from Shakespeare. The editorial introducing Miss Lindquist might well have had the same forward-looking caption.

Bertha's unwillingness to put her retirement into words may also have indicated the painfulness of her withdrawal from the magazine. For twenty-five years, consciously and subconsciously, her mind had been engaged with the planning, preparation, and improvement of *Horn Books* — number after number, 140 in all. The preoccupation had become an ingrained habit, a part of the fabric of her mental and emotional existence. That she was to become President of The Horn Book, Incorporated when she retired offered some consolation, but no presidency would ever take the place of being Editor of her beloved magazine. That had been her greatest joy.

A Gleaming Thread

"FOR HER UNIQUE CONTRIBUTION to the field of children's literature," Bertha received The Constance Lindsay Skinner Award for 1955 from The Women's National Book Association. A Citation accompanied the bronze plaque listing those accomplishments which the Award honored. The Citation pleased Bertha because it had been written by her friend, Frederic Melcher, and because it was simple, straightforward, and restrained in tone. The concluding sentence, about *The Horn Book,* gave her the greatest pleasure and satisfaction. She cited it repeatedly in answering her letters of congratulation, though always stopping short of the last words in praise of herself. ". . . In 1924 she launched *The Horn Book,* beloved guide and counselor from then to now to all who serve the reading interests of children, a magazine without parallel or precedent, a magazine which carries the distilled, potent spirit of Bertha Mahony Miller."

That spirit was to be found particularly in *The Horn Books* of the late 1930s and the 1940s when Bertha's editorial powers were at their peak. The table of contents of each issue revealed it, but it was most strongly evident in Bertha's own writing. May Massee likened that writing to a gleaming thread running through a tapestry, in the tribute she wrote for *The Horn Book* when Bertha received the Skinner Award. The gleam came from the spirit, then and now. Time has in no way dulled its glister.

Bertha's writing is also vibrantly alive today because, when she wrote about children and their books, she dealt with fundamental values and basic needs that have remained steadfast through the years. Indeed, many of her editorials seem to have more meaning today than when she wrote them twenty-five or thirty-five years ago. They have increased, rather than diminished, in relevancy. There is a modern ring to the final sentence of "The Children's World," which was the last regular editorial Bertha wrote before introducing her successor.

> And that, — the inherent presence of love, its integral part of the fabric of good children's books, — that is what makes them more important now than ever before.[35]

No lengthy explanation could give a clearer sense of the spirit of Bertha's writing, or present more adequately its timelessness, than the writing itself. The excerpts from her *Horn Book* editorials and articles that follow are offered for that dual purpose. Comment on the individual selections would be gratuitous: the meanings emerge with clarity from Bertha's urgent style, her intense feeling, and the depth of her thought.

* * * * *

> There is a life-long exploration in words — as thrilling to some of us as unknown seas or regions of ice, heat and height to others. As a little child's spirit expands in his wonder over strange words or ideas, so the spirit of the wisest continues to grow in his wonder and effort to grasp completely the works of the greatest poets. 1935.[36]

> There is today a new wide wandering of people; a new wide wandering of children. What sustains them in their pain, grief and homelessness? It is courage; courage nourished by those words which are symbols of greatness, endurance and faith. Many of the word symbols now serving the valiant were gathered in childhood. Some may have lain hidden in secret places of the soul awaiting today's crucial need.
>
> Those who plead for the introduction to children, by means of the spoken word, of the finest works of the imagination, do so because they believe that is the way to keep alive in the world goodness, truth, beauty and kindliness. 1939.[37]

> . . . Is not the occasion ripe for raising a fund for the encouragement of story-tellers and story-telling? Words lie at the very core of life. And story-telling of a noble order is the source of that wonder which stirs our imagination, makes us sensitive, makes us strong, and makes us creative. . . .

It is not through the reiteration of the familiar and the commonplace but through the poetic record of the strange, noble, brave and beautiful that men have grown down through the ages world without end. 1937.[38]

Never was story-telling more needed than now. Our leaders fill us with doubt and disappointment. Our citizenry, too, seems filled with small spirit; and bent upon small goals; incapable of thinking constructively for the common good. Why is it so? Partly because we have forgotten that men must have heroes. Reading, writing, arithmetic, even the social studies and the best courses in civics do not breed them. A hero to serve as exemplar cannot be presented in everyday terms. He can't be too near. He must stand in large proportions, at some distance, on a pedestal, with proper surroundings. He must be presented to the imagination in words which stir the senses. "The most mystic of all leading is by way of the senses to the soul, the touch of sense upon the spring of emotion."* The leading of the story-teller is of this kind. The soul of the listener is moved, he gazes in uplifted state at the image of his imagination. By that image he raises his stature then and thereafter. His perception of what is important becomes clearer. Matters small and mean drop away. He thrusts his head straight up, stretching his spine to its fullest length. So his hero stands. So all fine spires thrust up into the sky — and for the same reason.

But more fundamental even than its effect upon children as citizens is the effect upon them as fathers and mothers. In the imagination, that is, in the depths of fathers and mothers, are their hopes for their children. This is the generating force, the evolutionary power of the race. Let these hopes be high by presenting to those who are young the best there is in the best way. 1935.[39]

Mothers and fathers do not always realize the importance of their opportunity to create and encourage individual personalities. They can provide first of all that order in the home which corresponds to the order in nature and in art and helps to give little children peace and security. The little child's early contact with art is

*Cecilia Beaux in *Background with Figures.*

through stories, pictures and music, and a few great people have believed that art is the basis of real education. Not art as something remote but as close as nature itself and growing out of nature.

"A free and floating imaginative self"* — these are the words I have wanted this long time to better describe my "going up" in delight over a book. They also describe the sensation of children when they move from their external world into the world of the story to which they are listening. It is reflected in their faces as every storyteller and reader-aloud knows. 1949.[40]

What our children today need more than anything else is the assurance of parents, teachers, and all their elders *by example* that life is a precious gift worthy to be lived with virtue, integrity and honor, as individual and as citizen. 1949.[41]

Children are influenced most by what happens in the home. If parents show no neighborly interest and take no part in the welfare of their town, children will not suddenly become inspired citizens. If, on the other hand, fathers and mothers are clear on the simple principles by which they live and for which they will die, if necessary, then daily living takes on for children significance and vitality. With a vigorous facing of whatever life may bring, children's lives become so exciting and interesting that they do not need to turn to ephemeral and violent hideosities. 1941.[42]

Many things come between little children and their right to life, liberty and the pursuit of happiness; perhaps nothing oftener than systems of education in school or home. Childhood's antidote is the world of the imagination. It is the story that stirs and feeds that world; gives the magic interlocking of the seen and the unseen; develops understanding of mind and heart; and creates wonder, that core of growth. Every waking moment children explore with all their senses the here and now. What they make of it depends upon the imaginative background out of which they interpret it.

*Herbert Read in *Education Through Art.*

It takes imagination to be a good citizen. It takes imagination to appreciate other people's suffering. It takes imagination to understand what freedom means and why it is worth living and dying for. 1941.[43]

"Reading for thought is the major objective," wrote an Elementary School Supervisor. But is it? Is not the major objective the education of the human heart, which in turn lends understanding to thought? The unpredictable in each child's reaction to a book and the fact that one of the joys of reading is personal discovery should discourage too definite age or personality earmarking of books. 1944.[44]

"Lifu was six years old, and he liked to ask questions. He wanted to know everything, so he asked questions about everything in the world."* This Chinese boy is true to child life everywhere. Out of this ardent, eager interest comes in adult years the ability to blaze new trails and to solve problems. We need this ardency in our struggle to win the war. We need it in planning the kind of world to work for when all the destruction is over. Too often we have seen children's eagerness turn into apathy, and we know all too many grown-ups hard to interest in anything.

What kind of schools will give children hope, courage, skill, patience, and vision for all the re-building and new building? *The Little Red School House,* Agnes de Lima's history of twenty years of public school experimental classes in New York City . . . offers an inspiring answer. . . .

From schools like this children will issue with knowledge, strength and vision sufficient to create at long last a genuinely coöperative world where peace may exist. For peace is the fruit of the tree, not the tree itself. It is brave, freely creative, strongly constructive, and unprejudiced men and women who will be the real peacemakers, worthy to be called "the children of God." 1942.[45]

We hear much today about spiritual poverty. We hear much about children's difficulty in learning to read and

*Eleanor Lattimore in *Lifu's Questions.*

also how slowly and with what difficulty many boys and girls of high school age do read. . . . We read, also, even in our own *Horn Book,* of the need of adolescents for "voluntarily readable, compellingly entertaining, mind-stretching non-fiction with a social conscience"; and of the need for books presenting "serious questions in an easy, natural but exciting way" and written "well within the first ten thousand words in Thorndike's grading, with not more than five or six exceptions to a 300-word page."

Spiritual poverty and difficulty or slowness in reading on the part of normal boys and girls go back to the same cause: at an early age these children have not been exposed to the real and the best in literature and in pictures. They have not caught as tiny children the fun of words and the lure of the book. . . . The bright, gay, real books have not been present to lend their irresistible invitation. They have not had the real experience of reading.

Mind-stretching books — books which give perspective, a sense of true values — will be books of great stature out of the past, not books of current comment. Nor can books be mind-stretching if they are so "compellingly entertaining, voluntarily readable" as to demand no effort on the part of the reader. . . .

The experience of reading is more than the ability to recognize and pronounce words. It is the ability so to surrender one's self to the experience evoked by words as to make the experience one's own. 1940.[46]

. . . A procession of splendid boys and girls march through the pages of our finest children's books, young people bred to a sense of personal dignity and strength through independence and responsibility, and freedom — but freedom combined with order, for there must be in homes and in schools an order which corresponds to the order in nature. Otherwise there can be no freedom and no peace. 1937.[47]

Children in America today through their fine books live as friends with children all over the world. Authors and artists express in these books the universality of life, love and art, and thus quietly and unobtrusively share in bringing to mankind in the long last that unified conscience and unified consciousness symbolized in effective world government. 1940.[48]

In America, as in other countries these days, human affairs are bewildering and depressing. Everywhere we look in vain for a true sense of values. But in one place true values are to be found. That place is in children's books. This rich and colorful stream, covering every kind from picture books and folk and fairy tales to books about the universe, is unique in this country. It is made up of genuine pieces of artistic effort in which the arts of writing, illustrating and book-making have united to create a whole capable of giving joy not to children alone but to all ages. Because of its genius and sound values, this stream is like a crystal-clear mountain brook. . . .

By values, I mean those principles which determine the good conduct of life anywhere, any time. The first of these is the one which Sinclair Lewis's Babbitt missed after gaining so many desired THINGS, without understanding what it was he lacked — a sense of God. . . . A seeking after truth and beauty; a sense of wonder and reverence; the balance and proportion which humor gives; these are values in terms of the spirit which shape the design and form for living. 1936.[49]

We are engaged upon a great imaginative enterprise in this country, a demonstration that a free society can exist. . . . We find a great scientist and educator of our day claiming that it is to the artists, writers, musicians and scholars that we must look for stimulation of imagination from the earliest years. They are the humanists of our times. . . .

This issue of *The Horn Book* opens with a fantasy in which an artist-humanist of our times makes a plea for the freedom of the artist and for his protection from exploitation. *The Horn Book* begs for full understanding of the writer's and the artist's important contribution to the humanities. 1949.[50]

Let us be thankful this Christmas of 1947 for art in all its forms which, like beauty in nature, is always building in us fresh courage. Let us be thankful for the living characters in this and other countries who still proclaim conscience as the heart of freedom, the voice of God in each of us; and for those who value diversity and flexibility in human affairs. And let us be thankful for the promise of our children. 1947.[51]

Art flourishes where there is sound critical judgment to examine and appraise. The critic must, first of all, have a real point of view about his subject. The essential point of view grows out of acquaintance with the best children's books past and present, and also with the world's best literature for everyone. This point of view — this measuring stick — must also bear some relation to children themselves and their reactions to books today. The critic should have [the] experience of sharing books with children or of seeing them choosing and reading books for themselves. It is a truism — and yet it does not seem to be generally understood — that criticism is just as importantly concerned with pointing out excellence as weakness. . . .

Comment on children's books is valuable in exact proportion to the judgment, honesty, fairness, and skill expressed by their critics. 1946.[52]

In this issue of *The Horn Book* is the complete cycle of literature, its growth out of life, the way it grows, its power to reveal to us the depth, height, breadth and significance of life; and its miraculous power to give to us ever new and increasing life. . . .

The world talks much about the ways to brotherhood and peace. These books do for children what Miss Skinner wanted her Rivers of America volumes to do — what all fine books do — they kindle the imagination and reveal us to each other and to ourselves. Ever-increasing power to put ourselves in others' places, that is the way to brotherhood, to peace. 1939.[53]

In a collection of stories published long ago, Dr. L. P. Jacks' Mad Shepherd said, "You must get out of your skin to understand the stars." . . .

It is true that we have to form the habit of getting out of our skins in the name of God to be thoroughly good Americans, to be able to think what is good for the country as a whole rather than what is good for me a mill owner, me a coal miner, me a farmer, me a Legionnaire, me a New Englander, me a Californian.

And now we must widen our leaps out of our skins to consider what is best not only for Americans but for the whole world. Unless we can take these leaps — short and long — no plan for world order will succeed. . . .

Childhood and youth have an innate longing for God and for the pursuit of noble ends. It is we grown-ups, all bound up with our petty self-seeking, who discourage them; we with our God-estrangéd faces, we who miss the many-splendoured thing. 1944.[54]

Truth does not become less true, honor less honorable, nobility less noble, nor goodness less exciting when evil, cruelly and powerfully armed, stalks the world. That is the time when we know the values for which we are ready to die as well as to live. 1940.[55]

At a time of violent world transition, comparable only to volcanic eruptions of the earth, it is reassuring, recreating, even essential to life itself to reflect upon steadfast people and values that do not change. Nature teaches us many lessons, far more than we have wisdom to interpret. No lesson is more often repeated than that every end is only a new beginning. . . . 1941.[56]

When we gouge out the land in sore or ugly fashion, Nature, if left to herself, starts at once to repair the damage. In human relations, too, there is a process like this always at work. . . .

Today all over the world, in the midst of so much intolerance, brutality, cruelty, savagery, many quiet, strong and steadfast people are expressing day in and day out the very opposites of those evil traits. Everyday expressions of kindness, good will and gentleness are like the grasses, low shrubs, bushes and trees growing up the sides of quarries and pits, spreading their soft and lovely green over the torn sides. 1936.[57]

O God . . . Look down in pity upon all little children this Christmas season.

Where they are homeless, orphaned, suffering or needy, give them the happiness and comfort of dreams.

Let them dwell in their dreams in warm candlelighted homes where kindness and merriment abound; with glowing Christmas trees and books and toys piled high about them; fires on the hearth, and good things to eat.

Send to children in Thy loving-kindness a dream for each of the Twelve Days of Christmas.

Let every dream bear happiness; but while some bring especially ease, and some especially comfort and delight, let all build visions for the swifter coming of Thy Kingdom on earth, and the pattern of each child's part toward that coming. Let these dreams be so strong in the wonder, reverence and mystery of Thee, so strong in Thy creative currents that these children are enabled once more to burst bonds and to overcome evil; and are led in the paths of judgment, knowledge and ways of understanding. 1940.[58]

Publications of The Horn Book, Incorporated

The Horn Book Magazine would seem enough for one life achievement. But midway in its career, as Mrs. William Miller, Bertha Mahony incorporated The Horn Book and became a book publisher. . . . Now the Horn Book published its own books. Among them came, in 1944, Paul Hazard's *Books, Children and Men.*

Mrs. Miller's imagination, practical as well as idealistic, saw needs in our field which we ourselves had neither time nor resources to fill. Thus she produced the first and only book on the illustrated children's book, that noble history and biography, *Illustrators of Children's Books: 1744-1945.*

— From a Resolution saluting the record of Bertha Mahony Miller, presented by the Children's Services Division of the American Library Association at its annual meeting in Washington, D.C., on June 23, 1959. Louise Seaman Bechtel drew up the Resolution[1]

From Colonial Hornbook to *Horn Book Reflections*

BERTHA'S NATURAL RESILIENCY and common sense quickly made retirement a word only, not a fact. To divorce herself from the editorial responsibility of her magazine *was* a wrench, but there were other Horn Book matters demanding her immediate attention. Most pressing was a book about Margery Bianco which The Horn Book, Incorporated had scheduled for publication on May 1, 1951.

The volume was not the first venture of the company into the book publishing field. It had started in the late 1930s, and when Bertha retired from the editorship of *The Horn Book*, five books of major significance had been published, as well as several Christmas gift books, two important lists, the first of the annual Horn Book calendars, and an intriguing parcel of materials derived from the earliest reading matter of children.

As President of her company, and then as Chairman of its Board of Directors, Bertha saw thirteen more books published under the imprint of The Horn Book, Incorporated. Some of the thirteen she worked on herself; others came about because of her vision; all of them engaged her interest and benefited by her counsel. When she died in 1969, she left as her partial legacy to the children's book world eighteen handsome volumes, each one illuminating some phase of children's literature: its history, its criticism and appreciation, and its creators.

The making of that splendid legacy was not the easiest task Bertha ever set herself. The capital of The Horn Book, Incorporated was infinitesimal in its beginning years. Each of the early publications meant an interest-free loan from William Miller to cover printing, binding, and promotional expenses. Except for Mrs.

Bechtel, until Siri Andrews became a Director, Bertha's board members were not at ease with publishing cost estimates, and most hesitant about publishing risks. When Bertha wanted to bring out another title before the loan had been completely repaid for the previous book, she met especially stiff opposition — though never from William. Yet if Bertha "felt full of faith and conviction" about a book, as she expressed it to a friend, she fought for its publication until she won.

Bertha did not set out consciously to make The Horn Book, Incorporated a publisher of books as well as of a magazine. Happenstance had much to do with it, as did the same instinctive recognition of a book need that had already produced three notable books about children's literature.

Beulah Folmsbee began it really when "to the work of making bricks without straw, she brought her craft ability and reproduced"[2] a series of attractive articles, landmarks in the history of children's books. The first was "A Chart of Old Hornbooks" whose pictures and text were drawn from Alexander Tuer's definitive two-volume study, *History of the Horn-Book*. The chart was poster-size and was available either antiqued, hand-tinted, and framed, or more simply — and less costly — in a mailing tube, sans color and mounting.

In the same year, 1939, Miss Folmsbee began to make replicas of a wooden hornbook used by children in early New England days. Because of its origin, the reproduction came to be known as "The Colonial Hornbook." The following year, using a model thought to be Dutch, she produced "The Silver Hornbook." Her next project was the making of two battledores: "The Horse" and "Friendship." Battledores were threefold, cardboard, illustrated reading tools that replaced the hornbook and led to today's primer. Miss Folmsbee found the originals of her battledores in the Boston Public Library.

When Miss Folmsbee was sandpapering, staining, and tacking hornbooks, her desk resembled a kitchen table with cookies spread out for cooling. The tinting of the charts, and the antiquing of them and the battledores, used every available flat space in the office, and for some time, too, since the accumulation of a discreet amount of good Boston dust added to the authenticity of the antiquing. When Miss Folmsbee left the Horn Book, Esther Munro took over the finishing of the reproductions, with Duncan's carpentry help. "It's such fun, Esther!" Mrs. Miller told her, blue eyes bright and eager, when she brought the first supply of charts, paddles, and battledores and all the materials needed to finish them.

The first book to bear the imprint of The Horn Book, Incorporated was published in 1942: *A Little History of the Horn Book*, by Beulah Folmsbee. The *Little History*, as its name implied, was a small book and it wore its scholarship jauntily as befitted its size and its subject. It was a welcome supplement to the exhaustive Tuer volumes. Miss Folmsbee not only wrote the text of the book, but also assembled the illustrative material for it, and did the entire layout. Its charming format, so right in every detail, augured well for any volume published thereafter over the imprint of The Horn Book, Incorporated.

Although the publication of the next book came about by accident, it was nonetheless of primary importance to the company and to the children's book world. In a box of French children's books which Esther Averill sent to the bookshop from Paris in 1933, Bertha found a slim volume *about* children's books: *Les Livres, les Enfants et les Hommes*, by Paul Hazard. M. Hazard was on the Faculty of the Sorbonne and held the Chair of Modern Literature in the College of France. Bertha sent the book out to Sunny Fields for Marguerite Mitchell to read, knowing of Mrs. Mitchell's fluency with the French language from her years of living and painting in the Amboise country.

Mrs. Mitchell recognized the book for the minor classic it was, and the importance of having it translated into English — as much for its gaiety of spirit as for its thoughtful analysis of distinctive national traits as revealed in children's books. She determined to translate the book herself and, on her behalf, Bertha requested an option from M. Hazard and Ernest Flammarion, his publisher, for a translation of the book into English and its publication by an American firm. The six months granted, unfortunately, was woefully inadequate for the making of a worthy translation for so fine a book, and the option lapsed.

Undaunted, Mrs. Mitchell went ahead with her translation and finished it, polished and perfect, in 1940. Originally, Bertha had planned to interest a publisher in the book when the manuscript was ready. In the ensuing years circumstances had changed and in 1940 she had no further to look for a publisher than her own infant company. Moreover, after she read Mrs. Mitchell's superb translation of Paul Hazard's sparkling French, she knew that she had a book she could champion with "faith and conviction."

That faith and conviction, and Bertha's limited supply of patience, were sorely tried before the book was published four long years later. The complications were incredible, deriving primarily from the fall of France in 1940 and the entry of the United States in World War II in 1942. The one affected the permissions to publish; the other controlled the paper, ink, and binding cloth needed to produce the book.

Before Bertha could negotiate with M. Hazard for his permission, he had left Columbia, where he was lecturing as a visiting professor of French, and returned to France to share his countrymen's troubled days. She was able, however, to obtain the necessary authorization from Dr. Horatio Smith of the University's French Department and Paul Hazard's good friend. It was the one fairly simple transaction in the whole complex affair.

The publisher's permission was another matter entirely. Because of the Occupation, Bertha was unable to deal directly with Flammarion. After an unproductive and time-consuming correspondence with a South American firm purporting to represent the French house, Bertha abandoned it, on the advice of Harry Burnham, and addressed her request to the Office of the Alien Property Custodian in Washington, D.C. The Office was willing to grant the permission, but had to be directed to do so by the State Department, for by then the United States was in the war.

To get that needed directive, William Miller spent his days in Washington haunting the State Department offices. Finally, on November 19, 1943 the permission filtered through the hierarchy. Just in time, too, because the approved applications which Bertha had secured for the purchase of paper and binding cloth for the printing of the book were due to expire at the end of the year.

Books, Children and Men was published on March 30, 1944, beautifully designed by Beulah Folmsbee. It was hailed at once by the critics as a unique and imaginative contribution to the literature about children's books; as a scholar's holiday, free of dusty pedantry, full of Gallic wit and deftly turned phrases; as a wise book that saw beyond the national characteristics of children's books their universal qualities.

> Yes, children's books keep alive a sense of nationality; but they also keep alive a sense of humanity. They describe their native land lovingly, but they also describe faraway lands where unknown brothers live. They under-

> stand the essential quality of their own race; but each of them is a messenger that goes beyond mountains and rivers, beyond the seas, to the very ends of the world in search of new friendships. Every country gives and every country receives — innumerable are the exchanges — and so it comes about that in our first impressionable years the universal republic of childhood is born.[3]

From 1940 to 1943 there was actually little for Bertha to do in connection with the Hazard book, except to engage in endless correspondence on its behalf and try to compose her soul in patience as the letters filled folder after folder in her files. The frustration of the experience would have been harder to bear if she had not had another publishing project in hand to serve as a kind of counter-irritant. She described it in a 1942 *Horn Book.*

> In November, 1943, *The Horn Book* expects to publish a successor to *Contemporary Illustrators of Children's Books,* which . . . has been out of print for several years but continues to be ordered steadily.
>
> The new book is being compiled by Bertha E. Mahony and Beulah Folmsbee and will be typographically designed by the latter. The format will be similar to the first book but the contents will be greatly enlarged, for it is planned to provide a biographical reference book of those who have illustrated books for children from the beginning. This is not such a large order as it sounds, for it was not until about the middle of the eighteenth century that books were first made for children's pleasure. . . .
>
> While this volume will be devoted to artists, it will provide a brief text survey and picture review of the development of illustration and book-making in books for children. Pages will number more than twice those of the earlier book. Among the new chapters for which arrangements have already been made are the following: "Pictures in Books for Children before 1800," by Anne T. Eaton; "A. B. Frost, An American Illustrator of the 1800s," by Warren Chappell; and "Howard Pyle, American Illustrator," by Philip Hofer.[4]

The announcement came to haunt Bertha. The compilation of the book was a much larger order than it sounded, its length came to be three times that of the original volume, and it was not published until October 1, 1947.

Bertha did the biographical section of the book, using the collections of the Boston Athenaeum and the Fine Arts Museum largely for her research. The serene atmosphere of both institutions calmed her war-jangled nerves until the seeming endlessness of the task began to nag at her consciousness. As close as she had been to children's books for twenty-five years, she had not quite realized the dimensions — the mushrooming dimensions — in the field of book illustration. Then, as the contributing chapters for the various sections began to come in, Bertha discovered she would have to write prefaces to each for the sake of continuity and the avoidance of informational gaps. That, too, meant hours of research before any writing could be attempted.

By 1944 it was clear to Bertha that she and Miss Folmsbee could not do the book alone if they wished to publish it within the century. With her usual instinct for the right person for a job, she asked Louise Latimer, the Director of Work with Children of the Public Library of the District of Columbia, to join herself and Miss Folmsbee in the preparation of the volume. Miss Latimer's task would be the compilation of the selective bibliographies of the illustrators and authors, working from the 2,500 volume Illustrators' Collection in her library. The Collection had just been put in complete cataloging order in anticipation of its transferral to a new library building where it would be dignified with a room of its own. Because of the Collection and its perfect order, and because her associates volunteered their assistance, Miss Latimer agreed to do the bibliographies for Bertha.

The associates were by name Elsie Sinclair MacDonald, Evelyn Wainwright Turpin, and Nancy Lee Bradfield, but during the long, hot summer of their most concentrated labors on the book they signed their letters to Beulah Folmsbee, "The Sweat Shop Workers" or, if it was too hot for even that, just "The SSW's." The heat, though, had very little effect on the gay spirits of Miss Latimer and her irrepressible staff. The exuberance and good humor that they brought to the project was almost as important as their wide knowledge of children's books and their experienced bibliographical skills.

In the spring of 1947 the book was finished in all the important details. It was then that Beulah Folmsbee felt free to respond to D. C. Heath's offer and resigned from the Horn Book. She had designed every part of the book, working on weekends with layout and dummy on long tables in the Sunny Fields studio of Marguerite Mitchell. When the book was published, no reviewer failed to comment on its design, from its spacious pages to its lovely cover, as one of the handsomest pieces of bookmaking of the year. It had been printed, of course, by The Thomas Todd Company, with Mr. Todd taking a personal as well as a professional interest in its production.

Miss Moore considered *Illustrators of Children's Books: 1744-1945* to be "the most valuable contribution to children's books in the half century of my experience in the selection and reviewing of books."[5] Because the *Illustrators* volume was a unique reference book, and because of the magnitude of its coverage it was welcomed by libraries, art museums and schools, and bookstores. It also made a place for itself in the home library where its provocative text, beautifully designed pages, and lavish use of illustrative matter invited the browsing eye. In every way the book fulfilled the two purposes about which Bertha wrote in her Introduction to the volume.

> And so we come to the two purposes of this book. The first is to show that art in children's books is a part of all art, not an isolated special field. In every period the greatest artists have shared in it. The second purpose is to invite to further reading and study, to wider examination of picture books and illustrated books of the past and present, and to more conscious effort to understand all that is involved in fine bookmaking, for thus is pleasure in books increased; and thus is created a book public discerning in its appreciation, capable of judging pictures and format as well as text; the kind of public that encourages artists to greater heights and advances the bookmaking arts.
>
> The work of the artist — like that of the writer, poet, musician — enlarges the understanding and vision of men and quickens their imagination. And imagination is best quickened in childhood. In patient effort and with periods of joy and delight, in spite of all the discouragements life in the world presents, the artist goes on trying to better today his best of yesterday. Always he tries to see "beauty with keener perception and subtler understanding" and to serve it. That is why the artist sees what other men cannot see. The every existence of artists, with their unceasing effort toward perfection in their work, would seem a hope and a promise to the world; a

> symbol of man's spiritual struggle toward the source of truth, goodness, mercy and beauty; evidence that the struggle is the very heart of life. These creative people who use their talents for children's books are blessed, and far more important than they realize, for they are helping to build that "World Republic of Childhood" which, rightly built, will one day bring into being the ideal Republic of the World.[6]

Bertha took great personal satisfaction in her third major publication, for it reflected many of her interests and friendships. The book, *From Rollo to Tom Sawyer and Other Papers,* consisted of twelve essays by Alice Jordan about American children's books of the nineteenth century. Six of the essays were revisions of articles that had first appeared in *The Horn Book.* There was nothing of the raw earmarks of research about Miss Jordan's papers; instead they bore a mellow patina that came from years of using the material with her staff at the Boston Public Library and her library school students at Simmons.

The paper from which the book took its title had been, in 1947, the initial Caroline M. Hewins Lecture, delivered under the sponsorship of the New England Round Table of Children's Librarians. Mr. Melcher had suggested the establishment of the memorial lecture and provided a generous honorarium to sustain it. Miss Jordan had been one of the founders of the Round Table and a friend of Miss Hewins; it was right that she should have the honor of giving the first Hewins Lecture. Bertha, who belonged to the Round Table and strongly supported its activities, approved the choice.

Bertha asked Nora Unwin to design Miss Jordan's book. Miss Unwin had come to America after the war and made her home in Peterborough, just over the New Hampshire border from Ashburnham. Aware of Miss Jordan's Maine heritage, and of her great love for Grand Manan where she owned a summer home, Miss Unwin used for her endpaper design and page decorations blueberries, dunes, and an island cottage. *From Rollo to Tom Sawyer* was a serene book, as pleasant to look upon as it was easy to read, a graceful testimonial to the quiet fame of its author.

The book was not the first publication by Miss Jordan to come from Bertha's company. In 1947 she had contributed to the February *Horn Book* an article about children's classics and a list of sixty books which she considered to be such. Bertha had had the article and the list reprinted at once and issued as a pamphlet, "Children's Classics." From time to time the list was revised so that it has remained current and contemporary over the years.

The second Hewins Lecture, "The Travelogue Storybook of the Nineteenth Century," was delivered by Virginia Haviland, then the Librarian of the Phillips Brooks Branch of the Boston Public Library. Bertha was proud to use it as a three-part series in *The Horn Book* and then to publish it as a book, in a limited edition.

Just before Bertha left the editorship of *The Horn Book,* she launched the first of her company's annual Calendars which are derived from the children's book field. The 1951 Calendar presented twelve quotations from Walter de la Mare, chosen by Bertha for the month-long contemplation they could bear. The borders that framed the quotations and the monthly calendars with snowflakes, stars, roses, hearts, and other seasonal symbols, were made especially for the Calendar by Pamela Bianco in her delicate and precise style. Seldom have the Calendars of subsequent years surpassed that first one in quality of quotation or beauty of illustration.

When Bertha moved into the Presidency of The Horn Book, Incorporated, she carried with her the manuscript of a book almost ready for Mr. Todd and a May 1 publication: *Writing and Criticism: A Book for Margery Bianco.* Miss Moore and Bertha had prepared the volume together in honor of the critic, novelist, and writer of children's books. The book consisted of a selection of Mrs. Bianco's original and critical writings, following personal accounts of her by her daughter, Pamela, by her friend, Valenti Angelo, and by Miss Moore. Bertha wrote the biographical introduction to the volume and Mr. Angelo designed it and created its decorative details. The finished book was, in Pamela's words, "just like a jewel!"[7]

Bertha's next publication was termed "a distinctive and elegant book" by its *Horn Book* reviewer.[8] *Caroline M. Hewins: Her Book* had two parts. The first was a reprinting of Miss Hewins' *A Mid-Century Child and Her Books,* which Louise Seaman had originally brought out at Macmillan in 1926 in a charming lavender-and-old-lace format. The second part, "Caroline M. Hewins and Books for Children," was the third Hewins Lecture, delivered by Jennie Lindquist in 1950, the year before she became the editor of *The Horn Book.* Miss Lindquist had received the first Hewins

Scholarship which the citizens of Hartford had established in honor of their librarian. In her Preface to the book Bertha wrote of its purpose: ". . . so that young librarians might have a well-rounded impression of an unusual woman who found her way into library work for children when the route was uncharted and far more solitary than it is today."[9]

Bertha had been deeply involved in all the books published by her company but, except for the *Illustrators* and the Bianco volumes, her association had been primarily that of editor rather than contributing writer. That ended when she and Elinor joined forces once again, this time to produce *Newbery Medal Books: 1922-1955* and *Caldecott Medal Books: 1938-1957*. They worked on the material largely in the Florida homes they and their husbands shared during the winters of the 1950s. Each year a bound set of *Horn Books* went south with Bertha, and a room was set aside in the winter quarters where she and Elinor could work comfortably on their projects.

The nucleus of each book consisted of the acceptance speeches of the recipients of the Medals and biographies about them. In addition, the Newbery volume contained excerpts from the Medal books, to give some sense of their flavor and the writers' use of the language; the Caldecott, by reproducing an illustration from each honored book, demonstrated the way the artists told their stories with brush rather than pen. Each book concluded with a critical appraisal of the books which had received the Awards. Elizabeth Nesbitt, the Associate Dean of the Carnegie Library School and lecturer on children's literature, commented on the Newbery titles; Esther Averill, on the Caldecott.

Thanks to Bertha's foresight in acquiring permission from the American Library Association in 1937 to publish the acceptance speeches in *The Horn Book,* and after 1939 in running accompanying articles about the Award winners, the assembling of the material after those dates was a relatively simple matter. The difficulty came from the earliest days of the Newbery Award when no formal speeches were made, or, when they were, were not recorded anywhere in their entirety. Bertha and Elinor were therefore obliged to do considerable research for the Newbery book and some original writing so that, in the end, they were much more than just the editors of the volume, as they modestly called themselves.

Norma Fryatt selected the illustrations to be reproduced in both books, more importantly in the Caldecott — no easy thing to do when color had to be sacrificed and original size altered for a new page requirement. Miss Fryatt worked closely with Dorothy Abbe, the designer of both books, and with Thomas Todd, Jr., their printer. Mr. Todd had become head of the family business when his father retired in 1950. The combined efforts of the three skilled craftsmen brought an award to the Newbery volume: it was selected by the American Institute of Graphic Arts as one of the fifty books of the year 1955 notable for excellence of format.

Like the special issues of *The Horn Book*, the Newbery and Caldecott volumes are rich in primary source material. The serious student or the casual reader "may be startled to find an exciting human being instead of a collection of sterilized facts"[10] emerging from the biographical sketches. The acceptance speeches offer an understanding and an appreciation of the creative genius: how it works, what its inspirations are, and why it labors to write and illustrate books for children.

Back in 1942, in defiance of the war-darkened days and nights, Bertha had published in the December *Horn Book*, "Light the Candles! A List for Christmas Reading," by Marcia Dalphin, the Librarian of the Rye Free Reading Room in Rye, New York. The list had been immediately reissued as a pamphlet, revised from time to time, and is now supplemented by Sidney Long's equally joyful "And All the Dark Make Bright Like Day."

When, in the early 1950s, Bertha contemplated bringing out a supplement to the monumental *Illustrators* volume, she turned to Miss Dalphin for help. *Illustrators of Children's Books: 1946-1956* followed the pattern of the parent volume. Bertha assembled the papers for the text section and wrote the general introduction; Miss Dalphin compiled the bibliographies; and Ruth Hill Viguers, who would become *The Horn Book's* third editor in 1958, did the biographies. Like all of Bertha's so-called "reference tools," the second Illustrator book served more than just that utilitarian purpose. Its selective bibliographies offered guidance in the judgment of book illustration, and its articles strove to clarify a question that had haunted the children's book world for many a long year: "What *is* a picture book?"

The *Illustrators* volume, published in 1958, was the last publication of her company for which Bertha bore direct responsibility. The volumes that came after it were all done by other members of the Horn Book family, although Bertha was actively involved in their planning and followed their progress with undiminished eagerness.

She was especially delighted with Norma Fryatt's *A Horn Book Sampler,* a collection of papers from the first twenty-five years of the magazine's publication. In making her sampling, Miss Fryatt "looked especially for vivid, spare writing, for the expression of enduring truths about children and their books with the hope that these pages would speak to today's parents, librarians, authors and illustrators with the same urgency and point as when they were written."[11] That Miss Fryatt's *Sampler* reads as freshly today as when she compiled it, is a tribute to the sensitivity with which she made her selections. Bertha wrote an introduction to the book full of delightful bits and pieces of *Horn Book* history.

The Three Owls' Notebook appeared for the last time in the December 1960 *Horn Book.* On January 20, 1961, on the Inauguration Day of John Kennedy, Anne Carroll Moore died in her ninetieth year. It pleased Bertha to offer as an enduring memorial to her friend, the re-issuance of Miss Moore's *My Roads to Childhood* by The Horn Book, Incorporated. The book, originally published by Doubleday, Doran & Company, Inc., was drawn from the critical essays on children's books which Miss Moore had contributed to *The Bookman* from 1918 to 1939. In her Introduction for the Horn Book edition, Frances Sayers called the essays contemporary in substance and said they held an "exuberant invitation to throw open windows and doors for a wider view on the judgment of books for children."[12] The invitation has lost none of its exuberance with the passing of the years; the book is still contemporary in spirit.

The next publication of Bertha's company indicated how extensive her influence had been as the director of a bookshop and the co-founder of a magazine. Nine of the fifteen papers included in *The Hewins Lectures: 1947-1962* had been presented by staff members of the Bookshop for Boys and Girls or associates of the Horn Book. The volume, substantial in size and handsome in format, was edited by Siri Andrews, then a member of the Board of Directors of The Horn Book, Incorporated and herself a Hewins Lecturer. The lectures offered what is necessary for progress in any field of endeavor: an understanding of its past; the past being, in the case of the lectures, the reading matter of nineteenth-century New England children.

In 1963 Lee Kingman Natti became associated with the Horn Book as a member of its Council. Bertha's acquaintance with Mrs. Natti was more than casual. She had known her first as Lee

Kingman, an eager participant in the children's reading contests of the Bookshop and *The Horn Book*; as a teenage contributor to the magazine just before she entered the same school — today, Colby College, New Hampshire — where Bertha's mother had received her early musical training; as the children's editor at Houghton Mifflin, successor to Mrs. Hogarth; and as the wife of Robert Natti who, in 1966, became Principal of Gloucester High School which Bertha had attended. William and Bertha had admired the creative young couple and had delighted in visiting them at the home they built, largely with their own hands, on the edge of a Cape Ann water-filled quarry. The driveway to the house followed the roadbed of the old "Polyphemus" engine Bertha had known as a child.

To be able to have Mrs. Natti undertake the editorship of the next two Horn Book publications was a real satisfaction to Bertha. The books were *Newbery and Caldecott Medal Books: 1956-1965*, edited by Lee Kingman, and *Illustrators of Children's Books: 1957-1966*, compiled by Lee Kingman, Joanna Foster, and Ruth Giles Lontoft. In subject matter and format both books were distinguished supplements to the earlier volumes Bertha had worked upon.

In the summer of 1967 Bertha's eyes were bright with pleasure whenever she spoke of another supplement that was in the making. It was to be a collection of Horn Book papers, a companion volume to Norma Fryatt's *Sampler*, chosen from the 1949-1966 issues of the magazine. What pleased Bertha most was that Elinor was making the selection and editing the book. *Horn Book Reflections* was published in the fall of 1969; Bertha did not see the finished book for she died in the spring of the year. The expectation had been enough.

In her review of *Reflections*, Mrs. Sayers wrote of the joy of reading, quoting from one of the papers in the book, "the full and furious joy of it."[13] No one had experienced that joy more intensely than Bertha Miller. In a sense, to make the joy known to children had been the ultimate purpose of all her Horn Book publications. The books celebrated the genius of the writers and illustrators whose words and pictures were the source of the children's joy, and invited the perceptive judgment of the adults who led the children to the joy and shared it with them.

Years of Retirement

Life within us, life outside us, life beyond us — there is no end to any of them until the life, that is within us for earthly purposes, itself comes to an end: only to begin again, as it is believed.

— Walter de la Mare. From the introduction he wrote for his *Animal Stories.*

California: Rehearsal for Retirement

IN A KIND OF REHEARSAL for retirement, Bertha and William left New England in January, 1947, for a long, leisurely vacation in California. William's concern for Bertha's health had prompted the indulgence. Her bouts with bronchial pneumonia had become almost as regular as the northern winters that caused them. She would have been particularly vulnerable in 1947: the five years of intensive work on the *Illustrators* volume had drained her, and nursing Ruth through a long illness, after the death of Harry Burnham in 1945, had been an added physical and emotional strain. William hoped that the sunshine of the California winter would restore Bertha's spirits, and that the mild climate would spare her a debilitating illness.

In addition, both he and Bertha looked forward to visiting various members of the Dean, Jarmon, and Schoonmaker families who had come to make their homes on the West Coast for one reason or another. Bertha also expected, most eagerly, to meet the librarians of the area with whom she had been in correspondence about *Horn Book* matters over the years.

Their houses were in good order. The affairs of the W. F. Whitney Company could safely be entrusted to family and business associates. Copy for the *Illustrators* volume was in the hands of the printer and arrangements were complete for the special *Wanda Gág Horn Book* to be published in May. Mildred Barber, already retired, would live in the Ashburnham home during the Millers' absence to help Hanna and Duncan cope with any emergency that might arise. Mildred would also go into Boston from time to time to look after Ruth, who was still not well and whose tremor had worsened so that she could no longer work.

As her last pleasant task at home on January 27, Bertha sent off the orders for Duncan's flower and vegetable seeds, and then wrote a gay note of farewell to Marguerite Mitchell: "So with Beulah in charge at the Horn Book and Mildred here with an eye out for Ruth, I feel footloose and really like kicking up my heels."[1]

The Millers crossed the country by train to southern California. There they picked up their car, which had been shipped earlier by freighter, to drive to the cities on their itinerary: Vista, San Diego, Los Angeles, Santa Barbara, and San Francisco. William had been to the West Coast before; it was Bertha's first visit. She was fascinated by the mountains coming down so close to the sea, by the coast itself, by the unfamiliar flowers and trees, and by the lush growth of those she knew.

Her pleasure in the natural beauty of the state, however, was nothing like her delight in its librarians — or they in her. They welcomed Bertha as a friend, not a stranger, though few knew her personally. The source of their regard and affection was, of course, *The Horn Book* and more specifically Bertha's writings in it. Before she left southern California, however, there was scarcely a children's or school librarian who had not actually met Bertha at one of the breakfasts, luncheons, teas, or dinners arranged by their hospitable supervisors: Gladys English, Jasmine Britton, Rosemary Livsey, and Clara Breed. Bertha spoke at each of the occasions, but briefly; then she showed to the awed librarians the great bundle of page-proofs of the *Illustrators* book that had been mailed out to her from Boston, and answered their questions about its preparation and publication.

There were small private parties, too. A particularly happy one was an al fresco luncheon at Gladys English's home with Hannah Pederson, an exuberant eight-year-old, as the junior guest-of-honor. Hannah had been three when her mother's friends joined Bertha in preparing the memorial Rachel Field Pederson *Horn Book*. Then, when Bertha and Jasmine Britton discovered they had been born on the same day, a joint birthday party was arranged in the Green Room of the Chapman Park Hotel in Los Angeles.

William was courteously welcomed to all the parties given for Bertha, at first as the husband of the honored guest and then for himself as his dry wit and sturdy character became known. William was frankly astonished at the esteem in which Bertha was held, and decided that librarians who served children were among the world's most delightful creatures.

The Millers only spent one day at Santa Barabara instead of the week they had planned and they never reached San Francisco at all. Beulah Folmsbee's letter of resignation reached Bertha in Los Angeles and it seemed wise to make an earlier start for Boston to begin the search for a new business manager. They did not abandon their plan to drive home, though, stopping along the way to visit friends and libraries.

In Arizona they had a reunion with Carol and Whitton Norris, in whose small Ashburnham school they had been keenly interested. Mrs. Norris recalls that, in spite of Bertha's concern over the Horn Book crisis, both she and William seemed lighthearted, carefree, and full of fun. She also remembers that the mountainous heights fazed neither of the New England drivers and that they spun around hairpin curves with complete nonchalance.

At Tucson they had planned to visit Sophie Hart, a friend of Celena's and a distinguished former professor at Wellesley. A heart condition had hospitalized Miss Hart and visitation was not allowed. William and Bertha informed themselves thoroughly about Miss Hart's circumstances and were thereafter in constant touch with her doctors and nurses to make sure that nothing was lacking for her care and comfort.

The visits at public and school libraries were a revelation to Bertha. Familiar with the way New England city and town libraries served their young patrons, she was nonetheless astonished by the imaginative and dedicated service provided for Western and Southern children of city, ranch, farm, and mountain. She was so moved by her observations that on her return home she wrote a *Horn Book* editorial in praise of the "work where good people make homelike places for children and show them the way to realms of gold."[2]

Bertha and William went to California again in 1950. They entertained their 1947 hostesses with a gala dinner at the Chapman Park; otherwise, Bertha refrained from professional engagements. The visit was a private one, undertaken because of their concern for Alice Dean who had moved to the West Coast and was busy putting her new home and citrus grove in order. Bertha spent most of her days in old clothes, pushing a lawn mower or wielding a paint brush, happy with the new experiences, but less content with the results of her untrained hands.

When Bertha died in 1969 the memory of her California visits was still vivid in the minds of the librarians who had been exposed to her eager, enthusiastic presence. They sought some way to honor her and found it when they had drawn into the building plans for the new School of Library Science at the University of Southern California "The Bertha Mahony Miller Seminar Room."

The new building is expected to be completed and ready for classes in September 1973. The committee responsible for raising the funds for the room honoring Bertha plans a special dedicatory program after the building itself has been officially opened to use. Storytelling demonstrations, workshops, research projects, and exhibits of children's books will then be scheduled for the Seminar Room.

The Later Years in Winter Park and Ashburnham

TWO YEARS AFTER THEIR FIRST California visit, Bertha and William wintered in Florida. They were persuaded to do so by their good friends, Bertha and Henry Greene. The Greenes had made up their minds to sell their home in Petersham, had done so with characteristic dispatch, and had moved forthwith to Winter Park. Winter Park is in central Florida, adjacent to Orlando, and the home of Rollins College, the first institution of higher learning established in the state. On one of Winter Park's many lakes, the Greenes had a house built exactly suited to their needs and pursuits.

Once settled in, they had undertaken a thorough exploration and study of the natural Florida scene. With equal enthusiasm they had entered into the cultural activities of the college town: concerts given by an orchestra known for its interpretation of Bach, plays presented by such famed companies as the Dublin Players, art and craft exhibits held in private galleries and in the town's central park, flower shows arranged by local garden clubs, and programs sponsored by the Florida Audubon Society.

Henry Greene knew that the natural wonders and cultural advantages of Winter Park would interest the Millers and, of course, he was right. For some reason, though, Bertha was dubious about that first winter. Still, she made the drive south with William, comforted perhaps by a carful of Ashburnham linens, enough to run a small hotel, and a collection of hat boxes — "Bring *a* hat," Bertha Greene had advised, "to ward off the hot March Florida sun." Bertha Miller never took *one* of anything anywhere.

The drive down was uneventful except for the surprised people William left behind them by paying for small services with two dollar bills. "He always carries a supply of them on a trip," Bertha explained to a friend. "It is a little game he has for himself. I rather enjoy it myself."

Once established in the house the Greenes had secured for them, Bertha and William were well content. William was especially pleased with the boat at his disposal to fish from and to explore the lakes and the canals that connected them. Bertha, a little fearful of the housekeeping chores, learned delightedly how to use a dishwasher, a garbage disposal, an electric stove, a washer and a dryer. Indeed, they were both so pleased with the relaxed living, the Florida scene and the congenial atmosphere of Winter Park that a seasonal visit there came to be a part of the pattern of their retirement years.

To the pleasure of the Florida winters were added meetings with old friends and family members living in Winter Park or within easy driving distance from it. William's two sisters, Blanche Manthorne and Dorothy Burleigh, shared a home at New Smyrna Beach, just to the north of Winter Park on the East Coast. A niece of Celena's, with her family, lived in the Tampa area. Ruth Gainer, a Lane cousin of Bertha's from Cape Ann, lived in Winter Park.

At a flower show Bertha was discovered by another native of Cape Ann: Madge Haskell, the companion of her high school days and the early secretarial period at the Union. The two women had not met for years, but Miss Haskell heard Bertha's distinctive voice in the crowd, recognized it at once, and sought out her old friend. They never lost each other again.

Inevitably, many of the friendships were related to the book world. When Siri Andrews visited her sister in Orlando, she and Bertha had the opportunity to discuss Horn Book matters. The parents of Elizabeth Orton Jones were in Winter Park and Grace Allen Hogarth's mother was in nearby Mt. Dora. On occasion, Ruth Sawyer, of storytelling fame, visited the Millers from Captiva Island on the Gulf Coast where she spent the winter months. Mildred Lawrence and Kay Williams, both writers of children's books and both living in Orlando, were welcomed into the Miller circle, as was Clara Wendel, the young and able librarian of the Orlando Public Library.

The circle also included Blanche and Herbert Hirshberg, whom the Millers had met in Massachusetts through the Greenes, Henry Greene and Herbert Hirshberg having been boyhood friends in Worcester. Mr. Hirshberg, the retired Dean of the School of Library Science of Western Reserve University — now Case

Western Reserve — in Cleveland, was a nationally known figure in the library world. A warm friendship existed between Bertha and Blanche Hirshberg based on their mutual interest in books, for Mrs. Hirshberg, in addition to being the wife of a librarian, had had a distinguished library career of her own.

There were frequent visitors from the north to enlarge the circle of family and friends "in residence" in Florida, so to speak. Mary and Gordon Manthorne came occasionally and once Arnold Manthorne and a Cushing classmate made the trip alone. Bertha had the pleasure of providing suitable entertainment for the young boys and she did not fail them. There were spring-training baseball games with Uncle Will, boat trips through the lakes and canals, visits to New Smyrna Beach, and a performance of "The Gondoliers" at the Rollins theatre to remind them of the annual Gilbert and Sullivan presentations by Cushing students. When young Reggie Bradlee visited the Millers with his parents, Celena Dean and H. Gardner Bradlee, Bertha was delighted with the boy's very real interest in the Florida out-of-doors.

There was one constant in the seasons at Winter Park: the companionship of Elinor and Will Field. They spent a part of each winter with Bertha and William in their Florida home. The four lived together with the same harmonious and comfortable ease that had marked the long years of their friendship. Bertha and Elinor worked on Horn Book projects together and shared the housekeeping chores. Cooking was not easy for either of them, although they had progressed beyond stuffing chickens with cracker dressing. That they had once done at Mount Airy and the resultant swelling had almost floated the little house off the hilltop. It still took them time to cook and contrive, but there were fewer culinary disasters, and much chatter and laughter seasoned the dishes. "Often," Elinor wrote in her "Story of a Friendship," "one husband or the other would come out to the kitchen saying, 'What in the world is going on here? You are talking like magpies and laughing your heads off.' "[3]

Following their long-established custom, the four friends generally spent the evenings reading aloud, with Will Field doing most of the reading. The books read ranged widely from Washington Irving's *Life of George Washington* to *The Bible and the Common Reader* by Mary Ellen Chase, from Harsanyi's *The Star-Gazer* to the latest John Buchan yarn, from *The Violent Men* by Cornelia Meigs to Marjorie Kinnan Rawling's *The Yearling.* Bertha wrote of the last experience, a moving one, to Jeanne Jarmon.

While the Fields were here we had a wonderful time reading *The Yearling* aloud. Will Field did all the reading and he was so swept away with the book that his reading had a kind of emotional vibrancy and life, yet nothing came between us and the text. I could not help thinking how style and form and beauty of language come out in reading aloud."[4]

A lagniappe of each Florida winter was the opportunity to visit with friends on the drives down and back. One regular overnight stop came to be at the hospitable home of Elizabeth and Stanley Reed in Richmond, Virginia. Mrs. Reed had been an early *Horn Book* subscriber and, in 1944, wrote to the magazine for suggestions of books to read aloud to her young sons. Bertha answered the letter, responsive to a young mother who was interested in reading to her children. A warm friendship grew and flourished over the years dependent completely upon letters until the first visit of the Millers at the Reed home. Mrs. Reed recalls it vividly.

We did not meet until 1951 when she and Mr. Miller stopped for a brief visit with us en route to Florida. I still remember the shock of hearing for the first time her deliberate and tremulous voice on the phone when she called from the edge of town. Another surprise when I opened the door and found her to be such a short little person. But there she stood, backed by her handsome ruddy-brown William, her hair somewhat wind-blown, and her eyes eager and intense with the anticipation of friends meeting.[5]

That winter, the winter of 1951, was the first one the Millers spent in the new house which their young landlords, Jackie and Tom Sawyer, had built on Lake Maitland. It was a handsome two-floor structure with a pillared façade overlooking the lake. Great live oaks, green hedges, and orange groves surrounding the house assured its occupants peace and quiet and a real sense of solitude. Bertha and William found their new quarters agreeable in every way and William had no cause to regret the ten-year lease he had taken on the property. Henceforward, their time was divided between the comfortable old New England farmhouse in Ashburnham and "Glamor Manor" as they affectionately called their Winter Park residence.

Because of their new life pattern, the Millers determined to give up the Boston apartment they had taken with Ruth and Harry Burnham. Bertha had used the apartment primarily while working each week in the Horn Book offices and in caring for Ruth after Harry's death. Retirement eliminated the regular Horn Book visits and Ruth's deteriorated condition made it unwise for her to be so far from family and friends. She was persuaded to accept the accommodations William found for her in Ashburnham and, insofar as she was able, she helped Bertha close the Boston apartment. It was like pulling a tree up by its roots to get themselves out of the apartment, Bertha told a friend; they had lived in Boston for a lifetime.

The move was providential. On December 19, 1952 Ruth Mahony Burnham died, escaping at last from the tragic shadow the tremor had cast over her life. Her death was a release for Bertha, too; she had shared in the carrying of her sister's burden. Bertha grieved, but for her own loss, not her sister's death.

Death brought another change in the Millers' lives the following spring. When they returned from Winter Park in April, Mildred Barber met them at the door with the sad news that Hanna Kovanen had died of a stroke in the early morning hours. In consultation with Hanna's nieces and the Finnish community to which she belonged, Bertha and William arranged for the funeral of their housekeeper and friend. She was buried beside her daughter, Lilja Kovanen La Brack, who had died as a young woman.

For a year after Hanna's death, Bertha ran the house with only part-time help and a completely remodeled kitchen which included all the appliances she had come to know in Florida. Then, in August of 1953, Mary Lydia Nims — young, energetic, and cheerful — became the Millers' new housekeeper. With Mrs. Nims came her eight-year-old son, Johnny, and once more a child was at home in the Miller household.

Mrs. Nims was a graduate nurse, the sister of Dr. John Mason, the Millers' physician. One of Mrs. Nims' duties was caring for William's older sister, Blanche, whom he had brought, stricken, to spend her last days in his home.

Bertha and William were always responsive to the needs of family, friends and neighbors when they were in difficult circumstances. William saw to it that their financial resources yielded them the maximum of support; Bertha looked to doctors, nursing homes, and creature comforts. Their concern reached out to Sophie

Hart in Tucson and Madame Martin in Paris, in whose home William had lived while a student at the Sorbonne.

The Ashburnham home did not, however, become a place of death and mourning as it would sound, but remained vigorously and vitally alive. The slightest excuse brought the Horn Book staff out from Boston for a business discussion, followed by one of Mrs. Nims' delicious luncheons. Miss Moore and Miss Jordan were frequent house guests. Elizabeth Yates and her husband, William McGreal, visited from their home in Peterborough, New Hampshire. They often brought with them their friend and neighbor, Nora Unwin. Elizabeth Orton Jones drove down from Mason in New Hampshire to talk about the work she and Miss Unwin were doing at the new Rehabilitation Center at Crotched Mountain for the crippled children of the state.

Nieces and nephews were in and out informally, with their children visiting at weekends or during school holidays. The little girls who had loved the dolls into such comfortable shabbiness, and the small boys who had "farmed" with the toy box treasures, were students at Cushing or various New England colleges.

Bertha managed to gather some fourteen of them together in September 1955 to meet Peter Brooke, Leslie Brooke's oldest grandchild. Peter had been two when Bertha had met him during her London visit in 1936. He was in the United States on a travel grant from Balliol College at Oxford and had spent four months touring the country in his own car. He had been a keen observer of the American scene and talked easily of his impressions. Some of his conclusions, however, were challenged by the Miller young people so that the evening, to Bertha's delight, was a lively one.

The year before, Bertha had been pleased to introduce to her family and friends Momoko Ishii of Tokyo — journalist, editor, writer and translator of children's books. Miss Ishii, in the very early 1940s, had become concerned with the quality of Japanese children's books and the lack of library service available to the boys and girls of her country. She determined to do what she could to improve both conditions. She was encouraged and counseled in her early efforts by Bertha, to whom she had written for help in translating a Milne story into Japanese. She had taken Bertha's name from the title page of *Realms of Gold* which, with *Five Years of Children's Books*, she had found in a Tokyo bookstore. Bertha, seeing in the young woman the shadow of her own pioneering self, had given her help generously and gladly.

The war momentarily halted Miss Ishii's work, but she

picked it up as soon as it was economically possible to do so. In 1954 she secured a fellowship grant from the Rockefeller Foundation to visit America in order to observe library service to children and to investigate the publishing of juvenile books. Bertha was not convinced the Foundation understood Miss Ishii's purposes or how they might best be accomplished; therefore, with its approval and blessing, she undertook the planning of her protégé's schedule down to the last minute detail.

The itinerary ended in Boston with Bertha herself acting as Miss Ishii's guide in a five-day whirlwind tour of bookstores, libraries, publishing houses, and printing establishments. Like everyone else, Miss Ishii found it difficult to keep up with her septuagenarian hostess. "Mrs. Miller was very lively and walked about with springy steps for her age," Miss Ishii recalls. "When I told her so she said, 'Yes, William always says that I walk like a young girl.' "[6]

Fortunately, before sending her on to the Canadian part of her tour, Bertha drove Miss Ishii home with her for two weeks of rest. The easiest way into the Ashburnham house from the garage was through the kitchen and, after parking the Chevrolet, Bertha led Miss Ishii there.

> When we went in through the back door a little boy, Johnny, came out of the kitchen to welcome me.
>
> And in the kitchen I found a big smiling gentleman, just standing, saying nothing. Mrs. Miller introduced me to him. I didn't really expect him in the kitchen, but to find him there made me feel as if he were a very intimate person.
>
> He said something like, "So you are here at last. For some months Bertha has talked about nothing but Miss Ishii, Miss Ishii, Miss Ishii" — more or less humorously, and more or less resignedly, in his gruff voice. "Oh, are you being jealous with me, Mr. Miller?" I said, unexpectedly, even to myself. From that moment, we became friends.[7]

Indeed, Miss Ishii became friends with all the Miller connections, especially with Mary and Gordon Manthorne, with whom she stayed because of Blanche Manthorne's confinement at the Millers. Each day Miss Ishii went to visit Bertha, and the long talks they had under the pines and in the library established a genuine affection between the two women, so disparate in age, so alike in spirit. The echo of those talks and a treasured file of letters influence Miss Ishii to this day as she continues her work in behalf of Japanese children and their books.

While Bertha had been making the arrangements for Miss Ishii's tour, she had also been preparing the Caroline M. Hewins Lecture which she was scheduled to give at the 1954 October meeting of the New England Library Association at Swampscott. She had chosen for her subject "Eliza Orne White and Her Books for Children."

Bertha's interest in Miss White went back to 1915, when she was studying children's literature informally with Alice Jordan in preparation for the opening of the Bookshop for Boys and Girls. One of the first books Miss Jordan had assigned Bertha to read was Miss White's *When Molly Was Six*. It had come as a revelation to Bertha "that a book interesting to a six-year-old could also be so genuinely interesting to a grownup."[8] After the Bookshop opened, Miss White was a frequent visitor until confined to her Brookline home by the blindness and deafness that plagued the last third of her life. Then Bertha called upon her, greatly admiring the calm strength and dry humor with which Miss White accepted her handicaps.

The Hewins Lecture, then, was to be a tribute to an old friend, and an attempt to arouse fresh interest in Miss White's sturdy stories of family life. Bertha worked long and hard with her material, needing all of the two years allowed for the preparation of the Lecture. Her first diffuse and all-inclusive draft bore little resemblance to the organized, disciplined Lecture that she delivered at Swampscott.

As was its custom with all Hewins Lectures, *The Horn Book* printed Bertha's. The April 1955 issue that carried it, ran also the announcement of the awarding of the Constance Lindsay Skinner Medal to Bertha by The Women's National Book Association "for merit in the realm of books," and the tribute May Massee wrote for the magazine to celebrate the occasion. Miss Massee's kind words embarrassed Bertha, as all personal commendation did, but she could not deny the truth of one paragraph in particular in praise of *The Horn Book*.

> It is impossible to measure the influence of that beautifully printed and planned magazine. It reaches to the length and breadth of this country and other countries around the world. It is a living example of the power of

> an ideal given tangible substance through a lifetime of work of the head, heart and hands of one woman, Bertha Mahony Miller.[9]

The year 1955, that had begun so auspiciously for Bertha and William, ended on a dual note of sorrow. In the late summer Blanche Manthorne's life came to a quiet end, and shortly thereafter arrangements had to be made for Mildred Barber, who could no longer look after herself.

Then, in October, William suffered a severe coronary. He made a good recovery due to Dr. Mason's skills, the nursing care of Mrs. Nims, and the stratagems devised by Bertha to keep an active man content for a long month of hospital bed rest.

One of her most successful diversions was reading aloud, but with their usual roles reversed, as Bertha read and William listened. *Episode of Sparrows* and *Gods, Graves and Scholars* were accepted with grace and interest, but most successful was Claire Huchet Bishop's *The Big Loop.* The story concerned a poor Parisian student who longed for a bicycle to enter the famous Tour de France Bicycle Race that annually flings itself out in a great 2,556 mile loop across the French countryside. Bertha knew the book would remind William of his own student days in Paris; she was unprepared for another poignant memory it brought into sharp focus. As a boy in Haverhill, William, too, had wanted a bicycle. Indeed he had once saved enough of his own money to buy one, but then conscience would not allow him to spend it for such a self-indulgent and frivolous purpose. The first bicycle he ever had was the one he bought in Paris to ride to and from the Sorbonne.

After his recovery was complete, William was able to counsel Bertha about various changes in Horn Book affairs, changes vital to the company's future. In 1957 Ruth Hill Viguers was elected to the Board of Directors of The Horn Book, Incorporated. Mrs. Viguers' professional credentials were impressively cosmopolitan: as a children's librarian, she had worked on behalf of children and their books in Seattle, New York City, Boston, Paris, Madrid, and Wuchang, China. She was the mother of three daughters and had entered the New England scene when her husband became a hospital administrator in Boston.

Once established in her new home, Mrs. Viguers began to contribute to *The Horn Book* — with which, of course, she was well familiar — and was presently asked by Bertha to join her and Marcia Dalphin in the compilation of the first *Illustrators* supplement. When Jennie Lindquist retired in 1958 to give all of her time to creative writing, Bertha appointed Mrs. Viguers as her successor. Bertha and William were confident that Mrs. Viguers would bring to her responsibilities the same "unfailing understanding of the spirit and the faith of our Magazine"[10] that had characterized Miss Lindquist's editorship.

In 1957 Mary Manthorne had also become a Director of the Horn Book. Over the years, Bertha and William had noted with pleasure Mrs. Manthorne's deepening interest in their little company and her growing understanding of its operations. To have her join The Horn Book, Incorporated as an informed and able Director gave them the greatest satisfaction.

It also assured them of the continuance of the company in the years to come. When Bertha was ready, at a time of her own choosing, she would relinquish the presidency to Mrs. Manthorne. That Bertha, in personal letters, referred to Mrs. Manthorne as "my friend," as well as "the wife of William's nephew, Gordon," indicated the warm and affectionate relationship that existed between the older and the younger woman. It also suggested with what pride and confidence Bertha would make the transfer of office when the time was right.

It was well Bertha and William had provided for the future. William was hospitalized again in 1958, first with bronchial pneumonia and then with a second, milder coronary. While recovering from the heart attack in the hospital he suffered a slight stroke.

At the end of the year, however, he was feeling so well and so hopeful that he decided he and Bertha would go to Florida for the winter as usual. Bertha agreed, concealing her forebodings, and only letting the anguish of seeing her dear companion grown suddenly old spill over into letters to friends. They left on December 20, earlier than usual, and flew down, as they had done since William's first illness in 1955. The Fields went with them and Arnold drove the loaded car to Winter Park so their things would be waiting for them when they arrived.

Everything pleased William that December: a new room, added to Glamor Manor, provided a sunny place to rest on the first floor; the stair-chair he had had installed in order to use the second floor rooms, worked perfectly; the winter was predicted to be unusually mild, and the Florida sunshine was never warmer or more welcome.

Then, on January 5, while shopping with Bertha, William was stricken with his third, and fatal, coronary. Bertha tried to drive him home, as he wished, but he died in the car at her side. That valiant soul, almost sure of what had happened, managed to get the car out of traffic and into a service station where help was immediately available.

Bertha stayed on in Florida for the rest of the winter finding comfort in being with Elinor and Will. "The salt and savor has gone out of my life," she wrote to Nancy. "Will Field reads to us in the evening and I read to myself in bed and so stay away from the brink of desolation."[11]

Later, on June 6, William's ashes were interred in the New Cemetery in Ashburnham after a Memorial Service in the Ashburnham Community Church. Friends made the church beautiful with flowers and greens, and at the Service the Reverend Ben Roberts spoke about "my friend" with such simple directness as to recreate the spirit of a loved and respected man.

It was a grievous sorrow to Bertha that William could not share with her an honor that came to her in the same month as his burial. It was a resolution, "An Expression of Appreciation," presented to her by the Children's Services Division of the American Library Association at its 1959 annual meeting in Washington, D.C. The resolution, written by Louise Seaman Bechtel, began:

> We, the Children's Librarians of America, have passed our half-century mark; we are conscious of having a history. To mark high points in that history, we have honored some of our great professional standard-bearers. Today we wish to honor one, not a librarian, whose significant creative activity in our field has inspired us for forty-three years.[12]

After describing Bertha's career in the children's book world, the tribute concluded:

> On this twenty-third day of June, 1959, we propose a resolution saluting the record of Bertha Mahony Miller, a proud and vital part of the history of children's books in America and an integral part of the progress of library work with children.[13]

Bertha was overwhelmed by the generous resolution, particularly the ringing sound of that "We, the Children's Librarians of

America." William would have appreciated that too, for like herself he had held those who worked in libraries with children in great esteem. He would have valued the tribute as highly as she did.

Two years later Bertha was able to acknowledge publicly her appreciation of the work children's librarians did. Alice Jordan, at ninety, died in her sleep on March 9, 1960. To honor her friend and a pioneer children's librarian, Bertha edited and published on November 7, 1961 an Extra Memorial Issue, *The Alice M. Jordan Horn Book.* The number included a salute to "all children's librarians who strive with heart and mind to make reading an everlasting joy to children."[14]

As a further, continuing, memorial to Miss Jordan, Bertha established a Fund whereby a series of lectures might be given annually at the Boston Public Library for the benefit of the area librarians. She asked the New England Round Table of Children's Librarians to assume the responsibility of the lecture arrangements, and Mrs. Florence Sturges to chair the Fund. Mrs. Sturges had begun her library work under Miss Jordan's direction. The subject of the lectures, at first limited to storytelling, was presently left to the discretion of the Round Table so long as it related to library work with children. Over fifty librarians attended the first series of eight lectures in 1962.

After Bertha's death in 1969 the Round Table, wishing to honor her, the founder of the series, as well as Miss Jordan, established The Jordan-Miller Memorial Course in Children's Literature. The freedom that the original Fund gave to both lecturers and librarians continued to be enjoyed, and the inspiration that the series provided to all participants was doubled.

When Bertha was eighty in 1962, a heart attack indicated the eventuality had come for which she and William had so carefully prepared. Accordingly, at the end of the year, she placed the presidency of The Horn Book, Incorporated in the capable, and by then experienced, hands of Mary Manthorne. Bertha took for her own new title, Chairman of the Board, and was well content to have it so.

Following the doctor's orders, Bertha curtailed her activities to permit late risings and long afternoon rests, but between the risings and the restings she was as briskly energetic as ever. She looked increasingly frail, and the flyaway hair was white, but the blue eyes were still eager, the step still lively.

Indeed, the contrast between her appearance and her actions

provided guests at the Ashburnham and Winter Park homes with delightful studies in incongruity. She "rested" in the mornings on her Ashburnham sleeping porch by using a typewriter proficiently from her breakfast tray. In Winter Park, almost lost in a king-size bed, she worked on her memoirs, highly amused at the whole endeavor but kept at it by Elinor and Mrs. Manthorne. She obediently rode the stair-chair, which had been reinstalled in Ashburnham after one-level quarters were taken in Florida, but frequently carried with her the Sunday *Times* — weighing almost as much as herself — for reading in bed. The white head, scarcely topping the bar in one of the Florida homes, nodded vigorously as she dealt competently with a shaker of pre-dinner cocktails. If the dinner was to be at a restaurant, she no longer drove her guests there herself — Mrs. Nims was the chauffeur; but, once arrived, her dinner companions had to step smartly to keep up with the pace she set across the parking lot.

The little company of women that had come to revolve around Bertha in Ashburnham and Winter Park rejoiced for her when, in 1967, the Catholic Library Association bestowed upon her its Regina Medal in recognition of her "continued distinguished contribution to children's literature." Bertha had been very ill in Winter Park that year; much as she longed to go to Cleveland in March to receive the Medal at the Association's annual meeting, it was impossible for her to do so. She asked Mrs. Manthorne to represent her at the presentation luncheon, and Mrs. Viguers to make the acceptance speech in her name. By quoting extensively in her speech from Bertha's writings, Mrs. Viguers brought Bertha Mahony Miller into the award ceremonies almost as vividly as if she had been there in person.

Bertha never fully recovered from the 1967 illness. It left her suddenly and shockingly old, as she had not been before. The Florida winters were abandoned and, although friends were still welcomed at Ashburnham, their welfare devolved on Mrs. Nims and their entertainment on Mary and Gordon Manthorne.

Then, Bertha began to withdraw imperceptibly into a world of her own, aware of life moving around her, but too weary to venture out into the stir. Once when Mrs. Manthorne tried to interest her in a Horn Book matter, Bertha stopped her with: "Mary dear, I don't want to work my brain any more." May was Bertha's favorite month of the year. By May of 1969 the frail body found it increasingly difficult to support life. On the fourteenth of the month, gently, quietly, with no distress whatsoever, Bertha died.

Death was the corporeal ending only of Bertha's life experience. Her spirit is to this day vitally and urgently alive. It speaks from her writings on behalf of children and their reading pleasure. It is abundantly evident in the issues of *The Horn Book* that she edited with such joy. It informs the distinctive volumes about children's literature that her company published in her time. Reassuringly, it is to be found in the labors of those who continue her work, faithful to the fundamentals she established for her magazine and her publishing house.

In these ways, then, the children's book world which she had helped create and form and which had known her presence for half-a-century, continues to be influenced by "the distilled, potent spirit of Bertha Mahony Miller." That spirit, in the full vigor of its greatest creativity, will never know the finality of death.

Appendix

Original Sources

In addition to the published writings by and about Mrs. Miller, as listed in Miss Haviland's bibliography, the writer had access to her personal and business papers and to the unpublished material listed below.

Except for her diary, Mrs. Miller's manuscripts are on file in The Horn Book office.

Darling, Frances C. Bookshop Caravan Diary: 1920-1921.
In Miss Darling's possession.

Field, Elinor Whitney. "The Story of a Friendship."
An essay of appreciation in Mrs. Field's possession.

———, and Bertha Mahony Miller. Travel Diary of the 1924 Trip to France and Great Britain.
The diary, jointly kept, is in Mrs. Field's possession.

Miller, Bertha Mahony. An Account of the 1936 Trip to England with Her Sister, Ruth. In: Memoranda Notebook A.

———. Diary: 1914-1918.

———. Memoir MSS. A through K.
Untitled by Mrs. Miller, these were so designated by the writer for purposes of identification and reference.

———. Memoranda Notebook B.

———. "Rain on Metabetchouan."
An account of a fishing expedition in Canada with Bertha and Henry Greene.

———. Sketch of Bertha and Henry Greene.

References

Abbreviations:

BMM — Mrs. Miller as the author of unpublished manuscripts and published writings in *The Horn Book*

HBM — *The Horn Book Magazine*

THE CAPE ANN YEARS

1 BMM, Memoir MS. D, p.1
2 Ibid., B, pp.3,5-8 and C, pp.1-3
3 BMM, "The Joy of Reading," *HBM*, v.11, November-December 1935, p.327
4 BMM, Memoir MS. B, p.17
5 Ibid., G, p.4, Insert A
6 "The Joy of Reading," p.327
7 BMM, "Children and Solitude," *HBM*, v.2, June 1926, pp.3-4
8 Ibid., p.3
9 Ibid., pp.4,6-7
10 BMM, Memoir MS. B, pp. 18-20
11 Ibid., pp.21-22
12 Ibid., pp.14-15
13 Ibid., pp.15-16
14 BMM, "The Delicate Magic Machiney of Poetry: *The Winged Horse*," *HBM*, v.3, August 1927, p.5
15 Letter from Miss Abby Merchant to the writer
16 Kenneth L. Mark, *Delayed by Fire: Being the Early History of Simmons College*, n.p.: Privately printed, 1945. p.1

COLLEGE AND "UNIVERSITY"

1 Ibid., p.18
2 Ibid., p.17
3 Ibid., p.115
4 BMM, Memoir MS. E, p.6
5 Ibid., p.5
6 Ibid.
7 Ibid., p.6
8 Cornelia James Cannon, *The History of the Women's Educational and Industrial Union: A Civic Laboratory, 1877-1927*, Boston: [The Union, 1927] p.4
9 Bertha E. Mahony, "The Bookshop for Boys and Girls — Boston," *Publishers' Weekly*, v.91, May 26, 1917, p.1701
10 Earl Barnes, "A New Profession for Women," *Atlantic Monthly*, v.116, August 1915, p.234

THE BOOKSHOP FOR BOYS AND GIRLS

1 BMM, "Editorial," *HBM*, v.10, September 1934, p.275
2 BMM, Diary: 1914-1918. Entry for December 12, 1914
3 Letter from Marguerite Haskell to the writer

4 Diary: 1914-1918. Entry for August 28, 1917
5 BMM, Memoir MS. F, p.2 and G, pp.6-7
6 Ibid., F, p.7
7 Frederic G. Melcher, "Chapters from *Horn Book* History — I," *HBM*, v.38, April 1962, pp.192-93
8 Bertha E. Mahony Miller, "On the Twentieth Century John Newbery," in *Frederic G. Melcher. Friendly Reminiscences of a Half Century Among Books & Bookmen*, New York: The Book Publishers' Bureau, 1945. p.49
9 Ibid.
10 Annie Carroll Moore, "The Bookshop for Boys and Girls," *A. L. A. Bulletin, Louisville Conference Number, 1917*, v.11, July 1917, p.168

Later Miss Moore changed "Annie" to "Anne" to avoid confusion between herself and Annie E. Moore of Columbia's Teachers College.
11 BMM, "Caroline M. Hewins," *HBM*, v.29, February 1953, p.11
12 BMM, "Sidney Smith and the Bookshop's Colophon," *HBM*, v.9, May 1933, p.93
13 BMM, Memoir MS. F, p.4
14 Letter from Margaret Sayward to the writer
15 "The Bookshop for Boys and Girls," pp.168-69
16 "The Bookshop for Boys and Girls — Boston," p.1702
17 "On the Twentieth Century John Newbery," p.50
18 "The Bookshop for Boys and Girls — Boston," pp.1701-02
19 BMM, Memoir MS. F, p.14
20 BMM, "Editorial," *HBM*, v.10, May 1934, p.135
21 Lee Kingman, "Chapters from *Horn Book* History — VI," *HBM*, v.39, February 1963, p.93
22 Margaret Warren Brown, "Along the Road to Childhood," *HBM*, v.22, November-December 1946, p.483
23 Elinor W. Field, "Neighborhood Stories by Mrs. A. D. T. Whitney," in *The Hewins Lectures: 1947-1962*, ed. by Siri Andrews, [Boston]: The Horn Book, Inc., 1963. p.114
24 Ibid., p.113
25 Elinor W. Field, [Autobiographical Sketch] in *The Junior Book of Authors*, ed. by Stanley J. Kunitz and Howard Haycraft, 2nd ed. rev., New York: H. W. Wilson Company, 1951. p.297
26 "Neighborhood Stories by Mrs. A. D. T. Whitney," pp.108-09
27 Elinor W. Field, "The Story of a Friendship," p.1
28 Elinor W. Field, "Chapters from Horn Book History — III," *HBM*, v.38, August 1962, p.401
29 "The Story of a Friendship," p.1
30 Ibid., pp.3-4
31 Charles Messer Stow, "Parnassus without a Pegasus Tours New England," Boston *Evening Transcript*, Saturday, July 3, 1920, Part 3, p.5
32 Letter from Genevieve Washburn to the writer
33 "Caravan Schedule for North Shore and Maine." Typed copy noted in pencil as "BEM's Copy"
34 "Paranassus without a Pegasus Tours New England," p.5
35 From an informational letter about the Caravan which Mrs. Miller wrote to the President of the Union, Miss Marion Churchill, October 10, 1921. Mrs. Kehew had died in 1918.
36 "Report of the Book Caravan's Summer, July 5 to October 1." Mimeographed copy, p.2
37 Frances C. Darling, "Chapters from *Horn Book* History — VII, The Book Caravan," *HBM*, v.39, April 1963, pp.208-09

38 Frances C. Darling, Bookshop Caravan Diary: 1920-1921, various entries
39 BMM, Memoir MS. G, p.21
40 BMM, "The Bookshop and Its Relation to Schools," *HBM*, [v.2] January 1926, Extra Number: *Experimental Schools in England*, p.3
41 BMM, "Marguerite Mitchell of Sunny Fields," *HBM*, v.28, October 1952, p.299
42 BMM, Memoir MS. H, p.5
43 Milton Bryon, "A Venture in Poetry: Boston Bookshop for Boys and Girls," *Saturday Review of Literature*, v.8, July 25, 1931, p.14
44 Ibid.
45 BMM, A Hunt Breakfast Item, *HBM*, v.10, May 1934, p.132
46 BMM, "The First Children's Department in Book Publishing," *HBM*, v.4, August 1928, p.24
47 BMM, Memoir MS. F, p.8
48 In a letter from Miss Eliza Orne White to "The Dolls' Convention at the Bookshop for Boys and Girls, February 20, 1929"
49 Elinor Whitney, "A Friendly Spy," *HBM*, v.5, May 1929, pp.55-58
50 M. H., "Muriel, Rose and Mary Ann Have Wild Time at Hub Dolls' Convention," Boston *Sunday Post*, February 17, 1929, C-8
51 Elinor Whitney, "Puppet Parade," *HBM*, v.9, May 1933, p.59
52 BMM, A Hunt Breakfast Item, "The Power of Words," *HBM*, v.11, March-April 1935, p.66
53 "Alice-Heidi at Home," *HBM*, v.1, October 1924, p.16
54 "Alice-Heidi's House," *HBM*, v.1, November 1924, pp.25-26
55 Lee Kingman, "Chapers from *Horn Book* History — VI," *HBM*, v.39, February 1963, pp.92-93
56 Elinor W. Field, "Chapters from *Horn Book* History - VIII," *HBM*, v.39, June 1963, p.329
57 Elinor Whitney, "Realms of Gold Including Books," *HBM*, v.4, August 1928, p.72
58 "Chapters from *Horn Book* History — VIII," p.329
59 "Realms of Gold Including Books," p.72
60 Alice Jordan, "*Realms of Gold*," [book review] in "The Three Owls" page of Anne Carroll Moore, New York *Herald Tribune Books*, May 12, 1929, p.8
61 Anne Carroll Moore, "*Realms of Gold*," [book review] in her "The Three Owls" page, New York *Herald Tribune Books*, May 12, 1929, p.8
62 May Lamberton Becker, "*Realms of Gold*," [book review] *HBM*, v.5, May 1929, p.14
63 Padraic Colum, "*Realms of Gold*," [book review] *Saturday Review of Literature*, v.5, July 13, 1929, p.1180
64 BMM, A Hunt Breakfast Item, "The Bookshop for Boys and Girls Changes Management," *HBM*, v.12, July-August 1936, p.194
65 Letter from Mrs. Miller to Mrs. Thomas S. Perry, June 21, 1936
66 Letter from Eleanor Estes to the writer
67 "Chapters from *Horn Book* History — III," pp.401,403
68 Margaret E. Sayward, "Chapters from *Horn Book* History — II," *HBM*, v.38, June 1962, p.298
69 Mary Adeline Whitney, "Chapters from *Horn Book* History — V," *HBM*, v.38, December 1962, p.625
70 Members of the Staff of the Bookshop for Boys and Girls, "Chapters from *Horn Book* History — IV," *HBM*, v.38, October 1962, p.510
71 Ibid., p.511
72 Ibid., p.509

73 Alice Jordan, "The Bookshop That Is Bertha Mahony," *The Atlantic Bookshelf*, June 1929, pp.52-59

THE HORN BOOK: YEARS OF GROWTH, 1924-1935

1 BMM, [Statement of Purpose and Policy] *HBM*, v.1, October 1924, p.1
2 Elinor W. Field, "The Story of a Friendship," pp.1-2
3 Second page (carbon) of a letter from Mrs. Miller to a friend. No further identification possible because the first page is missing
4 Elinor W. Field and Bertha M. Miller, Travel Diary of the 1924 Trip to France and Great Britain. Entry for May 4
5 Postcard from Mrs. Miller to her sister, Ruth. Sent from Beddgelert, Wales, June 18, 1924
6 Travel Diary. Entry for May 15
7 "The Story of a Friendship," p.2
8 Travel Diary. Entry for June 22
9 Memoir MS. I, p.11
10 Ibid.
11 Elinor W. Field, "Our Twenty Years," *HBM*, v. 20, May-June 1944, p.151
12 "Chapters from *Horn Book* History — IV," p.510
13 Letter from Frederic G. Melcher. October 23, 1924
14 Statement by the editors preceding the advertisements, *HBM*, v.2, November 1926, p.53
15 A Hunt Breakfast Item, "From L. Leslie Brooke," *HBM*, v.3, May 1927, p.46
16 [Statement of Purpose and Policy] p.1
17 BMM, A Hunt Breakfast Item, *HBM*, v.10, January 1934, p.60
18 "Our Twenty Years," p.151
19 [Statement of Purpose and Policy] p.1
20 "Our Twenty Years," p.151
21 "The Horn Book's Future," *HBM*, v.2, June 1926, p.53
22 BMM, "Editorial," *HBM*, v.9, February 1933, p.1
23 Letter from Frances Clarke Sayers. September 19, 1957
24 BMM, "Reading with Children," *HBM*, v.16, July-August 1940, p.223
25 Letter from Anne Eaton. Undated
26 Letter from Cornelia Meigs. March 21, 1953
27 Letter from May Massee. January 2, 1953
28 BMM, Memoranda Notebook B. Various pages
29 Letter to Miss Folmsbee. March 10, 1943
30 Letter to Mary Lou Thompson. January 1, 1958
31 BMM, "Editorial," *HBM*, v.9. November 1933, p.173
32 BMM, A Hunt Breakfast Item, *HBM*, v.10, March 1934, p.66
33 BMM, "Praise to the Living," *HBM*, v.12, July-August 1936, p.197
34 BMM, A Hunt Breakfast Item, *HBM*, v.10, November-December 1934, p.336
35 BMM, A Hunt Breakfast Item, *HBM*, v.10, July 1934, p.212
36 Bertha Mahony Miller, "Introduction" to *A Horn Book Sampler*, ed. by Norma R. Fryatt, Boston: The Horn Book, Inc., 1959 p.[xv]
37 BMM, A Hunt Breakfast Item, *HBM*, v.10, November-December 1934, p.336
38 BMM, A Hunt Breakfast Item, "The White-Breasted Nuthatch," *HBM*, v.12, May-June 1936, p.183
39 BMM, A Hunt Breakfast Item, *HBM*, v.10, May 1934, pp.196,198
40 Letter from Professor R. E. Rogers. May 3, 1927
41 "*Horn Book Reflections*," [book review] (London) *Times Literary Supplement*, October 16, 1969, p.1205

42 BMM, "*Long Island's Story*—Why Not Other Regional Books?" *HBM*, v.6, February 1930, p.59
43 BMM, "A View Halloo," *HBM*, v.5, May 1929, pp.30-31
44 Letter to Ruth H. Viguers. February 21, 1959
45 Letter to Norma Fryatt. March 28, 1953
46 BMM, "Editorial," *HBM*, v.10, January 1934, p.7

THE EARLY YEARS AT ASHBURNHAM

1 Letter from Marguerite Mitchell. September 4, 1934
2 BMM, Diary: 1914-1918. Entry for July 3, 1918
3 Letter to Helen Rand Parrish. May 31, 1948
4 Letter from the Reverend Ben Roberts to the writer
5 Ibid.
6 BMM, A Hunt Breakfast Item in "The March Contributors," *HBM*, v.11, March-April 1935, p.118
7 Letter from Anne Carroll Moore. August 18, 1932
8 Letter from Mary Fitzgerald. September 14, 1932
9 Letter to the Staff of the Bookshop. Undated
10 Letter to Annis Duff. July 16, 1949
11 Anne Carroll Moore, "The Three Owls' Notebook," *HBM*, v.24, September-October 1948, p.347
12 Letter to Hilda van Stockum. December 28, 1943
13 Letter to Mary Manthorne from Carolyn G. Norris. August 19, 1969
14 BMM, "Guide to Treasure," *HBM*, v.16, May-June 1940, p.178
15 BMM, A Hunt Breakfast Item, "Book Week in Northern Massachusetts," *HBM*, v.15, March-April 1939, p.127
16 "Guide to Treasure," p.185
17 Memoir MS. B, p.1
18 Letter to May Massee. May 18, 1946
19 Letter from William Miller. Undated
20 Letter from William Miller. May 12, 1939
21 BMM, A Hunt Breakfast Item in "Personals," *HBM*, v.12, July-August 1936, p.252
22 Letter to Elinor W. Field, never mailed. September 5, 1939
23 BMM, "Rain on Metabetchouan," Various pages
24 BMM, Sketch of Bertha and Henry Greene, p.12

THE HORN BOOK: YEARS OF MATURITY, 1936-1950

1 "Citation for the Constance Lindsay Skinner Award for 1955," *HBM*, v.45, October 1969, p.623
2 BMM, A Hunt Breakfast Item, "The Horn Book, Inc." *HBM*, v.12, November-December 1936, p.322
3 BMM, An Account of the 1936 Trip to England with Her Sister, Ruth. In: Memoranda Notebook A, p.1
4 Ibid., pp.2-3
5 Ibid.
6 Ibid., p.10
7 BMM, A Hunt Breakfast Item, "The *Sunday Times* Book Exhibition," *HBM*, v.13, January-February 1937, p.64
8 An Account of the 1936 Trip to England with Her Sister, Ruth, p.10
9 Ibid., p.13
10 Ibid., pp.15-16
11 Ibid., p.18
12 Ibid., pp.6-7
13 Ibid., p.8
14 Ibid., p.9
15 Ibid., p.10
16 Anne Carroll Moore, "The Three Owls' Notebook," *HBM*, v.25, September-October 1949, p.435
17 "The Three Owls' Notebook," *HBM*, v.12, November-December 1936, p.344

18 BMM, "*The Horn Book's* Quarter Century," *HBM*, v.25, September-October 1949, p.353

19 BMM, "A New Chapter in *Horn Book* History," *HBM*, v.15, September-October 1939, p.277

20 "The Three Owls' Notebook," *HBM*, v.17, January-February 1941, p.24

21 Louise Seaman Bechtel, "I Long to Share It with a Child," *HBM*, v.17, January-February 1941, pp.21-23

22 BMM, "A Salute to Alice Jordan and Anne Carroll Moore," *HBM*, v.26, July-August 1950, p.243

23 BMM, "Anne Carroll Moore — Doctor of Humane Letters," *HBM*, v.18, January-February 1942, p.17

24 Margaret C. Scoggin, "Outlook Tower," *HBM*, v.24, January-February 1948, p.67

25 BMM, A Hunt Breakfast Item, "Outlook Tower," *HBM*, v.24, January-February 1948, p.2

26 "The Three Owls' Notebook," *HBM*, v.21, p.108

27 BMM, "Peter Rabbit and His Homelands," *HBM*, v.3, August 1927, p.18

28 BMM, "Beatrix Potter in Letters," *HBM*, v.20, May-June 1944, p.223

29 Ibid., p.215

30 Letter to Beulah Folmsbee. March 10, 1943

31 BMM, A Hunt Breakfast Item, "This Wanda Gág Memorial *Horn Book*," *HBM*, v.23, May-June 1947, p.138

32 BMM, "A Tribute to Beulah Folmsbee," *HBM*, v.23, July-August 1947, p.237

33 BMM, A Hunt Breakfast Item, "*The Horn Book's* Staff," *HBM*, v.26, November-December 1950, p.410

34 BMM, "*The Horn Book's* New Editor," *HBM*, v.26, November-December 1950, p.445

The following writings of Mrs. Miller from *The Horn Book Magazine* are editorials, unless otherwise noted.

35 "The Children's World," v.26, September-October 1950, p.345

36 "Editorial," v.11, July-August 1935, p.201

37 "Greatness Sown Broadcast," v.15, May-June 1939, p.137

38 "A Shedlock Fund for Story-Tellers," v.13, September-October 1937, p.265

39 "Editorial," v.11, May-June 1935, p.133

40 "Free and Floating," v.25, July-August 1949, p.257

41 "*The Horn Book's* Quarter Century," [article] v.25, September-October 1949, p.358

42 "Salute to Laura E. Richards," v.17, July-August 1941, p.245

43 "Time Voyages in Trust," v.17, September-October 1941, p.341

44 "Contrariwise," v.20, September-October 1944, p.345

45 "The Children of God," v.18, September-October 1942, p.313

46 "Guide to Treasure," [article] v.16, May-June 1940, pp.178-79

47 "What Makes Us Strong," v.13, January-February 1937, p.5

48 "Thy Kingdom Come," v.16, March-April 1940, p.81

49 "Children's Books in America Today," [article] v.12, July-August 1936, pp.199,204

50 "Artists and Writers, Humanists," v.25, May-June 1949, p.185

51 "Christmas, 1947," v.23, November-December 1947, p.409

52 "Criticism of Children's Books," v.22, May-June 1946, pp.175,224

53 "Life and Literature," v.15, July-August 1939, p.199

54 "Ultimate Goals," v.20, January-February 1944, p.5

55 "Reading with Children," v.16, July-August, 1940, p.223

56 "To Alice M. Jordan: A Tribute," [article] v.17, January-February 1941, p.15

57 "Good Will and Christmas," v.12, September-October 1936, p.265
58 "A Prayer for Children: Christmas, 1940," v.16, November-December 1940, p.395

PUBLICATIONS OF THE HORN BOOK, INCORPORATED

1 [Louise Seaman Bechtel], "A Salute to Bertha Mahony Miller," *HBM*, v.35, August 1959, pp.278-79
2 BMM, "A Tribute to Beulah Folmsbee," *HBM*, v.23, July-August 1947, p.237
3 Paul Hazard, "The Soul of Man: The World Republic of Childhood," in his *Books, Children and Men*, 3rd ed., Boston: The Horn Book, Inc., 1947. p.146
4 Announcement on Cover 4 *HBM*, v.18, July-August 1942
5 Anne Carroll Moore, "The Three Owls' Notebook," *HBM*, v.23, November-December 1947, pp.433-34
6 Bertha E. Mahony, "Introduction," to *Illustrators of Children's Books: 1744-1945*, compiled by Bertha E. Mahony, Louise P. Latimer [and] Beulah Folmsbee, Boston: The Horn Book, Inc., 1947, p.xvi
7 Pamela Bianco, A Hunt Breakfast Item, "Comments on *Writing and Criticism: A Book for Margery Bianco*," *HBM*, v.27, July-August 1951, p.280
8 Madelyn C. Wankmiller, "*Caroline M. Hewins: Her Book*," [book review] *HBM*, v.31, April 1955, p.128
9 Bertha Mahony Miller, "Preface" to *Caroline M. Hewins: Her Book*, Boston: The Horn Book, Inc., 1954. p.v
10 Leah Carter Johnston, "*Newbery Medal Books, 1922-1955*," [book review] *HBM*, v.32, February 1956, p.46
11 Bertha Mahony Miller, "Introduction," to *A Horn Book Sampler*, ed. by Norma R. Fryatt, Boston: The Horn Book, Inc., 1959. p.[v]
12 Frances Clarke Sayers, "Introduction," to *My Roads to Childhood*, by Anne Carroll Moore, Boston: The Horn Book, Inc., 1961. p.xii
13 Frances Clarke Sayers, "*Horn Book Reflections*," [book review] *HBM*, v.45, December 1969, p.659

YEARS OF RETIREMENT

1 Letter to Marguerite Mitchell. January 27, 1947
2 BMM, "Where Good People Are —," *HBM*, v.23, September-October 1947, p.321
3 Elinor W. Field, "The Story of a Friendship," p.4
4 Letter to Jeanne Jarmon. March 29, 1951
5 Letter from Elizabeth Reed to the writer. 1970
6 Letter from Momoko Ishii to the writer. April 29, 1970, p.6
7 Ibid., p.8
8 Bertha Mahony Miller, "Eliza Orne White and Her Books for Children," in *The Hewins Lectures: 1947-1962*, ed. by Siri Andrews [Boston]: The Horn Book Inc., 1963, p.155
9 May Massee, "For Merit in the Realm of Books," *HBM*, v.31, April 1955, p.87
10 BMM, "Salute to Jennie D. Lindquist," *HBM*, v.34, June 1958, p.171
11 Letter to Nancy Dean Kingman, May 17, 1959
12 [Louise Seaman Bechtel], "A Salute to Bertha Mahony Miller," *HBM*, v.35, August 1959, p.278
13 Ibid., p.279
14 Eulalie Steinmetz Ross, "An Accolade and an Obligation," *HBM*, v.37, November 7, 1961, Extra Memorial Issue: *The Alice M. Jordan Horn Book*, p.59

Selected Bibliography

Compiled by Virginia Haviland

The Writings of Bertha Mahony Miller

Book Lists

Mahony, Bertha E. *Books for Boys and Girls — A Suggestive Purchase List.* Boston: Women's Educational and Industrial Union, 1916. 110 pp.

———. ———. 2nd ed., rev. 1917. ?pp.
No copy was found for examination.

———.———. 3rd ed., rev. November, 1919. [1919]. 95 pp.

———. ———. 4th ed., rev. September, 1922. 1922. 146 pp.

———, and Elinor Whitney, comps. *Books for Boys and Girls.* Boston: The Bookshop for Boys and Girls, Women's Educational and Industrial Union, [1924]. 39 pp.
"Supplement for 1924 to *Books for Boys and Girls — A Suggestive Purchase List,* 4th ed., rev. 1922."

Books

Mahony, Bertha E., and Elinor Whitney, comps. *Contemporary Illustrators of Children's Books.* Boston: Bookshop for Boys and Girls, Women's Educational and Industrial Union, 1930. 135 pp.

———. *Five Years of Children's Books.* A Supplement to *Realms of Gold.* Garden City, N.Y.: Doubleday, Doran, 1936. 599 pp.

———. *Realms of Gold in Children's Books.* Garden City, N.Y.: Doubleday, Doran, 1929. 796 pp.
Designated by its compilers as "The Fifth Edition of *Books for Boys and Girls — A Suggestive Purchase List.*"

Mahony, Bertha E., Louise Payson Latimer [and] Beulah Folmsbee, comps. *Illustrators of Children's Books: 1744-1945.* Boston: The Horn Book, Inc., 1947. 527 pp.

Miller, Bertha Mahony, and Elinor Whitney Field, eds. *Caldecott Medal Books: 1938-1957.* With the Artists' Acceptance Papers & Related Material Chiefly from *The Horn Book Magazine.* Boston: The Horn Book, Inc., 1957. 329 pp. (Horn Book Papers, v.2)

———. *Newbery Medal Books: 1922-1955.* With Their Authors' Acceptance Papers & Related Material Chiefly from *The Horn Book Magazine.* Boston: The Horn Book, Inc., 1955. 458 pp. (Horn Book Papers, v.1)

Miller, Bertha Mahony, Ruth H. Viguers [and] Marcia Dalphin, comps. *Illustrators of Children's Books: 1946-1956. A* Supplement to *Illustrators of Children's Books: 1744-1945.* Boston: The Horn Book, Inc., 1958. 299 pp.

Moore, Anne Carroll, and Bertha Mahony Miller, eds. *Writing and Criticism: A Book for Margery Bianco.* Decorations by Valenti Angelo. Boston: The Horn Book, Inc., 1951. 93 pp.

Chapters, Forewords, Introductions, Prefaces

Andrews, Siri, ed. *The Hewins Lectures: 1947-1962.* Introduction by Frederic G. Melcher. [Boston]: The Horn Book, Inc., 1963.

"Elizabeth Orne White and Her Books for Children," by Bertha Mahony Miller, pp.151-62.

Caroline M. Hewins: Her Book. Containing *A Mid-Century Child and Her Books,* by Caroline M. Hewins [and] *Caroline M. Hewins and Books for Children,* by Jennie D. Lindquist. Boston: The Horn Book, Inc., 1954.

Preface by Bertha Mahony Miller, pp.v-vi.

Frederic G. Melcher: Friendly Reminiscences of a Half Century Among Books & Bookmen. N.Y.: The Book Publishers' Bureau, 1945.

"On the Twentieth Century John Newbery," by Bertha E. Mahony Miller, pp.48-54.

Fryatt, Norma R., ed. *A Horn Book Sampler: On Children's Books and Reading.* Selected from twenty-five years of *The Horn Book Magazine,* 1924-1948. Introduction by Bertha Mahony Miller. Boston: The Horn Book, Inc., 1959.

Introduction, pp.[xiii-xv]. Mrs. Miller's writings included are: "The Honey Heart of Earth," pp 4-7; "Criticism of Children's Books," p.95; "Twenty Years of Children's Books," pp.104-10; "Editorial," pp.118-19; "Tir-Nan-Oge and Tir Tairngire," pp.120-24; "Beatrix Potter and Her Nursery Classics," pp.228-33.

Hazard, Paul. *Books, Children and Men.* Translated by Marguerite Mitchell. 3rd ed. Boston: The Horn Book, Inc., 1947.

This edition has Mrs. Miller's "Publisher's Preface to the Third Edition" (pp.xxi-xxiii) and the "Publisher's Preface" she wrote for the first, 1944, edition, (pp.v-vii)

Potter, Beatrix, *Wag-by-Wall.* With decorations by J. J. Lankes. Boston: The Horn Book, Inc., 1944.

"The Story of This Story," by Bertha E. Mahony, pp.[1-4]

Material for Children

Diaz, Mrs. Abby Morton. *Polly Cologne.* Illustrations by Morgan J. Sweeney ("Boz"). Introduction to new edition by Bertha E. Mahony. Boston: Lothrop, Lee & Shepard, [1930]

Introduction, pp.7-12.

Field, Eugene. *Some Poems of Childhood.* Selected by Bertha E. Mahony. Illustrated by Gertrude A. Kay. N.Y.: Scribner, 1931. 128 pp.

Also: Foreword, by Bertha E. Mahony, pp.v-vi.

Our New Wonder World. Rev. ed. Chicago: George L. Shuman & Co., 1932, 11v.

Foreword, "Why Read Books," by Bertha E. Mahony to *Story and Art,* v.5.

PERIODICAL

The Horn Book Magazine. Founded, October 1924, by Bertha Mahony, editor, and Elinor Whitney, assistant editor. Quarterly through 1933; bi-monthly thereafter. Boston: Women's Educational and Industrial Union, v.1, no.1, October 1924 through v.12, no.5, September-October 1936; The Horn Book, Inc., v.12, no.6, November-December 1936 through v.26, no.6, November-December 1950.

The Horn Book Magazine, in 1973, is in its forty-ninth year of publication. The Horn Book, Inc., continues to publish the magazine, and Paul Heins is the present editor.

Mrs. Miller's writings in *The Horn Book* consist of articles, editorials, and Hunt Breakfast columns of news and comment. Until Alice Jordan began to edit the Booklist in September 1939, Mrs. Miller and Mrs. Field, with occasional guests, reviewed all the new children's books. Since September 1950, the Booklist has been prepared by a staff of reviewers comprising the editor of the magazine and area librarians.

ARTICLES IN *The Horn Book Magazine*

"Abbie Farwell Brown," v.3, May 1927, p.15.

"Adventure," v.5, August 1929, pp.35-40.

"Adventures Among New Books," v.2, November 1926, pp.22-30.

"Alice M. Jordan: Her Life and Work (Part I); Her Quiet Fame and Influence on the Future (Part II)," *The Alice M. Jordan Horn Book,* v.37, November 7, 1961, Extra Memorial Issue, pp.5-17.

Mrs. Miller edited the Memorial Issue. Part I was a reprint of her article, "To Alice M. Jordan: A Tribute," first published in *The Horn Book,* v.17, January-February 1941, pp.7-15.

"Anne Carroll Moore — Director of Humane Letters," v.18, January-February 1942, pp.7-18.

When Miss Moore died, Mrs. Miller's article was reprinted in *The Horn Book,* v.37, April 1961, pp.183-92.

"Anne Parrish's Memorable Nonsense Story" [*The Story of Appleby Capple*] v.27, January-February 1951, pp.20-23.

"*Another Here and Now Story Book* [by Lucy Sprague Mitchell]" v.13, May-June 1937, pp.164-66.

"Artists Triumph," v.14, July-August 1938, pp.201-08.

Dorothy Lathrop and the first Caldecott Award.

"Beatrix Potter and Her Nursery Classics," v.17, May-June 1941, pp.230-38.

"Beatrix Potter in Letters," v.20, May-June 1944, pp.214-24.

"The Bookshop and Its Relation to Schools," [v.2] January 1926, Extra Number: *Experimental Schools in England*, pp.3-5.

"Boys at School and at Work: The Books of William Heyliger," by Bertha E. Mahony and Elinor Whitney, v.10, November-December 1934, pp.382-84.

"Children and Solitude," v.2, June 1926, pp.3-7.

"Children's Books in America Today," v.12, July-August 1936, pp.199-207.

"The Delicate Magic Machinery of Poetry: *The Winged Horse*," v.3, August 1927, pp.3-5.

"Eliza Orne White and Her Books for Children," v.31, April 1955, pp.89-102.

The Seventh Caroline M. Hewins Lecture.

"Eliza Orne White: Her Books for Children," v.1, June 1925, pp.3-9.

"A Fairy Village on a School Green," v.5, August 1929, pp.59-62.

"The First Children's Department in Book Publishing," v.4, August 1928, pp.3-24.

"*The Golden Name Day*," [by Jennie Lindquist] v.31, October 1955, p.380.

"Guide to Treasure," v.16, May-June 1940, pp.177-85.

Storytelling experiment in the Ashburnham schools.

"*The Heart Is the Teacher*," [by Leonard Covello with Guido D'Agostino] v.36, February 1960, pp.60-61.

" 'The Honey Heart of Earth' in the Books of Anne and Dillwyn Parrish," v.7, February 1931, pp.61-67.

"*The Horn Book's* Quarter Century," v.25, September-October 1949, pp.351-58.

"Ingri and Edgar Parin d'Aulaire," by Bertha E. Mahony and Marguerite M. Mitchell, v.16, July-August 1940, pp.257-64.

"Introduction," v.26, October 19, 1950, Extra Number: *Thomas Schofield Handforth: Artist, Illustrator, Author*, pp.3-4.

"Laura Mackay — A Maker of Little Folk," v.4, November 1928, pp.68-71.

"Little Brother and Sister," v.12, May-June 1936, pp.167-74.

Review of Eleanor Farjeon's *Portrait of a Family*.

"*Long Island's Story* — Why Not Other Regional Books?" v.6, February 1930, pp.55-61.

"May Lamberton Becker and Her *Adventures in Reading*," v.4, February 1928, pp.9-12.

"New Books," v.3, February 1927, pp.41-44.

"Newburyport Storyteller," [Ethel Parton] v.20, May-June 1944, pp.227-28.

"*North America*, by Lucy Sprague Mitchell," v.7, August 1931, p.235.

"Of Rachel Field and Letters," v.18, July-August 1942, pp.237-50.

"Other Children's Book Departments Since 1918," v.4, August 1928, pp.74-76.

"Peter Rabbit and His Homelands," v.3, August 1927, pp.18-19.

"*The Poet's Craft*," [by Helen Fern Daringer and Anne Thaxter Eaton] v.11, March-April 1935, pp.114-16.

"Primitive Hearths of the Pyrenees," v.3, November 1927, pp.72-76.

" 'A Quick Ear for Silver Bells': *Cross Roads to Childhood, Books for Middle-Aged Children*, by Anne Carroll Moore," v.3, February 1927, pp.16-19.

"Randolph Caldecott," v.14, July-August 1938, pp.218-23.

"A Rampancy for Romance," v.4, November 1928, pp.30-37.

"*Saturday's Children* and Those of Other Days and Ways," v.3, May 1927, pp.23-28.

"Sidney Smith and the Bookshop's Colophon," v.9, May 1933, pp.91-93.

"Some Outstanding Books on 1928 Fall Lists of Children's Book Departments," v.4, August 1928, pp.77-85.

[Statement of Purpose and Policy] v.1, October 1924, p.1.

"Tir-Nan-Oge and Tir Tairngire," v.10, January 1934, pp.31-36.

"To Alice M. Jordan: A Tribute," v.17, January-February 1941, pp.7-15. Reprinted, after Miss Jordan's death, as "Alice M. Jordan: Her Life and Work (Part I)" in *The Alice M. Jordan Horn Book*, v.37, November 7, 1961, Extra Memorial Issue, pp.5-13.

"Toujours Gai," [book reviews] v.7, August 1931, pp.190-94.

"Twenty Years of Children's Books," v.14, November-December 1938, pp.343-50.

"A View Halloo," [book reviews] v.5, May 1929, pp.26-36.

" 'What's Past Is Prelude' " v.20, May-June 1944, p.248.

"*Why Do They Like It?*" v.3, May 1927, p.57.
A review of a book by E. L. Black, an English boy of sixteen.

Articles in Other Periodicals

"Apprentices to Life," *Saturday Review of Literature*, v.10, December 9, 1933, pp.340-41.

"As a Bookseller Sees Children's Book Week," *Publishers' Weekly*, v.100, October 22, 1921, p.1397.

"A Bookshop for Boys and Girls," *American Review of Reviews*, v.56, December 1917, pp.657-58.

"The Bookshop for Boys and Girls — Boston," *Publishers' Weekly*, v.91, May 26, 1917, pp.1701-03.

"Caldecott's Picture Books," *Publishers' Weekly*, v.132, August 28, 1937, pp.674-77.

"Choosing Books for Boys and Girls," [R. R. Bowker] *Book Review*, November 1929, pp.20, 22, 24, 26.

"The Companionship of Books," *Parents' Magazine*, v.15, November 1940, pp.19, 79-81.

"Fairy Tales and the Spirit," *Child Life*, v.9, November 1930, pp.543, 568, 585.

"Far Horizons in Spring Books for Boys and Girls," *Elementary English Review*, v.6, June 1929, pp.143-46.

"Realms of Gold: Five Centuries of Children's Books," *Publishers' Weekly*, v.115, March 2, 1929, pp.975-79.
Based on the introductory chapter of *Realms of Gold in Children's Books*.

"Social Workers and Children's Books," *The Social Worker: Children's Work Number* [Alumni, Simmons College, School of Social Work] v.7, December 1930, pp.7-9.

Writings About Mrs. Miller

"Acceptance of The Regina Medal for Bertha Mahony Miller," by Ruth H. Viguers, *Catholic Library World*, v.39, September 1967, pp.35-40.
Reprinted in *The Horn Book*, v.45, October 1969, pp.516-24.

"Bertha Mahony Miller: 1882-1969," by Paul Heins, *The Horn Book*, v.45, August 1969, p.371.

"Bertha Mahony Miller: 1882-1969," *The Horn Book*, v.45, October 1969.
A Memorial Issue, the October 1969 *Horn Book* included: "Bertha Mahony Miller," by Elinor W. Field, pp.467-68, 622 [reprinted from *Catholic Library World*, v.38, February 1967, pp.359-62]; "Looking Backward and Looking Forward," [an editorial] by Elinor W. Field, p.495; A Portrait, p.496; "In Remembrance: Bertha Mahony Miller," by Elizabeth Orton Jones, pp.497-515; "Acceptance of The Regina Medal for Bertha Mahony Miller," by Ruth H. Viguers, pp.516-24 [reprinted from *Catholic Library World*, v.39, September 1967, pp.35-40]; "*Horn Book* Articles (1951-1969) about Bertha Mahony Miller," p.524; "A Unique Sense of Communication," by Norma R. Fryatt, Frances C. Darling, Elizabeth Yates, Nora S. Unwin, Jennie D. Lindquist, Annis Duff, Lynd Ward, pp.556-65; "Bertha Mahony Miller and Horn Book Publications," by Siri Andrews, pp.566-69; "Mrs. Miller Remembered," by Jasmine Britton, pp.466, 623; Citation for the Constance Lindsay Skinner Award for 1955, p.623.

"The Bookshop for Boys and Girls," by Annie Carroll Moore, *A. L. A. Bulletin, Louisville Conference Number, 1917, v.11*, July 1917, pp.168-69.

"The Bookshop from the Outside," by Alice M. Jordan, *The Horn Book*, v.1, October 1924, pp.12-15.

"The Bookshop That Is Bertha Mahony," by Alice Jordan, *The Atlantic Bookshelf* [News of the Book World, Book Reviews and Advertisements from the June *Atlantic Monthly*] June 1929, pp.52-59.

"A Bookstore Entertains the Nation's Dolls," *Publishers' Weekly*, v.115, March 2, 1929, p.985.

"Chapters from *Horn Book* History," *The Horn Book*, v.38: I — by Frederic G. Melcher, April 1962, pp.192-93; II — by Margaret E. Sayward, June 1962, pp.298-99; III — by Elinor W. Field, August 1962, pp.401-03; IV — by Members of the Staff of the Bookshop for Boys and Girls, October 1962, pp.509-11; V — by Mary Adeline Whitney, December 1962, pp.624-25. v.39: VI — by Lee Kingman, February 1963, pp.92-93; VII — "The Book Caravan," by Frances C. Darling, April 1963, pp.207-10; VIII — by Elinor W. Field, June 1963, pp.327-30; IX — by Louise Seaman Bechtel, August 1963, pp.412-15.

"For Merit in the Realm of Books," by May Massee, *The Horn Book*, v.31, April 1955, pp.86-87.

The Constance Lindsay Skinner Award.

"Medals and Magic," by Ruth H. Viguers, *The Horn Book*, v.43, February 1967, pp.24-25.

The Regina Medal Award.

"Our Twenty Years," [an editorial] by Elinor W. Field, *The Horn Book*, v.20, May-June 1944, p.151.

"Presentation of the Regina Medal Award," by Margaret Long, *Catholic Library Award*, v.39, September 1967, p.34.

"A Salute to Bertha Mahony Miller," by Louise Seaman Bechtel, *Top of the News*, v.16, October 1959, pp.45-46.

A resolution presented by the Children's Service Division of the American Library Association at its annual meeting in Washington, D.C., on June 23, 1959. Also in *The Horn Book*, v.35, August 1959, pp.278-79.

"Take a Bow: Bertha Mahony Miller and Fannie Butcher," *Publishers' Weekly*, v.167, March 5, 1955, pp.1469-71.

The Constance Lindsay Skinner Award.

"To B. E. M." by Jennie D. Lindquist, *The Horn Book*, v.27, January-February 1951, p.11.

"A Tribute from the Coast," by Jasmine Britton, *The Atlantic Bookshelf*, June 1929, p.59.

Accompanied Miss Jordan's article, "The Bookshop That Is Bertha Mahony," in the same issue of the magazine.

"A Venture in Poetry: Boston Bookshop for Boys and Girls," by Milton Bryon, *Saturday Review of Literature*, v.8, July 25, 1931, p.14.

The Amy Lowell Memorial Poetry Series.

Index